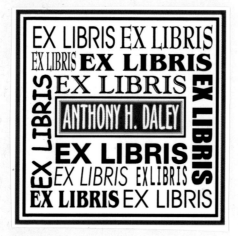

Killing No Murder

When should we or must we kill a politician? *Killing No Murder* is a provocative, stimulating study which takes a completely fresh look at assassination, placing it in a historical perspective. Among the examples Mr Hyams analyses and speculates on are Caesar, whose death had the opposite effect to that intended, Lincoln, whose killing was a tragedy which still carries its aftermath, the assassination of Franz Ferdinand, the Phoenix Park murders, the death of Lord Moyne at the hands of Israeli nationalists, and the extraordinary case of Walter Rathenau, the Jewish Finance Minister in the Weimar Republic.

Considering each of these in depth, Mr Hyams is led to pose some questions which some will find extremely controversial but which none can deny are highly pertinent. A *Times* first leader, discussing the alarming implications of the assassinations within the last five years of John F. Kennedy, Martin Luther King, and Robert Kennedy, concluded that these began 'to make much more serious the prospect of a return to political assassination as a resort for the political extremist'. A radical reassessment of assassination and its place in society along the lines Mr Hyams suggests would seem to be a priority.

THE NATURAL HISTORY OF SOCIETY

EDITOR: ALEX COMFORT

EDWARD HYAMS

Killing No Murder

A STUDY OF ASSASSINATION
AS A POLITICAL MEANS

'[Assassination] exists to further by force or the threat
of force civil policies which cannot
be furthered by any other means'

– with apologies to the *Staff College Manual*

NELSON

THOMAS NELSON AND SONS LTD

36 Park Street London W1
P.O. Box 2187 Accra
P.O. Box 336 Apapa Lagos
P.O. Box 25012 Nairobi
P.O. Box 21149 Dar es Salaam
77 Coffee Street San Fernando Trinidad

THOMAS NELSON (AUSTRALIA) LTD
597 Little Collins Street Melbourne 3000

THOMAS NELSON AND SONS (SOUTH AFRICA) (PROPRIETARY) LTD
51 Commissioner Street Johannesburg

THOMAS NELSON AND SONS (CANADA) LTD
81 Curlew Drive Don Mills Ontario

THOMAS NELSON AND SONS
Copewood and Davis Streets Camden New Jersey 08103

First published 1969
Copyright © 1969 by Mary Bacon

17 138012 6

Printed in Great Britain by
WESTERN PRINTING SERVICES LTD
Bristol

Dedicated to the memory
of the twenty million war dead who, since the author's birth,
have sacrificed their lives for the score of leaders
who might, at the cost of their own,
have saved them

'. . . it is lawful to call to account
a tyrant or wicked King and after due conviction
to depose and put him to death. . . .'
— JOHN MILTON,
The Tenure of Kings and Magistrates

CONTENTS

ACKNOWLEDGEMENTS

The author is grateful to the following for their kind permission to include quotations from the books indicated:

Messrs A.B.P. International and Messrs Harper & Row, New York: Norman Cohn, *Warrant for Genocide*; Messrs Jonathan Cape Ltd and Messrs A. M. Heath & Co.: Sir Bernard Pares, *A History of Russia*; Messrs J. M. Dent & Sons: *The Travels of Marco Polo* (Everyman's Library edition); Messrs Faber & Faber Ltd: Margaret Murray, *The God of the Witches*; Mr Robert Graves and Messrs A. P. Watt & Sons: Suetonius, *The Twelve Caesars* (Penguin Classics translation by Robert Graves); Messrs MacGibbon & Kee and Messrs Simon & Schuster Inc., New York: Vladimir Dedijer, *The Road to Sarajevo*; Messrs Frederick Muller Ltd and Messrs Funk & Wagnalls, New York: J. M. Cottrell, *Anatomy of an Assassination*; Messrs Penguin Books Ltd: Plutarch, *The Fall of the Roman Republic* (Penguin Classics translation by Rex Warner); Messrs Routledge & Kegan Paul: Alex Comfort, *Darwin and the Naked Lady*.

INTRODUCTION

THE object of this pamphlet is to put forward, with examples from several parts of the world and several periods of history, some of the arguments for and against using assassination as a useful expression of domestic or foreign policy and as a means of promoting the greatest good of the greatest number. In view of the revival, since 1963, of this means of trying to advance or to prevent particular policies, it becomes desirable to examine this means of advancing political ideas in a spirit of enquiry and without emotion. Why and by whom President John Kennedy was assassinated is not yet clear. Dr Luther King was assassinated as a leader of the struggle of the American blacks for first-class citizenship; and it is possible that his death may have served his cause even better than his life by shocking the whites into granting more, more swiftly, than they would otherwise have done, and the blacks into the use of effective force. Robert Kennedy was assassinated by an Arab, as a friend of the Jews and of Israel, to prevent a friend of the enemy from becoming the most powerful man in the world.

The first reaction of any ordinary man to the proposition that assassination may, in certain cases, be justifiable and useful, is revulsion and rejection. This does more credit to his heart than to his head. He ought, unless he be a pacificist who also rejects war unconditionally, to use his head more, and deny his heart so much indulgence. For where, as I shall show can be the case, assassination can be an alternative to war, there can be no question of its worth and justice.

When, in November 1963, President John Kennedy of the United States was assassinated, the civilized world was shocked. As for politicians – even Soviet politicians – they were appalled; and well they might be since the second best guarded chieftain in the world had proved killable. Yet half a century ago, while the loss of such a man would doubtless have been felt as grievous, and the failure of his police defence as disconcerting,* the event would hardly have come as a shock: political assassination was then far too commonplace to cause surprise, let alone shock. Between 1865, when Abraham Lincoln was assassinated, and 1914, when it was the turn of the Archduke Ferdinand, heir to the Austro-Hungarian Empire, that is within a period of less than fifty years or the middle part of a man's lifetime, assassination as a political means, and one which, as I shall try to demonstrate below, had some support from monumentally respectable legal and religious authorities, enjoyed a sort of 'golden age'. There have been, of course, numerous political assassinations of great importance in our own lifetime before 1963: for example, the assassination of Leon Trotsky by the emissaries of J. V. Stalin; of King Alexander of Yugoslavia and the French Foreign Minister, M. Barthou; and of the Mahatma Gandhi. Others are the subjects of study in later chapters of this book. But there has not, since 1914, been anything to equal that forty-four years of assassinations between 1870 and 1914.

It should be fairly easy for the English reader to consider the subject of assassination as a political means, dispassionately; and, indeed, as we shall presently see, English thinkers, the English courts, and the House of Commons have, in the past, done just

---

* The failure of Abraham Lincoln's police guard has occupied as much of the historians' attention as the assassination itself (see Chapter Four).

that. For the American reader it is much less so; in fact it is going to be difficult. Not only have a number of United States Presidents been assassinated; not only is one of those assassinations still fresh in our minds; not only was there the case of Dr Martin Luther King and the killing of Senator Robert Kennedy, but the atmosphere of immanent violence in the country is so alarming to all men of good will that Americans are bound to condemn without hesitation the very idea that political assassination can, in any circumstances, serve a useful purpose or be justified by any consideration. I suggest that they put aside for the time being the feelings which must influence their judgement, and use that judgement coldly, uninfluenced by emotion, even, if possible, heartlessly.

The first important victim in the golden age of assassination was Juan Prim, the Prime Minister of Spain. This remarkable man was a liberal and generous-hearted gentleman who distinguished himself by fighting, both in elections and with arms, first against the dictator Espartero, whom he defeated, then against the ultra-reactionary Prime Minister, Narváez. Despite the hatred and fierce resistance of the extreme right, Prim was triumphant. But by that time the right had realized that in Prim they had a political enemy too strong for them and they took the only remaining way of getting rid of him by having him assassinated in December 1870, with results entirely satisfactory to their cause.

The next assassination worthy of note was that of the Viceroy of India, the Earl of Mayo, in 1872. This was not a true political case, but may fairly be described as a social one. The Viceroy was on a visit of inspection to a convict settlement at Port Blair in the Andaman Islands when he paid the price of power. One of the convicts seized the opportunity to avenge his misery, the misery of a majority class, by assassinating Lord Mayo. Doubtless the man had long laboured under that terrible sense of injustice which, where there is organization of the lower classes, leads to revolution; and, where there is not, to such individual protests.

The President of Ecuador, Gabriel Moreno, was done to death by an assassin in 1875, and one year later it was the turn of the Sultan Abdül Aziz of Turkey.

This potentate had been relatively liberal at first but after 1870 he turned against the West and its ideas and allied himself to Russia. Trouble in his Slav provinces spread to his Moslem subjects, and in 1876 he was deposed by an anti-Russian and anti-Absolutist faction which, four days after the deposition, did away with him and put it about that he had committed suicide. This probably averted some kind of civil war and a great deal of bloodshed.

Eighteen eighty-one was a bumper year; the assassination of Tsar Alexander II of Russia is dealt with at some length in Chapter Four. The other victim was President James Garfield of the United States. Garfield was a Stanton man, that is, a Republican opposed to Lincoln's policy of treating the defeated South magnanimously and favouring Stanton's policy of treating it punitively and as a colonial territory. Opposition to Garfield was embodied in the 'Stalwarts' and Garfield's assassin was a 'Stalwart' named Guiteau who was tried and executed for his deed.

Less than a year after the Russian tsar and the American president had been disposed of by assassins came the Phoenix Park assassinations, the victims being Mr Burke and Lord Frederick Cavendish: I have given an account at length of this case in Chapter Eight. For the next few years assassins were successful only against lesser victims, but in 1894 came the assassination of President Sadi Carnot of France.

Sadi Carnot was the fourth President of the Third Republic and his assassination is a particularly interesting one in the context of this work because he was what I call (see below) a pure scapegoat. Certain leaders, as I shall try to show, are put to death not for their crimes but, as representatives, for ours; the crimes being such only, of course, in the eyes of some anti-establishment movement. As a politician Carnot was less obnoxious than many others of his time: he was reasonably liberal and exceptionally honest. But all this was beside the point of his assassin, the Italian Anarchist, Casero, for whom Carnot was evil not in himself but in his office. He was a ruler and was condemned not for what he did but for what he was, a vessel of political power.

Two years after Carnot was assassinated in Lyon came the

Shah of Persia's turn. Nasr-ed-Din's accession to the throne was bitterly contested, chiefly by the followers of a religious reformer – or lunatic – known as 'El Bab'. This man was a Shi'ite mystic and leader of a sect whose members were persuaded to believe that he was the Imam Mahdi, the expected Shi'ite messiah. Two years after becoming Shah, Nasr-ed-Din was able to arrest El Bab, put him to death, and massacre a considerable number of his sectaries. This failed to exterminate the sect and, led by El Bab's young successor, the Babites tried to assassinate the Shah in 1852. Their failure cost them more massacres and more ruthless persecution which still failed to extinguish their zeal, and forty-four years later, in 1896, one of their number succeeded at last in assassinating the Shah, thereby fulfilling a religious obligation he could not have repudiated without damning himself.

Another Spanish prime minster, Cánovas del Castillo, fell to the Anarchists in the following year, and, in 1898, Juán Barrios, President of Guatemala, to his political opponents; and the Empress Elizabeth of Russia to the Nihilists, concerning whom more will be found in Chapter Five. The new century began with the assassination of King Umberto I of Italy.

This monarch was an authoritarian by temperament; and by training a narrow-minded and virtually uneducated soldier without culture or sensibility. It was obvious to a great many people in Italy that the sooner they were rid of Umberto the better, and a first attempt on his life was made by one Passanante in 1878; the king survived it because he carried a sword and was quick with it.

It is worth breaking off here to consider for a moment the curious difference between those victims of an assassin who defend themselves and those who, as if they felt themselves predestined victims, hardly do so at all. Both Caesar and Lincoln seem, in the light of every bit of evidence available carefully studied, to have been aware of what was going to happen to them; and read, in this context, the last speech made by Martin Luther King before he died. What is the significance of such apparent foresight: not, if one is a rationalist, premonition; there remains, by way of explanation, guilt. Why guilt? Because, as I shall show, the great leader is necessarily a criminal, doing for the people necessary crimes so that they can remain guiltless by repudiating him. But there is more to it than that: the leader is constantly striving to retain control of the evil in him (as in all men, but in him given a chance to become explicit and active), and which tries to drive him to abuse his power, to torture and kill not only for the people, but for the satisfaction of the ego manifest in his will-to-power.

Returning for a moment to Umberto of Italy. As Umberto grew older he became increasingly absolutist and opposed to any kind of liberty of the subject, and by 1898 he had so subverted the democracy that he had manipulated the premiership and five other key ministries into the hands of generals and admirals who had taken an oath to serve not Italy, but Umberto. As a result the Republicans were provoked at last to violent protest and applauded when, on 29 July 1900, the Anarchist, G. Bresci, rid the nation and people of this royal incubus, with a revolver.

The evil in the heart of the leader is probably (from the Freudian point of view quite certainly) a manifestation of the evil in the heart of the father which Shelley had the insight and courage to express explicitly in *The Cenci* long before any scientific psychologist had understood it.

> If when a parent from a parent's heart
> Lifts from this earth to the great Father of all
> A prayer. . . .

> One supplication, one desire, or hope,
> That he should grant a wish for his two sons. . . .

> And suddenly beyond his dearest hope
> It is accomplished, he should then rejoice. . . .

> I thank thee! In one night thou didst perform
> By ways inscrutable, the thing I sought.
> My sons are dead. . . .*

This should be read side by side with those passages of Elias Canetti's *Crowds and Power*† in which Canetti, with brilliant and

† Elias Canetti, *Crowds in Power*, Gollanez, 1962.
* Percy Bysshe Shelley, *The Cenci*.

alarming insight, shows that, deep, deep under all the Leader's (to get the full weight of the word, put it into German and say *Führer*'s) explicit wish to serve the people, lies a drive to rape all the women of his crowd and kill all the men, to experience the ultimate satisfaction of the ancient and lonely 'I' by being alone, alive, on a vast heap of corpses. Cenci, in his hatred, his wild suspicions *in which he himself as a rational creature does not believe*, is Bonaparte, is Hitler, is Stalin; but all leaders, all father-figures, are, in a measure, and with the most dangerous elements of those composing the Leader-Father character, under control. Bonaparte; Hitler and Stalin – and, therefore, Cenci. Shelley saw very deep: consider his pope, who supports the monster Cenci against his oppressed children:

> He holds it of most dangerous example
> To weaken the paternal power,
> Being, as 'twere, the shadow of his own.*

It is the Church-and-State gang-up against the people; and the revolt, too, must go deep, for clearly not only is it true that, in Giacomo Cenci's words in the poem:

> ...Well
> Are no more, as once, parent and child,
> But man to man, the oppressor and the oppressed;
> The Slanderer to the slandered; foe to foe. ...†

– but beyond Cenci and the Pope is God-the-Father, God-the-enemy. For God is on the Führer's side; there's holy writ for that. And Shelley's other hero at this time was Prometheus, God's gloriously rational and deeply feeling enemy. Prometheus is the arch-assassin, the proto-assassin:

> Why scorns which informs ye,
> How to commune with me?
> Me, alone, who checked,
> As one who checks a fiend-drawn charioteer,
> The falsehood and the force of him
> Who reigns supreme. ...‡

* Shelley, op. cit.
† ibid.
‡ Percy Bysshe Shelley, *Prometheus Unbound.*

Daddy; or the King; or the President. Did Julien Benda consult Shelley, or his own intelligent insight or perhaps Freud, when he wrote:

'Il existe, par dessus les classes et les nations, une volonté de l'espèce de se rendre maîtresse des choses. . . . On peut penser quelquefois qu'un tel mouvement s'affirmera de plus en plus et que c'est de cette voie que s'éteindront les guerres interhumaines; on arrivera ainsi à une "fraterniteé universelle" mais qui, loin d'être l'abolition de l'esprit de nation, avec ses appetits et ses orgueils, en sera au contraire la forme suprême, la nation s'appelant l'Homme et l'ennemi s'appelant Dieu.'*

In 1901 the principal victim of assassination was President McKinley of the United States, who was by no means, as politicians go, a man who deserved to be assassinated for his deeds. He was, like Sadi Carnot, a victim of the Anarchist (Shelleyan) conviction that, as manifestations of evil, personification of that political power which no man had a right to, rulers are fair game. His assassin, who killed the President in Buffalo after a banquet and public address on the occasion of the Pan-American Exposition, was an American-Polish Anarchist named Leon Czolgosz, who shot McKinley in the belly and paid for the deed with his own life.

There was a zero year in 1902, but it was amply made up for by the spectacular assassination of King Alexander and Queen Draga of Serbia in 1903. Alexander Obrenovich became king as a boy following his father's forced abdication. Before his majority he dismissed the Council of Regency and began ten years of personal rule, to which end he abolished the liberal constitution of 1869 and harked back to an earlier and authoritarian one. His puppet governments – there were seventeen in all – put up with it when he appointed his abdicated father Commander-in-Chief of the Armed Forces, but, oddly enough, jibbed when he married a widow of dubious reputation, ten years his senior, Draga Masin. Unable to find a new government and aware of a very menacing atmosphere in the army, Alexander restored the 1869 Constitution, or something like it. But he had no sooner done so than he suspended it to gratify a personal whim to remove from office

---

* Julien Benda, *La Trahison des Clercs*, Bernard Grasset, Paris, 1927.

some judges and civil servants whom he himself had appointed; whereupon one of the radical secret political societies, deciding that Serbia had suffered enough at the King's hands, assassinated both the King and the Queen and threw their bodies out of a window, thus extinguishing the Obrenovich dynasty. Politically and socially this assassination was justified in its results. The King had made war on his people; the people had reacted by making war on him. Locke and Aquinas (please see below) would have found Serbia's Black Hand assassins justified by 'natural law'.

There were two major assassinations in 1907: those of Pettkov, Prime Minister of Bulgaria; and Delyannis, Prime Minister of Greece. And in the following year, King Carlos of Portugal and his son and heir, the Crown Prince Luis, were put to death by an irritated people. He tried to be an absolute monarch. As a consequence he was held personally responsible for national misfortunes which were not really his fault, and in 1891 the Republicans of Oporto broke into open revolt. This came to nothing, and following another revolt in 1906, the King made the arch-conservative Jaõa Franco dictator; his repressive measures predictably strengthened the radical secret political societies, which managed to provoke a violent rising in 1908. Carlos was in the country on holiday; he hastened to Lisbon with his son and heir, the Crown Prince Luis, and both were shot dead by a Republican radical shortly after reaching the city. A 'pure' political case; and justified in law to this extent, that had the assassin contrived to take refuge in, e.g. England, his extradition (see page 24 below) would have been refused. But in another sense, this was more than a political case.

For it would be difficult to find a more beautiful case of throw-back to primitive priest-king slaughter, of a king dying because it is 'expedient that a man die for the people' to atone for, and by extension to cure, the national troubles. It is hardly going too far to claim that King Carlos of Portugal was sacrificed to improve the crops. The only question is *why* should we think to better our condition by killing our father-leader? It goes back a long way – beyond man to hominid, to pithecanthropine, and even, perhaps, australopithicine. Consider this:

'The Oedipal reversal involved the need to divide the mind into compartments, albeit far from watertight, and to keep the contents of those compartments actively separated. . . .'*

Because, otherwise, mother-rape and father-killing – and by extension leader-killing – become inconveniently frequent. But a reversal has been involved: from time to time, under strain, we refuse to go on standing on our heads; and a leader *is* killed.

In 1910 the Egyptian Prime Minister, Butrus Pasha Gali, was assassinated; in 1911 President Caceres of the Dominican Republic; in 1912 yet another Spanish prime minister, Canalejas y Mendes. In 1913 President Francisco Madero of Mexico was the most important victim; and in 1914 the Archduke Franz Ferdinand, whose case, precipitating the First World War, is studied in Chapter Six.

These are not all; they are only the major items in a list which, for that half-century, was twice as long. And if one were to add the attempts which failed, the mere list of names would occupy a couple of pages.

*

In order that they shall be governed and enabled to live and work peacefully, men are obliged to set other men in authority over them. These leaders, raised to greatness by election or born to it under systems of hereditary monarchy, are our scapegoats.

Lord Acton's dictum that power corrupts sounds, like so much philosophy and history, more impressive than it is, for it is beside any political point of importance: any man who believes himself fit to lead and direct other men is, fortunately for those of us who repudiate the job with real or feigned disgust, corrupt before he even begins; someone has to do the dirty work.

But it is vitally important to face the fact that, where the methods of ridding ourselves of these doers of dirty work, evolved by social and political scientists from Aristotle to Marx, fail, we have literally no recourse but assassination; and today this truth has become much more important than ever in Man's

---

* Alex Comfort, *Darwin and the Naked Lady*, Routledge & Kegan Paul, 1961.

history. Consider this passage from Alex Comfort's *Darwin and the Naked Lady*:

'. . . the behaviour which evolved to keep primitive hominids from killing their parents has made us able to think. Vulnerable to symbolism, prone to anxieties of which we do not know the nature, and prone to express them concretely. . . .'*

Thus though our psyches are rigged to avoid actual killing, it is still fairly easy for us to give expression to the ancient parricidal urge, in tyrannicide, even though the leader-father be not, strictly speaking, a tyrant. But since we have a rational side to our nature, we usually need a reason for killing to justify the wish to kill. That, of course, is why every modern war is given a reason by the leaders responsible for waging it. Does the modern assassin also seek reasons? Almost invariably, yes.

'. . . conceptual thought has given us science, but the accessory consequences of the same psychological pattern have given us the neurotic behaviour which is employing science in projects which threaten human survival. Man's ability to employ his mind in the hard-centred control of mind may prove, in our time, the supreme example of an adaptation making possible the survival of a species – '†

This is a passage which I implore the reader, and especially the American reader, to bear in mind whenever I ask him to consider the pros and cons of leader-killing without regard to his own shrinking from violence.

Towards the end of his life Tolstoy, one of the very few secular saints (except to his unfortunate wife) in the history of mankind, said that he regarded '. . . all governments as intricate institutions, sanctified by tradition and custom, for the purpose of committing by force and with impunity the most revolting crimes . . . national governments whose evil, and above all whose futility is in our time becoming more and more apparent'. And if we consider, first carefully putting off those sanctifying rosy-tinted spectacles of tradition and custom, what the national governments of the world have done, are doing, and will continue to do,

* Comfort, op. cit. 　　　　　　† ibid.

in our own lifetime, it is impossible not to agree with this opinion.
Now clearly only criminals are attracted to the task of manning a
criminal institution. It is, therefore, not unreasonable to put this
argument forward as a justification for assassinating, i.e. executing,
political chiefs.

There is another powerful argument which also leads to this
conclusion. Alex Comfort, whom I have already quoted, says:

'There is no private outlet for irrational aggression compatible with
our own self-respect. The proper alternative is to transmute it into
rational direct action, purposive and if possible level-headed resentment
against abuses, which will bring the rest of society into line with its
own moral pretensions.'*

On the other hand, the argument which follows below may be
used to urge that assassination of politicians is unjust, for, by the
definition I am going to adopt, the criminal politicians, and all
politicians are more or less and necessarily criminals, are no more
than personifications of the criminal element in ourselves: the
great Anarchists, from Proudhon to Tolstoy and Kropotkin, and
even as far back as Godwin, regarded man as naturally good, so
that evil in the leader could not be excused as a reflection of evil
in the led. I am unable to agree with this, but there is also this to
be said: in so far as men of good will try to root out the evil in
themselves and behave gently, and in so far as most ordinary
people are men of good will, are we not at least entitled, and
perhaps even bound, to destroy the representatives of evil in our
public life, the users of force, the wagers of war?

It is surely the case that as the personification of a *crowd*† –
nation, party, religious or political sect – the incarnation of the
crowd-mind or crowd-spirit, the leader is obliged to break tabus
which govern the individuals composing that crowd, when it is
expedient to do so. He must kill (as a judge or soldier), though the
law condemns killing; he must lie and cheat (as diplomat or

---

* Comfort, op. cit.
† Throughout this book I use this word in the sense of Elias Canetti in *Crowds and Power*
already cited. A crowd is a more or less dense collection of men gathered together as a
nation, sect, or party and displaying psychologically peculiar 'crowd' behaviour. Canetti's
book should be read by everyone who has a vote.

finance minister), though strong custom condemns lying and cheating; he must be merciless, though the crowd's religion calls for mercy. In short the leader, be he monarch, president, prime minister, or wazir, pope, presbyter, or rabbi, is there to enable his crowd to survive by continuing to obey the 'natural law' of ruthless competitiveness which the crowd, in the striving of its nobler elements towards a higher level of culture and courtesy, towards justice and mercy and good manners and such other unnatural goods, is trying to repudiate.

Anthropologists say that in the past the scapegoat role of the priest-king was explicit; he was put to death because it was expedient that a king die for the people. The rite of killing the king, or a substitute king, is usually represented as fertility magic; the king died but he was reborn in his successor and thus set an example to the corn which was accordingly also reborn so that the people could eat. There is another explanation: the king took all the sins of the people on himself and by dying atoned for them; that, according to Christians, is what Christ did for the people, and if it was so, then Christ, as priest-king of the Jews, was following a very ancient precedent.

But dying is not the only service which a leader can render: a politician or a soldier who does such evil work as declaring and waging war; a judge or an executioner who takes blood-guilt on his head by putting a man to death – these and other servants of the people commit sins for the people; it is beside the point whether they do so because they are exceptionally noble or because they are exceptionally ignoble. But such great men are no longer killed as a matter of ritual course to cleanse the soul of the people; on the contrary, unless the assassin, appointing himself as a sort of priest for the people, take a hand, they are apt to survive into a tiresome old age in excellent health, and to be buried at long last in Westminster Abbey or in the Parthenon; and, there-after, to be deified like Alexander, Caesar, Napoleon, Lenin, and, as in due course he doubtless will be, Adolf Hitler. Nor is this surprising: for, in time, we come to realize that the wickedness done by our heroes was no more than what was in our own souls; in the souls of the crowd which the hero ruled and served.

But from time to time the old sacrifice of the leader is still made and great men are put to death for the very reason that they do personify a crowd and act for it – be it nation, sect, or party. They are slain not as persons but as powers; in other words, they still occasionally fill the ancient role of scapegoat. It is expedient, and good political sense, to choose as such scapegoat a man who has committed one of the two most pernicious abuses of power: he who, like Shelley's Cenci, has allowed his role as incarnate safety valve, as outrager-in-ordinary of the moral code to the people, to get so out of hand that he becomes merely and solely a criminal, freed by the headiness of great office from all controlling inhibitions (Hitler is the obvious case in point, but there have been innumerable others); and he who lives too long and will not renounce his power. As William Faulkner wrote in *Intruder in the Dust*, 'No man can cause more grief than one clinging blindly to the vices of his ancestors.'* Such is the leader who accomplishes a reaction by appealing to the traditions of his crowd.

In our own time brave and self-sacrificing men have sought by turning assassin to rid us of a burden of evil by killing a single man.

The attempted assassination of Chancellor Adolf Hitler may perhaps have been a manifestation of 'conscience' finding expression in the assassin's act. Whatever the manifest intention of the assassins, there was perhaps also a latent one: to cleanse the crowd of sin by sacrificing a scapegoat. It seems to me an oversimplification to talk of the would-be assassins of Adolf Hitler as trying only to save the German people from the further consequences of their Führer's wickedness: his evil was their evil; the would-be assassins were surely trying to rid themselves and their fellow Germans of the scapegoat on whose head they had succeeded in accumulating the sins which, as ordinary cowardly individuals, they would have committed, but dared not commit, until he released the evil in them.

Common murder which has been premeditated is the basest and most revolting of crimes, if only because it reveals in the murderer unawareness of another life as real, that unawareness

---

* William Faulkner, *Intruder in the Dust*, Chatto & Windus, 1949.

which, I have read, the Buddhists regard as the unforgiveable sin. But it does not seem to me that we should regard the dedicated assassin in a disinterested cause, as a criminal; or political, religious, or nationalist assassinations as crimes of murder. I shall not so consider them in this book. The leader or chieftain of a crowd, whether that crowd be nation, sect, or party, accepts and perhaps glories in a situation outside ordinary humanity. In Britain and America we try to pretend that this is not so; we pay to democracy the empty tribute of calling a president by his initials, a prime minister by his Christian name.* But, in fact, the power of glamour, of that 'divinity which doth hedge a king', inflates even little men, enlarges a Neville Chamberlain, a Khrushchev, or a Harry Truman; while such considerable men as Winston Churchill, Stalin, or Charles de Gaulle are blown up past recognition as human beings. That is why the man in great office, alone of mankind, is capable of giving expression in his life to the idea and feeling we call *tragedy*. The great tragedies of the Greek, the English, and the French dramatic literatures are all concerned with men in great places. Strive though we may to admire the common man, ourselves, to write novels and plays about him, he cannot be and never is a figure of tragedy; not enough is staked on him, and as the great comic writers of our time have depicted him, Joyce, for example, Proust and Becket, he lives and dies ridiculous and in vain.

While, therefore, I do not urge going to the lengths of the Nechayev–Bakunin *Revolutionary Catechism* – 'Between the revolutionary and society there is war to the death, incessant, irreconcilable. . . . He must make a list of those who are condemned to death and expedite their sentence according to the order of their relative iniquities. . . .' – still I do not believe that it is wrong to assassinate a chieftain in the sense that it is wrong to murder your wife's lover or your rich aunt. There is a good analogue: by ancient and general consent a soldier who kills as an act of war is not guilty of any crime although homicide is against

---

* The ablest tyrants always know this: the emperor and god Augustus, enjoying the substance of supreme power, was always scrupulous in avoiding the monarchial titles; and J. V. Stalin was simply Secretary of the Communist party of the U.S.S.R.

the law in all civilized countries; the priest of his religion will
absolve him in advance and bless his weapons. Now assassination
of the only kind which *is* of interest is an act of war and should be
judged by the same standards. Moreover, it spares the guiltless.
In practice it very often is so judged, and, for example, William
Tell is a hero to the Swiss, and Gavrilo Princip, assassin of the
Archduke Franz Ferdinand, a hero to the Serbs and Croats.
Cromwell and the Commonwealth regicides (the cases here are of
judicial assassination, for neither Charles nor Louis had broken
capital law), and the French Revolutionary regicides, are far from
being seen as criminals except by a few extreme monarchists.
To some they were political heroes, to others military heroes since
their killings were acts of war; for others the assassins were doing
for them the act of parricide they could not accomplish for themselves. For if Freud was right in his Oedipus argument, the
mental shift from tyrannicide to parricide cannot be difficult.

I do not write these things as mere assertions and without good
authority: great and much honoured leaders and thinkers have
very often called upon their followers to use assassination as a
political means, and they have done so openly and proudly, without any of the shame which would have been natural to them had
they felt that they were calling for a base criminal act, a sin
against humanity, a mere murder. Priests, poets, and philosophers
have done this, as well as politicians. Alfieri, prophet of Italian
freedom and unity, exalted tyrannicide and propounded the
'theory of the dagger' as a valid political method. His theory was
adopted, developed, and put into practice by the secret political
society formed to restore liberty and called the Carbonari;* and
the Carbonari influence was strong in introducing assassination
into Russian revolutionary politics. Both the Italians and the
Russians, the leading exponents and practitioners of assassination
in modern times, had good philosophical, theological, and even
saintly authority for the right to assassinate; the Italians in the
writings of St Thomas Aquinas which greatly influenced, for

---

* It means 'coal merchants'; the business was used as a cover for the conspiracy; among
distinguished Carbonari were Lafayette, and, it is probable, Louis Napoleon Bonaparte
as a young man.

example, Mazzini. St Thomas Aquinas held that an individual had the right of resistance to tyranny based on natural law, even to the extent of assassinating the tyrant for the common good; such an act was, in certain defined conditions, an act of noble self-sacrifice.*

I gather that modern thinkers do not recognize any 'natural law'; and the concept is very difficult to define; but both the Catholic and the humanist rationalist thinkers who referred to it in all cases of difficulty believed in its existence and thought of it as something fundamental and excellent. For example, Abbot Yosif Volotsky also took his stand on natural law when he gave the Russians the same licence as Aquinas gave the Latins, towards the end of the fifteenth century.†

The important thing for these and other thinkers was purity of heart; the assassin must be disinterested and ready to sacrifice his own life. In his *Road to Sarajevo*,‡ Vladimir Dedijer says that before Mazzini gave Antonio Gallenga his consent to assassinate King Carlo Alberto of Sardinia, he was careful first to examine Gallenga personally, to ensure that the would-be assassin had no personal grudge against the King. The spirit in which this examination was made is clear, for Mazzini has left us a very forthright statement of his own attitude to assassination in a letter (1865) to Daniele Manin:

'Holy in the hand of Judith is the sword which cut the life of Holofernes; holy is the dagger which Harmodius crowned with flowers; holy is the dagger of Brutus; holy is the poinard of the Sicilian who initiated the vespers; holy is the arrow of Tell. When justice is extinguished and the terror of a single tyrant denies and obliterates the conscience of the people and God, who wished them free, and when a man unblemished by hatred and base passion, solely for the Fatherland and for the external right incarnate in him rises against the tyrant, and exclaims: "You torture millions of my brothers, you withhold from

---

* Tyrannicide: '. . . the killing of a tyrant by a private person for the common good' – *Catholic Encyclopaedia*. But this work parts company with Aquinas; it concedes the right of a whole people to active resistance, thus sanctioning revolution, but not of the individual to assassinate the tyrant.
† V. Valdenburg, *Drovnie Russkie Ucheniya o Predalakh Tsarkoi Vlasti*, Moscow, 1910.
‡ Vladimir Dedijer, *The Road to Sarajevo*, MacGibbon & Kee, 1967.

them that which God has decreed theirs, you destroy their bodies and corrupt their souls; through you my country is dying a lingering death; you are the keystone of an entire edifice of slavery, dishonour and vice; I overthrow that edifice by destroying you," I recognize in that manifestation of the tremendous equality between the master of millions and a single individual, the finger of God. Many feel in their hearts as I do, and I express it.'*

The dagger which Harmodius crowned with flowers, and the dagger of Brutus, executed men who had done great and necessary work for their countries, but work which, because it entailed abuse and breach of the laws and customs sacred to those countries and to their people, called not merely for a great man but for a great criminal. This argument can best be understood if we take a man of our own time as a case in point, a man who was not, but certainly deserved to be, assassinated.

J. V. Stalin was unquestionaly a great criminal. But, doing the work of re-creating a nation and laying the foundation of a new civilization, he was, equally, without doubt, by far the greatest creative statesman of the twentieth century, the first to work on the scale of Julius Caesar's task, or rather on a much greater one, since Caesar's time. Reading even the brief account of his work in, for example, Sir Bernard Pares's *History of Russia*, one realizes that he did the things that had to be done; and that no good gentleman could have done them. Later, smaller, kinder men have heaped upon his head the guilt of the Russian nation for those necessary crimes. Stalin was the perfect assassinee, the leader who ought to have been destroyed the moment his work was done, who was not, as far as we know (but that is not very far), assassinated.

The kindly and probably gentle reader, shrinking from the contemplation of such acts of bloody violence as we are here discussing so coldly, will probably ask, 'But why *assassinate* the leader whose work is done, to prevent him from ruining it? Why not remove him from office by decent constitutional means?' There are a number of reasons, and the first is that, as a

* Quoted in Valdenberg, op. cit. It is important to emphasize that this is from the pen of a respectable middle-class politician.

rule, such removal is impossible without violence. In 1945–7 the British, with awe-inspiring political sense and levelheadedness, got rid at once of their victorious war leader; and it is significant that the Americans, the French, and the Russians, who all cherished theirs, were deeply shocked. Eisenhower, de Gaulle, and Stalin all wrought evil in their several ways which the war-glamour enabled them to do. Secondly, the violent death of a leader at the end of an epoch or of a crisis serves a valuable psychological purpose, is, as it were, cathartic; it puts a that's-that to the conclusion of the epoch or crisis in question and clears the air for the next stage in the society's struggle.

The German Romantics were not at all behind the Italians in their enthusiasm for assassination, and their chief and eloquent spokesman in the cause is Schiller, to whose *William Tell* the reader is referred. The act of Karl Ludwig Sand in assassinating Kotzbue (Jena, 1819) was in the very spirit of that poem. Thus priests, poets, and philosophers license the dagger in the assassin's hand as readily as they license the bayonet or the H-bomb in the soldier's.

American readers may well find these truths disagreeable and painful and be anxious either to deny the truth of what I have written and am about to write, or to repudiate the thinkers whose opinions touching this subject I have tried to give or shall try to give. I believe it to be as necessary for them to resist these feelings, natural and praiseworthy though they be, as it is necessary, according to their own and my own respected leaders of church and state during many centuries, to overcome and even to reverse their equally natural distaste for war in which not one or two, but one or two million, men are apt to be killed. As for English readers, they may perhaps, even in 1969, be inclined to dismiss all this as very alien to the English spirit, conduct confined rather to the more excitable peoples; and to feel complacent about English compassion and good sense, those qualities which they are all sure they possess and which enable them to eschew such excesses. They would be mistaken; for we do not have to look to romantic Germans, excitable Americans, and passionate Italians for vindication of assassination in a good cause. We have an excellent authority at home and may fairly claim that the English showed other Europeans the way to justify assassination, in practice in the judicial assassination of Charles I; in theory in the writings of Milton and John Locke. Locke, for example, in *Of Civil Government*, wrote this: 'Whoever uses force without right . . . puts himself into a state of war with those against whom he uses it, and in that case all former ties are cancelled, all other Rights cease and everyone has a right to defend himself and resist the aggressor.'

Locke himself had an authority to refer to, other than Aquinas, or rather the Natural Law which he, too, revoked: for the sub-title of Milton's *The Tenure of Kings and Magistrates* published earlier in the century was: 'Proving that it is lawful and hath been held so through all ages to call to account a tyrant or wicked king and after due conviction to depose and put him to death, if the ordinary magistrates have neglected or denied to do it. . . .'

It is true that in the English, as opposed to the Italian and German cases of justification, it is *the people*, not an individual, who are vested by natural law with the right to kill the tyrant; there is not quite so clear a licence to assassinate. But there is an element of quibbling, of that evasiveness and moral shiftiness which makes the English spirit so difficult for simple-minded Latins and simple-hearted Slavs, bluff Germans, honest Americans, and logical Frenchmen to understand: for, by the laws of England, the Cromwellians had no more right to put Charles I to death than had Princip by the laws of the Austro-Hungarian empire to kill Franz Ferdinand. To put it in a less critical way, so strong is our feeling for democracy that we feel that what the majority decides is right, *is* right. Nor, in a very large and not fully integrated society, is an absolute 'consensus' required to make a very 'sensible' difference between mere murder and assassination. No consensus of the whole people of the United States 'justified' the killing of either John Kennedy, Martin Luther King, or Robert Kennedy. But can it seriously be denied that in each case there were enough people – millions, perhaps tens of millions who, secretly or half-secretly, approved with all their hearts of these assassinations – to remove the acts from the sector in which we place ordinary common murder, and put them into a special category: the category of acts, whose terrible aspect is, if not 'justified' (in the theological sense), at least mitigated by a very strong symbolic attribute which gives them nearly the quality of a rite? It is, indeed, because of this attribute that we can properly regard these killings as 'tragedy'; whereas an ordinary murder of an ordinary man – the author or his reader – can never be tragic because it is socially and politically and even 'spiritually' meaningless; is, in brutal fact, only a kind of uninteresting accident.

But no jurist or moralist could honestly and unequivocally agree to regard as legitimate an unlawful act merely because a lot of people and not merely one man or a small caucus of men consent to it. The physical executioner of Charles I and the man who operated the guillotine when the head on the block was Louis XVI's were neither more nor less guilty than Princip, who was the self-appointed but nationally approved executioner, for his particular 'crowd', of their particular 'scapegoat'.

Morally, no line can be drawn between tyrannicide outside the law by an individual and the same act committed by a caucus, a mob, a constituent assembly or a committee of public safety; in short, by a crowd. In practice we simply condemn the assassin whose cause fails to triumph; and either forget or honour the assassin whose act brings his cause success.

*

In this book I do not propose to pay any attention to mere murder, that is to homicides of political leaders committed for personal reasons or by lunatics. I shall confine myself to two main classes of homicide: socially or politically motivated assassinations; and assassinations designed to forward the cause of oppressed peoples. And I shall show that it is not difficult to distinguish the useful and profitable cases from the useless and unjustifiable. That there are 'useful and profitable' cases is surely not in doubt. For we have to face the fact that we have a permanent battle with our own rulers, for life and liberty, on our hands; and although there are objections to working off unconscious aggressions on the Establishment, there are much worse things we could do with them. Nothing is easier than to call active resisters to

authority lunatics; but can any man disturbed to the point of
violence by political and military trends really be called mad?
Revolt against abuse of power can fairly be considered an adaptive
character favouring survival, given the dominance behaviour of
world leaders.

This argument calls for some enlargement. What I mean by it
comes to this: that one of the hazards which have threatened, and
which continue to threaten the survival of our species, is the
dominance behaviour of its leaders (remember Canetti's crowd-
leader desiring, in his heart of hearts, to be the only man left alive
on top of a pile of corpses); that natural selection endows species
with 'adaptive characters' enabling them to ensure the survival of
the species; that there is, consequently, in civilized man a 'natural'
capacity to react violently to prevent a leader or leaders from continuing to behave in a manner which endangers the species. (From
the point of view of any particular group of men, who can only
judge 'genotypically', their group *is* the whole species; cf. a single
individual animal fighting for its life is fighting, willy-nilly, to
preserve the species.) So the assassin – the genuine assassin, not the
murderous lunatic – is, as it were, that particularly sensitive cell
of the social body which reacts first and most quickly to preserve
the social body.

Since there is a loose and vague but very general objection to
'justifiable' homicide excepting in a state of war, I should say
something about where I stand morally. The fact is, I don't: I
resist, with, I confess, very little difficulty, the temptation, which
is slight, to strike moral attitudes of any kind. My argument, if
reproached, would be as follows: I have myself killed a quite
considerable number of fellow men in war and have been com-
mended for it; I believe myself incapable of murder. But I refuse
to pretend that after what I have done for my country, and seen
other men do for theirs, that I can still hold human life sacred.
The fact is that from 25,000 B.C. to about A.D. 1850 men were not
aware of what, in the human race's strife to control its environ-
ment and its own nature, was happening to other men elsewhere,
not aware of the hundreds of thousands dying in wars, famines
and pestilences. But since the rise of the press, radio, and TV the

eye sees and the heart must grieve. The fact remains, the very ugly fact, that mass dying is part of the human condition. If we do not like this fact we now have the means to change it, by over-throwing every old institution and by taking control of ourselves psychologically and biologically. It remains true and terrible that a man's death – and therefore the deaths of millions – is, in nature, and under the aspect of eternity, a completely insignificant and, indeed, meaningless event, unless we make it significant and meaningful by putting it into a social context. And I note that there are large exceptions to the rule against homicides: for example, in some countries the *crime passionnel*, and in all formerly and most still, judicial killing as punishment, are admitted. In England the abolition of the death penalty – judicial homicide – was bitterly opposed by the entire judiciary. In all countries without exception, homicide in the course of warfare is honoured and rewarded. Both morally and logically the kind of assassin-ation I am interested in should benefit from the same dispensation as killing in war. For Locke's point cannot be denied – and we have seen that he had saintly authority for it – the oppressor, the tyrant, puts himself in a state of war with his fellow citizens and his servants: to kill him is not an act of civil murder; it is a military act; it can be an act of law; it can even be an act of religion.*

Granting all this, can we admit the would-be assassin's right (granting him also to be disinterested and even noble in his determination) to judge, condemn, and execute? Most people would say '*No*', though we do concede the right of an individual to judge, condemn and order execution; for example, to Presi-dent Johnson to judge, condemn, and put to death the Vietcong. I do not propose to argue this point, for I hope that an answer will emerge in the course of the following narratives. But it is at least worth noting that so strongly did the British feel about this in the past that an attempt to take away the right to judge, condemn, and execute a chief-of-state from the individual citizen (or even refugee foreigner), once led to the fall of an

---

* We should never forget that the Christian mass is a symbol for cannibalism, for god-eating or hero-eating.

English government led by a popular statesman. When, in 1858, the Italian patriot Orsini attempted, with Mazzini's *a posteriori* approval, to assassinate Napoleon III, the French government, on the grounds that Orsini had manufactured his bombs in England, publicly declared that: '. . . the law of England affords an improper degree of shelter and countenance to foreign refugees and incendiaries and that in neglecting to take means of preventing such conspiracies as that which has nearly proved fatal to the emperor's life, England has not acted the part of a faithful and sincere ally'.*

The prime minister was Palmerston; and as a result of this reproof he introduced a Bill to amend the law touching the crime of conspiracy to commit murder. The House of Commons, in those days still an effective and independent part of the government and not, as it is now, a slightly absurd though occasionally well-meaning cipher, threw the Bill out by a narrow majority (234 to 215), whereupon Palmerston, having been told that 'for the sake of mankind we should do nothing to circumscribe the liberties of England', resigned.

*

Where, finally, does English law stand on this question? Section 3 (1) of the Extradition Act of 1870 reads:

'A fugitive criminal shall not be surrendered if the offence in respect of which his surrender is demanded is one of a political character, or if he prove to the satisfaction of the police magistrate or the court before whom he is brought on habeas corpus, or to the Secretary of State, that the requisition for his surrender has in fact been made with a view to try or punish him for an offence of a political character.'

The legal light I have consulted tells me that the phrase 'an offence of a political character' has attracted much litigation and the judges have consistently refused to lay down a hard-and-fast definition. But consider the precedent created by the first case to be tried under this section, *In Re Castioni* (1891) 1 Q.B. 149: a

* *Annual Register.*

number of Swiss being dissatisfied with the government of their canton, rose in rebellion, attacked and took by force the local government building, disarmed the gendarmes, and established a provincial government of their own. One of the rebels killed a member of the old government during the fighting, and escaped to England. The court refused to extradite him, on the grounds that the murder for which he was wanted by the Swiss government was 'incidental to and formed part of a political disturbance and therefore was an offence of a political character'. Denman, J., observed: 'The question really is whether upon the facts it is clear that the man was acting as one of a number of persons engaged in acts of violence of a political character with a political object and as part of the political movement and rising in which he was taking part.'

Nothing could be clearer than that; and consider a pronouncement made by Lord Goddard, C.J., in a subsequent case under the same section:

'Let me try to illustrate this by taking a case of murder. The evidence adduced by the requisitioning state shows that the killing was committed in the course of a rebellion. This at once shows the offence to be political; but if the evidence merely shows that the prisoner killed another person by shooting him on a certain day, evidence may be given . . . to show that the shooting took place in the course of a rebellion.'

In short, English courts will not give up to a foreign government a man who, having committed a clearly and demonstrably *political* assassination on behalf of a recognized political cause, has fled to England for sanctuary.*

* I feel obliged to issue a clear and specific warning to all British Commonwealth citizens that they must not, and cannot, rely on these legal rulings. They are, in this as in other respects, worse off than aliens. If there is a Bantu rising and a Bantu assassinates the South African prime minister and takes refuge in Britain, he should not be surrendered to the South Africa police, because South Africa is not in the Commonwealth. But supposing the rising to be of Australian aborigines and the victim the Australian prime minister, since extradition between Britain and Commonwealth countries is governed by the Fugitive Offenders Act of 1881, the courts would have no power to refuse extradition of the refugee Aboriginal assassin. It should, further, be added that, law or no law, so strongly, albeit tacitly, organized is the 'International' of boss politicians, that the assassin of the most villainous rascal of a leader in any non-Communist country would be as unwise to

So it is hardly going too far to claim that the would-be assassin in a socially or politically admissible cause has a licence from St Thomas Aquinas, John Locke, the British House of Commons, and the highest court in the English judicature, four ponderously respectable authorities.

rely on safe asylum in the U.K. as the assassin of the most saintly leader in a Communist country would be safe in doing so.

Part One

1

RELIGIOUS WAR BY ASSASSINATION

WHEN a nation goes to war, the men who are safest from the prospect of being wounded or killed are the political leaders – kings, presidents, or prime ministers – who declare war, and the generals and admirals who direct the fighting. They put the lives of millions in jeopardy but are themselves usually safe. Even the most modern war weapons are less likely to kill them than any of their subjects, constituents, or administrees, because they are provided with the most resistant and sophisticated shelters, even if nobody else is. It was not always so; kings and generals led their own men into battle; but they have learned wisdom. It is natural enough that the great men of a crowd should use their power to save their own skins by respecting a tacit agreement with the leaders of alien crowds not to make war on each other personally. But there is a justification for it, too, for in theory at least their work of managing the nation at war and directing the fighting once a state of war exists is of vital importance to their people. In truth, of course, it would very rarely make much difference to the progress and outcome of a war if the government were replaced by a different one and all the generals replaced by other men. But there are sufficient exceptions in history to make most of us feel that our leaders' lives are more valuable to the nation than our own.

Arthur Koestler has suggested (originally in a lecture delivered in Copenhagen) that we stand in greatest danger of totally destructive war not because of our aggressiveness but because of some of our (conventionally considered) noblest sentiments: love of our own crowd, loyalty to it and its leader. Gallantly, heroically, moved by love, we are ready to die for our side and its captain. Elias Canetti, in the work I have referred to, long since went deeply into and identified this passionate desire of men to come together in denser and denser crowds and to lose individual identity in them. This makes it quite easy for the leader, who is himself a product of the same propensity (either the nucleus about which the crowd forms, or the element of it secreted, as it were, to give expression to the crowd's will-to-action), to go to war.

Let us, at all events, agree for argument's sake with the mighty men in high places that their lives must be preserved at all costs – at the cost, for instance, of our own. In that case, since the same must be as true for the enemy crowd as for our own, the most terrible and paralysing blow we could strike against an enemy in war would be to destroy his leaders – not his common soldiers helpless without a commander-in-chief, but the commander-in-chief himself and the general staff; not his ordinary men, women, and children cowering under our mutilating high explosives, our blinding and flesh-searing napalm, our genocidal H-bombs, but his heads of government departments without whom his country would, we are presuming, fall into chaos and despair; just as, in communities of rats, social rules fail, vice triumphs, and the individual rats become degenerate unless there be one old male among them accepted by all as the leader.

In short, and obviously, the proper target for a government at war is the enemy government. And I believe that this ought to be recognized and acted upon, that we should prepare and train commandos to wage war by assassination on the enemy's leaders; and that this should be a military priority. Admittedly such a war would be difficult to wage; the national leaders would protect themselves even more carefully and more strongly than they already do. But it is unlikely that determined, brave, self-sacrificing men, trained and equipped by and with every resource of modern technology, would fail to destroy the enemy leadership. I find it very difficult to believe that a commando of dedicated assassins could not have been trained by the British or Russians or Americans to kill Hitler, Himmler, and Göring; or by the Germans to kill Stalin, Churchill, and Roosevelt, not to mention the generals on both sides.

It has been suggested to me by a reader of this book (in MS.), who should know what he is talking about, that the United States and the Soviet Union certainly, and other powers probably, do, already, through their Intelligence and Security forces, use assassination when necessary. But at that level I would rather call it common murder. The sort of men they employ –

> I know two dull, fierce outlaws
> Who think man's spirit as a worm's and they
> Would trample out for any slight caprice
> The meanest or the noblest life . . . .
> They sell
> What we want.*

– and the shady, shameful gloaming in which they work will not do at all. Our assassins of the other crowd's leaders must, if we are not to lose our self-respect, benefit from the same nobility-and-self-sacrifice mystique as do our soldiers.

There is not really anything against this in our traditions of chivalry: as I've said, kings and generals formerly exposed their lives by leading their troops. In fact, political leadership as an institution derives from war-leadership, from the idea of the hero of great prowess elected to bear the brunt of battle. And in any case, we have long since reverted to primitive behaviour in war, to waging war on women and children, as well as on the enemy's soldiers, and no holds are barred.

Since it seems that, despite reason, despite good will, despite economic pressure and all the other forces which ought by now

* Percy Bysshe Shelley, *The Cenci*.

to have made war a thing of the past, we are to go on using war as one of the means of regulating our foreign relations, at least until Julien Benda's dream can be realized, I advocate this innovation of waging war by assassination of the enemy's leaders because I believe it would save millions of lives and untold suffering. To put the argument in the most cynical terms, political and military leaders, no longer reared in a tradition of leader self-sacrifice, no longer accepting the idea and feeling that the chieftain must fight in front of his people, and not behind them, would naturally be far more anxious to keep the peace if their own lives were the first to be endangered by war, and their survival unlikely. And to put it in terms more honourable to these mighty men, the assassination, one after another, of leaders as they rose courageously to take the places of the already assassinated, could not but bring war to an end much sooner if it be true, as such leaders themselves believe, that the number of men capable of effective leadership is very limited.

To the best of my knowledge only one government in the history of mankind has used the means of assassination, deliberately, and in preference to the war which is so much less economical of life and treasure, in its strife with foreign powers. Many governments, including those of Napoleon I, Benito Mussolini's Fascist Italy, the Third Reich, and the U.S.S.R. have used assassination occasionally in war; and possibly that of Great Britain, for certainly the French believe that a British government hired assassins to kill Napoleon Bonaparte, a perfectly sensible course if true. As for the United States, it is, as I have said, believed in some circles that various government agencies and quasi-official agencies have repeatedly made use of assassination against Socialists, directly or indirectly. But there has, on the whole, been a kind of tacit agreement between top men not to shoot at each other, even in war, even on the battlefield. And only the Ismaili Old Men of the Mountains,* with their trained *Hashashi* (whence our word *assassin*), made exclusive use of assassination, to the great benefit of their people who thus for

* Old Man of the Mountains is from Sheikh-al-Jebal and is more correctly translated Prince or Chieftain of the Mountains.

centuries escaped one common misery of mankind, the suffering, waste, and agony of war.

It is not unusual to see the history of that Ismailian sect founded by Hasan ibn-al-Sabbah, the first Old Man of the Mountains, and of the Assassins, treated as legend. In fact, however, it is well-documented history. It is, briefly, as follows:

A sect of Moslems, the Ismaili Shias, held that the descendants of Mahomet's cousin and son-in-law Ali ended with the seventh Imam, whose name was Ismail. Consequently, Ismail was the last Imam they recognized. Their prosperity as a sect dates from their establishment, in the Fatimid dynasty (named after Fatima, the Prophet's daughter and Ali's wife) as rulers of North Africa and Egypt, whence they sent out missionaries all over the Dar-al-Islam. The most active and able of these missionaries was Hasan ibn-al-Sabbah, whose field was Persia. And there, in 1090, he set up an independent sovereignty dominated by mountain fortresses in the neighbourhood of Alamut, his headquarters; and there founded his independent sub-sect of fanatical Ismailis.

It was only two centuries later, and in their new centre in Syria, that they became known to Europe as the 'Hashashi', that is hashish-eaters. This is the only part of the story which may be merely legendary: it is said that the young men chosen and trained to assassinate the public enemies of the Alamut Ismailis were promised paradise by their leaders; that they were given a foretaste of paradise by being doped with hashish; and that their dependence on the drug made them utterly subservient to their masters, the Old Men of the Mountains.

Hashish is *Cannabis sativa*, Indian hemp, better known to us as marihuana or, vulgarly, pot. Hashish-eating or smoking is very common in our great cities today; some of my own friends have tried it. I can find no evidence that it ever gives its consumers a foretaste of paradise; it appears to be a fairly mild, relatively harmless, slightly anaphrodisiac stimulant. In Turkey, among other countries, hashish is regarded as much less harmful than alcohol. In short, it does not seem to be sufficiently delightful in its effects, or sufficiently habit-forming, to be useful as a means of blackmailing its 'addicts'.

However, whether or not the emissaries of the Old Men of the Mountains were or were not given hashish, does not really matter. They were, doped or sober, the first consistently trained and politically used assassins in history. As a matter of fact, Marco Polo, as good an authority as any, says nothing of hashish but says that opium was the drug used. I give his account of the way the assassins were trained for what it is worth; it was written shortly after they had been exterminated by the Western Horde of the Mongol Khan, Hulagu.

'He was named Alo-eddin★ and his religion was that of Mahomet. In a beautiful valley enclosed between two lofty mountains, he had formed a luxurious garden, stored with every delicious fruit and every fragrant shrub that could be procured. Palaces of various sizes and forms were erected in different parts of the grounds, ornamented with works of gold, with paintings and with furniture of rich silks. By means of small conduits contrived in these buildings, streams of wine, milk, honey and some of pure water were seen to flow in every direction. The inhabitants of these palaces were elegant and beautiful damsels, accomplished in the arts of singing, playing upon all sorts of musical instruments and in all kinds of amorous allurement. Clothed in rich dresses they were seen constantly sporting and amusing themselves in the garden and pavilions, their female guardians being confined within doors and never suffered to appear. The object which the chief had in mind in forming a garden of this fascinating kind was this: that Mahomet having promised to those who would obey his will the enjoyments of Paradise, where every aspect of sensual gratification should be found, in the society of beautiful nymphs, he was desirous of its being understood by his followers that he was also a Prophet and the compeer of Mahomet, and had the power of admitting to Paradise such as he should choose to favour. In order that none without his licence might find their way into this delicious valley, he caused a strong and inexpugnable castle to be erected at the opening of it, through which the entry was by a secret passage. At his court likewise this chief entertained a number of youths, from the age of twelve to twenty years, selected from the inhabitants of the surrounding mountains, who showed a disposition for martial exercises and appeared to possess the quality of daring courage. To them he was in the daily practice of

★ The penultimate Old Man was, in fact, Ala-ed-din. The correct name of the last, the one Marco Polo is telling about, was Rukn-ed-din ben Ala-ed-Din.

discoursing on the subject of the Paradise announced by the prophet, and of his own power of granting admission; and at certain times he caused opium to be administered to ten or a dozen of the youths; and when half dead with sleep he had them conveyed to the several apartments of the palaces in the garden. Upon awakening from the state of lethargy, their senses were struck with all the delightful objects that have been described, and each perceived himself surrounded by lovely damsels singing, playing and attracting his regards by the most fascinating caresses, serving him also with delicate viands and exquisite wines; until intoxicated with excess of enjoyment amidst actual rivulets of milk and wine, he believed himself assuredly in Paradise, and felt an unwillingness to relinquish its delights. When four or five days had thus been passed, they were thrown once more into a state of somnolence, and carried out of the garden. Upon their being introduced to his presence and questioned by him as to where they had been, their answer was, "In Paradise, through the favour of your highness": and then before the whole court who listened to them with eager curiosity and astonishment, they gave a circumstantial account of the scenes to which they had been witnesses. The chief thereupon addressing them, said: "We have the assurances of our prophet that he who defends his lord shall inherit Paradise, and if you show yourselves devoted to the obedience of my orders, that happy lot awaits you." Animated to enthusiasm by words of this nature, all deemed themselves happy to receive the commands of their master and were forward to die in his service. The consequence of this system was, that when any of the neighbouring princes, or others, gave umbrage to this chief, they were put to death by these his disciplined assassins; none of whom felt terror at the risk of losing their own lives, which they held in little estimation, provided they could execute their master's will. On this account his tyranny became the subject of dread in all the surrounding countries. He had also constituted two deputies or representatives of himself, of whom one had his residence in the vicinity of Damascus, and the other in Kurdistan; and these pursued the plan he had established for training their young dependants. Thus there was no person, however powerful who, having become exposed to the enmity of the old man of the mountains, could escape assassination.'*

From this it is clear that (if we believe in every word of Marco Polo's account) opium, not hashish, was the drug employed; and

* Marco Polo, *The Travels of Marco Polo*, J. M. Dent (Everyman's Library), 1954.

that it was used solely to put the young men to sleep during their transport to and from 'paradise'.

The Old Men of the Mountains waged war by assassination against those leading men of their time who stood as obstacles to the propagation of their religion. That, chiefly, was the 'umbrage' which Marco Polo refers to. They raised no armies, but they put their young men through a sort of commando course in assassination which included the learning of foreign, including European, languages; the endurance of fatigue; the use of disguise; the study of alien religions; and the use of arms. In this highly specialized type of military training they were far in advance of European governments. Like the Japanese *kamikazi*, these trained assassins did not expect to return alive, but to meet the most honourable of deaths after their missions, usually carried out in public and with deliberate ostentation, had been accomplished.

To give some idea of their thoroughness; when the reigning Old Man of the Mountains decided that the great crusader Conrad of Montferrat must die, the assassins whom he sent off on that mission disguised themselves as Christian monks, entered, and were welcomed into the Crusaders' camp and stayed there, unsuspected, for six months, waiting the opportunity to kill the marquis in public. It was an important part of the Alamut Ismaili policy that their political assassinations should be publicly performed. And this is a significant fact worthy of emphasis here: the assassination was, in the first case, a religious act, and as such must be publicly performed; in the second case, if it was to be effective in its military, or rather political, object of striking terror into the hearts of leaders of crowds hostile to or hated by the Ismaili, it was important to demonstrate that the Ismaili assassins were dedicated, selfless heroes totally indifferent to their own safety. And this was equally important for the self-respect of the Ismaili crowd which must be able first of all to revere its terrible emissaries as heroes, and in the second place to be cleansed of their guilt of employing them to kill by the death of those same heroes. The Ismaili assassins, in short, united in their persons the several scapegoat roles which I have sought to show are those of the war-leader, and also took all the killing upon themselves. The Assassins must have spoken the Frankish languages correctly, been fully conversant with the Christian ritual and practices, and been men of extraordinary nerve. There can be no doubt that such able secret agents could have killed Conrad in circumstances which would have enabled them to escape with their lives; had they done so they would have been reviled as cowards and religious back-sliders when they returned home. What they actually did was to assassinate Conrad in church on a Sunday; and pay with their lives: as a jurist Aquinas might have acquitted them; as a Levite he would surely have understood them.

Certain points about the policy and methods of the Old Men of the Mountains should be made here. Does the idea of assassination as foreign policy continued in other terms horrify you? If so, it is worth while asking yourself why. Granted that men ought not to engage in killing each other, for the Ismailis the alternative to a policy of assassination was a policy of war. It is important to realize that their religion did not permit them to refrain from ridding the world of infidels and propagating their faith, any more than that of the Catholic Christians a few centuries later permitted them to refrain from torturing and burning infidels at the stake. The Ismailis were in much the same moral dilemma as the Protestants and Catholics of the seventeenth century who slaughtered each other by tens of thousands in order to save their souls. The policy of assassination meant that a small number of very important leading men were put to death by the Old Men of the Mountains during the two centuries of their history. Had they, instead, waged war, the loss of life and treasure would have been several thousand times as great.

The most distinguished victim of the Ismaili assassins, an assassinee quite as important in his day and place as was President Kennedy in our own, was the great Seljuk political economist and statesman, the Wazir Nizam ul-Mulk, author of the *Book of Government*, one of the earliest and best post-Hellenic works of political economy.

Nizam ul-Mulk rose to power under the Seljuk Sultan Alp Arslan by having his predecessor as first minister of the empire, the Wazir Kundruri, assassinated with the full knowledge and approval of the sultan. Before he died, Kundrui was able to send this message to Nizam ul-Mulk: 'An evil innovation and an ugly practice you have introduced into the world by putting to death dismissed ministers. I pray you may experience the same in your own person. . . .' Which was all very well; but Nizam knew what grave disorders in the empire might arise from faction; he was acting not as a spiteful or vengeful man, but simply as a politician who understood his ruthless trade: politics are about power.

The Seljuks were orthodox Moslems and they regarded the Fatimids, and still more the extremist Ismaili Shias, as wicked and dangerous heretics. They were, therefore, the natural enemies of the Assassins; and especially so after the Sultan Alp Arslan, and his wazir, Nizam ul-Mulk, had recovered the holy places, Mecca and Medina, from the anti-Khalifs.

In 1078 Alp Arslen was murdered: I use the word deliberately for this was not a political assassination but the outcome of a violent personal quarrel with one of his high-ranking officers. He was succeeded by Malik Shah, his son, who had the greatest reverence and affection for the Wazir Nizam. Minister and sultan worked harmoniously together to raise the living-standards, culture, and education of their subjects; one of Nizam's great works was the founding of universities in both Baghdad and Nishapur. But a statesman's domestic well-doing has never, to my knowledge, endeared him to the leading statesmen of foreign and hostile powers.

The power of the Assassins had been growing steadily. And they could not fail to realize that the man to destroy, if they were to overthrow the infidel Seljuk, was Nizam ul-Mulk. And they were right. The great Wazir's semi-disgrace had already been contrived by Malik Shah's Sultana, Turkan Khatun, whose son's claim to the succession he had opposed. His great work had thus already been checked when he was assassinated; but he was far too able a man not to have over-reached Turkan Khatan in the end. As it was, the baleful influence of Turkan Khatan became paramount with the Sultan; and although the empire held to-gether during his lifetime, it went to pieces after his death. Nizam ul-Mulk had not been given time enough to make its foundations enduring and to give it the impetus which might have carried it forward for centuries.

Thus, by the assassination of one carefully chosen man the Old Man of the Mountains' assassins can be said to have accomplished what several considerable wars waged by both Moslem and Christian enemies of the Seljuks had failed to do.

It is a case which statesmen should dwell upon. If we consider that it was inevitable that war of some kind be waged against the Seljuk empire, which of its enemies used the better means; the Christian Crusaders; the Fatimid anti-Khalifates; the Turkish khanates of Samarkhand and Bokhara, all of whom spent the lives of many thousands of men on both sides? Or the Ismaili assassins who spent the lives of one enemy and half a dozen of their own people?

The assassination of Nizam-ul-Mulk was beyond question the most important achievement of the Alamut Ismailis. But they continued to terrorize the rulers and ministers of the Dar-al-Islam, and to refrain from waging war on common men, until the year 1256, when Hulagu, chief of the Western Horde of the Mongol Empire created by his father Jenghiz Khan, undertook to extirpate them: it was a mission in which all chiefs-of-state could join with enthusiasm; in that matter, at least, they were of one opinion. Within a short time the reigning Old Man of the Mountains was dead, his fortresses in ruins, his Assassins no more.

But the Old Men of the Mountains had given a new word to the languages of Europe; and to the leaders of militarily weak countries and other crowds an interesting example. And it is a curious instance of the perversity of mankind that while we think of the mass slaughterer Jenghiz Khan, and his son Hulagu as heroes, we think of the Alamut Sheiks, whose policy of planned assassination spared so many thousand lives, as monsters; that we think of the mass-slaughterer Harry Truman, with his H-bomb, as a great war leader; of the man who shoots a single president as a villain.

2

HIPPARCHUS: THE USE OF GLAMOUR

ONCE it is conceded that there can be no moral objection to
assassination as a political act (and no less of course) than to war as
a political act, no more (and again, no less) revulsion against
sacrificing one great life to a cause the crowd feels to be a good
one than to sacrificing a thousand or a million little lives in that
cause, it is important to distinguish useful from futile assassinations; and to distinguish both from those which are pernicious
in their consequences. The only valid criterion by which we can
judge one case from another is that of the common good.

It is not, of course, always possible to identify the common
good in advance. An assassination planned and carried out by a
minority group to forward their own cause, by a small crowd
which has hived off from one of the greater crowds, may turn
out beneficial to the greater crowd. And when the assassination is
of the sacrificial type, is the assassination of a great symbol-
figure, it may have quite unexpectedly beneficial results. I have
already referred to the premonitory note in the speech by Dr
Martin Luther King before his assassination; and I have suggested
that the apparently premonitory feelings manifest in the words

and behaviour of many great assassinees may perhaps be due to guilt; they recognize the measure of primitive evil mingled with the good intentions of their political ambitions and feel the need to be punished and forgiven. Psychologists will, I think, agree that this is not as far-fetched as it sounds. But there is another possible explanation: the leader may – even if only obscurely and subconsciously – recognize that a moment has come when he can best serve his cause by dying, a scapegoat sacrifice. I do not here suggest that he thereupon arranges for his own assassination; only that these deep and obscure feelings may make him seem to be prepared for it. Shortly after King was assassinated, it began to be suggested that the pity roused in millions of white people, and their revulsion from what one of their number had done, could result in a quickening of the pace at which civil rights legislation was being put through the Congress. And, indeed, some such quickening did occur. However, as a rule it will be necessary to try to judge the worth of assassination, the political death of one man, as we try to judge the worth of war, the political death of millions: by calculation.

That assassination is useful and justifiable which relieves misery, emancipates the enslaved, decreases the sum of injustices in the world, advances a cause generally conceded to be good; a case of rare clarity which I shall come to, in point, is the assassination of the Tsar Paul I of Russia. It would, by this evidence, have been good and useful to assassinate the late Adolf Hitler, the late Benito Mussolini, and the late J. V. Stalin and a number of tyrannical dictators now living and suffering from the occupational disease of sadism; for their death could not fail to benefit their wretched peoples and all mankind, which is the rule to judge by.

There are some cases which are more difficult to judge; from the point of view of the assassins and their party, no assassination was ever more completely successful than that of the Archduke Franz Ferdinand of Austria. It did what it was intended to do, procured freedom for the Serbs and Croats. For the world, of course, the consequences were different: was there more or less injustice after than before the war of 1914–18? The question may be beside the point, since it is not likely that but for that assassination the war would never have been fought. I therefore place the assassination of Franz Ferdinand among the justified cases, as historians place the war of 1939–45, with its 16 million victims, among the justified wars.

That assassination is apparently futile which brings about no social or political change whatsoever: two cases I shall advance as examples are those of Julius Caesar and the Tsar Alexander II of Russia. And that assassination is pernicious, but may have valuable side-effects, which is bound to replace the assassinee by worse men – the case of Abraham Lincoln, for example, or President Kennedy.

When one comes to consider the case of manifestly useful assassination, we run into a very curious difficulty; there have been a number of killings which were mere murder in fact but, in their subsequent consequences, might as well have been the most nobly inspired of political assassinations. There can, for example, be very little doubt about the usefulness, in Athenian history, of the murder of Hipparchus: it was a mere murder, the motive a base personal one; but because of its grandeur in Athenian history, it is well worth a few minutes' consideration.

*

Some of the Greek democracies had such a horror of demagogic tyranny, which has always been a mortal disease of democracies, that they used to send a town-crier about the streets offering a reward in money and honour to any man who would assassinate any citizen whose conduct seemed to be designed to raise himself up as a tyrant. For over 2,000 years, most people who have heard of them believe that the Athenians Harmodius and Aristogeiton were champions of liberty who assassinated the tyrant Hipparchus. But:

'Men do not discriminate and are too ready to receive ancient traditions about their own as well as other countries. For example most Athenians think that Hipparchus was actually tyrant when he was slain by Harmodius and Aristogeiton. They are not aware that Hippias was the eldest of the sons of Peisistratus and succeeded him and that Hipparchus and Thessalus were only his brothers.'*

* Thucydides, translated into English by Benjamin Jowett, Clarendon Press, 1881.

Thus Thucydides; it should be remembered that he detested the democracy of his own country, but the fact remains that he was a writer of monumental integrity who can be relied on to tell the truth which he took pains to discover.

What the Athenians of Pericles' time believed was that two heroes of democracy, Harmodius and Aristogeiton by name, moved by a passionate determination to restore liberty and government by the people to their city, assassinated the tyrant Hipparchus and accomplished the liberation of Athens from the tyranny of the family of Peisistratus. This Peisistratus became tyrant of Athens by the usual mixture of ability and cunning backed by money. He was a dictator, but a benevolent one, somewhat in the manner of President Charles de Gaulle. He and his family did, indeed, violate the old Athenian customary law of free election to the Archonship, and law-making by the assembly of the citizens; and they did offend Athenian pride in freedom when they retained all the important offices by a combination of fraud and force; and, above all, by substituting the hereditary principle for election. But they respected the ancient laws and they were, by Thucydides' account, moderate in their tyranny. Peisistratus died in 527 B.C. and was succeeded in the tyranny by his eldest son Hippias. It should be noted that even the word tyranny was not necessarily a pejorative one at the time.

One of the most important elements of success in politics, success, that is to say, in terms of the ultimate reputation of the man of action and of what people come to believe about him and what, therefore, becomes history, is glamour. For instance, it is a fact, but not history, that Mary, Queen of Scots, was a raw-boned woman six feet tall who engaged in a squalid conspiracy to murder her husband; we have all heard her spoken of by her countrymen as if she had been a mixture of the romantic mistress of every man's dreams and Mary the mother of God; truth has been masked by glamour. And this is as well; for our own well-being the truth is pernicious and, believing in the nobility of the past, we may behave less ignobly in the present. Thus, too, glamour may transform a basely motivated murder into a nobly motivated assassination. Athenian 'morale' a century after the

murder of Hipparchus was raised in every crisis by what the
Athenians believed touching their 'heroic' liberation. They did
their best to live up to the glorious act, as they believed it to have
been, of their ancestors Harmodius and Aristogeiton.

What are the facts? The Athenians were 'liberated' by the
Lakedaimonians on behalf of their clients the Alcmaeonidae, rivals
of the Peisistidae. Hipparchus was not a tyrant, he was a younger
brother of the tyrant Hippias; and although as a member of the
Peisistidae he was certainly a man of consequence and power, he
never became the reigning tyrant. He fell in love with a young
man of his own class, Harmodius, whose affections were, however,
engaged elsewhere, and who, therefore, repelled Hipparchus'
amorous advances. Furthermore, Harmodius, as was natural, told
his lover Aristogeiton, a rich member of the rising middle class,
about Hipparchus' wooing. Aristogeiton was afraid that Hipparchus would use violence, backed by the power of the ruling
family, to gain his amorous ends. And for that reason – his
passionate love of Harmodius – began plotting to overthrow the
tyranny. Thus, neither he nor his lover were disinterested assassins; and therefore what, because of purely personal feelings, they
plotted and contrived, was not the overthrow and destruction of
a tyrant, but the elimination of a rival in love, who happened to
be the tyrant's brother.

Hipparchus, having made another attempt on the virtue, or at
least on the fidelity, of Harmodius and been again repulsed,
became resentful and made up his mind to insult Harmodius
publicly. He arranged for the young man's sister to be invited to
take part in a ritual procession; and when the girl arrived, rejected
her on the grounds that she was unworthy; we are not told what
kind of unworthiness she was accused of, but it was probably
unchastity. Harmodius, and for his sake Aristogeiton, were
furious. They had already decided to raise a revolt against the
tyrant's whole family; they now chose, for the occasion, the
festival of the Panathenaea. Their reason for this was that on that
occasion Athenian citizens taking part could carry arms without
attracting police attention, so that Harmodius, Aristogeiton, and
the other conspirators could go about armed without looking like

suspicious characters. The number of conspirators had deliberately been kept small to minimize the risk of delation; and in any
case, Aristogeiton appears to have believed that when the conspirators made their attack on Hippias and his brothers, the whole
crowd would rise, 'and assist in the recovery of their own
liberties. . . '. Thus Thucydides, who goes on:

'The day of the festival arrived, and Hippias went out of the city to
the place called Ceramicus, where he was occupied with his guards in
marshalling the procession. Harmodius and Aristogeiton, who were
ready with their daggers, stepped forward to do the deed. But seeing
one of the conspirators in familiar conversation with Hippias who was
readily accessible to all, they took alarm and imagined that they had
been betrayed and were on the point of being seized. Whereupon they
determined to take their revenge first on the man who had outraged
them and was the cause of their desperate attempt. So they rushed
just as they were, within the gates. They found Hipparchus near the
Lecorium as it was called and thereupon falling upon him with all
the blind fury, one of an injured lover, the other of a man smarting
under an insult, they smote and slew him. The crowd ran together,
and so Aristogeiton for the present escaped the guards; but he was
afterwards taken and not very gently handled. Harmodius perished
on the spot.'*

The result of this *crime passionnel* which history has falsified
into a political assassination in a noble cause, was that Hippias,
hitherto a liberal dictator as tyrants go, lost confidence, became
suspicious, and therefore oppressive in his government; and the
Athenians, until they were 'liberated' by the Lacedaimonian
intervention on behalf of the Alcmaeonid family, were worse off
than ever.

Yet within a century, and because any 'crowd' which possesses
real pyschological density and temporal continuity will always
tend to believe whatever favours the power of its collective spirit,
the Athenians were contriving to believe that Hipparchus, the
murdered man, had been tyrant at that time; and that he had
died a sacrifice to the spirit of liberty in their forefathers. There
can be no doubt about the value of this belief: political and social

* Thucydides, op. cit.

morale has no more massive buttress than faith in the noble deeds
of the past. The murder of Hipparchus, once it had been transformed by tradition, glamourized and written into history as an
assassination done by brave men in a noble cause, unquestionably
supported the spirit of Athens in moments of great trial. Moreover, as we have seen, it inspired liberators like Mazzini a couple
of thousand years later. Hipparchus and his murderers died in a
vain love quarrel; but they certainly did not die in vain.

★

But although it is true that Hipparchus, and for that matter
Harmodius and Aristogeiton, did not die in vain, the case is an
unusual one: the practical man weighing the pros and cons of
assassination as a political means, is bound to dismiss it as, at best,
inconclusive evidence, and at worst as evidence against the usefulness, to the citizens in general, of assassination.

For although it is true that by glamour this sordid murder was
turned into a source of inspiration, strength, and honour among
the Athenians for many centuries, that was a stroke of luck. It is
not possible to be sure that a crowd and its historians will glam-
ourize a murder into a noble political assassination done in a noble
cause. Such transformations wrought by time and by the fictions
industriously propagated by historians are not uncommon; but it
would be absurd to rely on one happening just to suit us.

Moreover, glamour does not always work in a useful sense.
The transformation by glamour of Brutus and his fellow conspirators from interested party-political assassins into heroes of
liberty is a case almost as outrageous as that of Harmodius and
Aristogeiton, and pernicious rather than useful in its effects. Not
Brutus but Caesar was the social progressive, the people's man.
Perhaps in all history only the assassination of Abraham Lincoln
was more squalid in its motivation than that of Julius Caesar
whose case I put forward as the supreme and instructive example
of abuse of assassination. Yet, as we shall see, even this assassination served a very useful political purpose, since not only did the
assassins fail to advance their own cause, they ensured, in the
event, the triumph of the opposing side.

3

JULIUS CAESAR: PARTY POLITICAL ASSASSINATION

GLAMOUR is not the only imponderable which can transform an ignoble killing into a useful assassination; the gods (that is, the enormous number of incalculables, creating the illusion that our affairs are governed by a gifted satirist), ensure that misconception of a political idea can do as much as glamour: for example, in the case of Caesar.

The assassination of Gaius Julius Caesar remains one of the most interesting in history. On the face of it, it accomplished absolutely nothing whatever; in fact, it ensured, as nothing else could have done, the complete success of Caesar's policy: the last and greatest service he could render in his own reconstruction of the Roman state was to let his life be sacrificed to it by its enemies. The case appears to fall into the class of futile assassinations: there is no point in assassinating a man if it is the social and political situation, and not the man himself, which makes your cause a hopeless one; by the time Caesar was assassinated the replacement of the Roman aristocratic republic by a democratic monarchy had become almost inevitable; by killing Caesar, its architect, his assassins made it quite inevitable.

The Roman Republic was an aristocratic one, an oligarchy. Its government can in some ways be compared to that of England after the Revolution of 1688 in that the franchise was limited to a relatively small number of owners of real estate, power in the hands of a Senate of landowners, and an executive drawn from a small number of noble or gentle families.

In the decadence of the Republic the dictator Marius had set up a sort of popular, radical government by appealing to the people over the heads of the Senate. The oligarchy reasserted its power in the person of the next dictator, Sulla, who overthrew the Marian reforms and set up what we should call a Fascist government which, though it took power away from the Senate of aristocrats as well as from the people and their almost powerless Tribunes, governed in the sense and interests of the old oligarchy. We, in our own time, have become familiar with this sort of thing.

Caesar, like Marius, served his personal ambition by appealing to the democracy over the heads of the oligarchy; to the left against the right. The policy of the oligarchs or Patrician party, the party of the old Senate, was, of course, designed to preserve the very great privileges of their own class. It does not follow that the senators were all selfish cynics: all conservative parties tend naturally to equate the national good with their own; and in assassinating a radical tyrant, men may be acting – subjectively speaking – nobly. Thus when they, the rightists, are represented as defending liberty and the Republic against Caesar's monarchical ambitions, an entirely misleading impression is conveyed to us. In modern terms, the senatorial oligarchs were General Motors declaring that what was good for them was good for the country: the best of them really believed this, but the liberty they were defending was that of their minority class, the Republic their own instrument; and they abhored and strove against the democracy and the very idea of the franchise and rights for the common people and the provincials.

Gaius Julius Caesar was born in the year 102 B.C.* He was an aristocrat by birth and while still in his teens married Cornelia,

---

* See Theodor Mommsen, *The History of Rome*, J. M. Dent (Everyman's Library), London, 1906. Mommsen's arguments for this date are convincing.

daughter of another aristocrat, Cinna. Sulla was dictator or, as he is called by most historians, Regent, at the time. For political reasons which need not trouble us here, the dictator ordered the young Caesar to divorce his wife. Caesar refused, and as a result he was stripped of his office as priest of Jupiter, an aristocratic sinecure; of his wife's dowry; and of his own patrimony. In short, and as Suetonius puts it, Sulla treated the young man, 'as if he were a member of the people's party', a comparison which makes vividly clear how the politicians who, for whatever reason, took the people's side, were being dealt with under the Sullan constitution. For a time Caesar had to 'go underground' and was hunted for his life by the secret political police. Meanwhile several influential noblemen among Caesar's kinsfolk, and even the Vestal Virgins, were pleading his cause with the dictator, chiefly because Caesar was, after all, a Julian, and therefore a gentleman, 'one of us'. In the end Sulla pardoned him; but he seems to have known that he was doing something foolish. Suetonius puts it thus:

'Whether he was divinely inspired or showed peculiar foresight is an arguable point, but these were his words: "Very well then, you win! Take him! But never forget that the man you want me to spare will one day prove the ruin of the party which you and I have so long defended. There are many Mariuses in this fellow Caesar."'*

Caesar served with the army in Asia, where he earned himself a reputation for courage and military daring on the one hand, homosexual debauchery on the other.† When the news of Sulla's death reached him, he returned hastily to Rome to see if the time had come to start satisfying his political ambitions. The government was temporarily in the hands of a politician named Lepidus who made Caesar some tempting offers: Caesar declined and withdrew; he liked neither the man, nor the situation, which was as follows:

The oligarchs or Patricians, operating the Sullan constitution,

---

* Suetonius, *The Twelve Caesars*, translated by Robert Graves, Penguin Books (Penguin Classics), 1957.
† Like all sophisticated Greeks and most Romans, Caesar was sexually catholic. He took his pleasures where he found them, but was not, in our sense, 'queer'.

were still in power but without a head. Opposed to them, and
equally headless, was an opposition of diverse interests very
loosely associated. They ranged from the old, tradition-worship-
ping families to the right of Sulla's conservative radicalism,
through the small party of liberal conservatives in the Senate
which wanted a compromise with the Plebeians and the non-
Roman municipalities of Italy; the great capitalists who resented
state controls; the burgess class in the non-Roman cities who
were still unenfranchised (compare, for example, Manchester and
Birmingham before the Reform Acts and Britain's American
colonies before the War of Independence); to the left-wing
Radicals leading the Plebeians or Populares, the urban mobs their
'proletariat', who aimed at restoring the 'democratic' tribunician
prerogatives which Sulla had abolished, and at climbing to power
on the shoulders of the common people.

In the absence of a unifying head and a really unifying, positive
policy on either side, effective power was in the hands of the
political clubs or unions known as *Hetaeriae*. They fixed the elections, bought judges, maintained para-military gangs, and so
dominated the cities. In their manifest existence and activities they
were legitimate unions; their vicious secret trading in votes,
justice, and power were winked at. Crooked senators of respectable family and position, such as Publius Cethegus, acted as go-
betweens or brokers between the Establishment power centres
and these louche and scabrous sources of real power. Constitutional
government was superseded by the basest 'horse-trading' between
the *Hetaeriae* bosses; and between them and the senatorial caucuses.

In this state of affairs, even a man of very ordinary abilities but
possessing that mysterious attribute, star quality, or glamour, was
likely to become important. One such man was Gaius Pompeius,
whom we call Pompey. In 78 B.C., when Sulla died, he was about
twenty-eight, had already a considerable military reputation, an
impressive body and handsome head, remarkable ability at trim-
ming his sails and even running with the hare and hunting
with the hounds, very little mind of his own, radiant health and
flawless courage. He was, in short, the sort of man who gets the
ordinary citizen's vote.

The temporary left-wing opposition leader whose prospects of success had not impressed Caesar, Marcus Aemilius Lepidus, had been an extreme Sullan rightist; but that had been merely a matter of expediency. He was a man without convictions; and as governor of Sicily he had so viciously plundered the people and province entrusted to him, that even his fellow Senators, most of whom took bribes in one way or another, could not stomach his behaviour and he faced impeachment. Salvation lay in office; he took the leadership of the Populares, they won him the consulship, and his election made bloody revolution certain.

The series of revolutions and civil wars which were Caesar's opportunity began. But it was not a case, merely, of an ambitious man seizing the chance to grasp at supreme power, but also one of a political vacuum filling itself; the state had fallen into near-anarchy, and the hopeless incapacity of the old Republican constitution to rule a world empire was demonstrated. A man was needed to destroy it and make a new one.

The first round was won for the right by Pompey, first in Spain and then at home. Hence, a Sullan restoration, during which Caesar discreetly went to Rhodes. The Sullan restoration lasted, uneasily, ten years. But the Senate was incapable and corrupt at home and abroad and had not even the sense to keep Pompey and the millionaire usurer-soldier, Crassus, who had put down the revolt of the slaves under Spartacus, happy; it quarrelled with them about the overseas empire. Who was to govern (and loot) the provinces? The Senate or the generals?

To strengthen their hand, the two generals sought leftist democratic support, and got it; on condition of totally dismantling the Sullan constitution.

Julius Caesar returned to Rome, was elected to office by the people, and took a very active part in anti-Sullan pro-democratic agitation. But while doing so he was also building up a great fund of popularity with the Roman people. He gave them, for example, the most magnificent gladiatorial games they had ever seen, in which even the cages of the wild beasts were of solid silver. Caesar was, then, at once a shrewd and able demagogue, a clever politician, a dashing and brilliant soldier, and a profligate and amusing leader of the young smart set in Roman society. This complex feat is the more remarkable in that it was all done on borrowed money; his debts were colossal and they were rising fast.

Caesar had, too, the great art of playing politics, but with statesman-like moves. For example, his measures, or those he supported rather, for he was not yet the master by any means, might be aimed to annoy and hamper the right wing; they were nevertheless always sound ones, and usually liberal. His combined policies of courting popularity on the one hand, and supporting popular measures on the other, paid a handsome dividend in the year 63 B.C. when he stood for election to the supreme pontificate against two very distinguished members of the Patrician party, who should have won easily, and beat them.

*

It would be tedious to follow, in detail, the struggle between the shifting political parties and their shifty leaders during the years of Pompey's absence conquering and restoring order in the east and creating for himself the army, the reputation, and the glamour which, with the democracy to back him, might make a monarch of him. The aristocratic party, on the defensive, was no longer capable of governing the empire; at most it could strive to retain its class privileges. As an instrument for governing a great state, on the other hand, the democratic party did not even exist. Government was certain to be in the hands of small caucuses, or of an individual, a monarch in all but name.

Caesar grasped at every opportunity to increase his personal power: he bought votes, he flattered and amused and bribed the citizens, and he took a hand in every plot designed to undermine or corrupt or overthrow the senatorial power.

His next public service was a military appointment in western Spain. He scored a couple of quick and complete victories against the tribes which were harrying the province, and then came rushing back to Rome to stand for the consulate. There was a legal difficulty about this candidature – soldiers could not stand for office – and he was obliged to resign his military rank so that he could enter Rome as a civilian, which meant that he had to forego the triumph due to him for his Spanish victories. Caesar was elected Consul by the usual method of buying more votes than the other side. Although Crassus had by this time paid his debts for him, he had not the means to buy so many votes out of his own pocket; but the money was put up by his very rich fellow democratic candidate. The aristocratic party had a nasty vision of Caesar as Consul with a weakling of like views as his colleague; they therefore put up the money to buy votes for the right-wing candidate, Bibulus. Caesar and Bibulus were elected.

Bibulus was no match for his consular colleague. When, in the interests of the right, he sought to block a popular and perfectly sound Agrarian Bill introduced by Caesar, Caesar used his lictor to '. . . drive him from the Forum by force of arms'. The method used by Bibulus had been to declare the omens bad; Caesar, although capable of manipulating the omens himself, never had any time for such nonsense. After his humiliating defeat, the Consul Bibulus stayed at home and sulked, leaving all consular business in Caesar's hands. Caesar used his chance thoroughly. With the people he dealt openly and frankly; with their leaders he used bribes; with the Senate he dealt sardonically, always polite, always showing a proper regard for senatorial manners, but always ready to use threats and even to implement them if their lordships stood in his way.

The aristocratic or oligarchic party seemed bent on self-destruction in any case. It made the elementary mistake of opposing all that the democratic leaders proposed simply on party political grounds. When, on those grounds, Marcus Cato, the honest, shallow-minded, brave, and priggish leader of the right, tried to talk out a useful and just Bill, Caesar had him arrested; he was sent to the east to introduce some order into the finances of Pompey's provinces. Cicero, another pertinaceous but less courageous opponent of the new 'democracy', was simply banished.

By this time the old Republicans could clearly and with horror see a monarch in sight; and an end to their privileges. But far from putting himself forward, Caesar was bringing Pompey increasingly to the fore. He began calling upon Pompey, rather than Crassus, to open debates in the Senate, and by custom that conferred a sort of precedence. He married his daughter Julia to Pompey. He was not yet ready to try for the supreme place himself, and he may have been making sure that the obvious claimant was a man whom he knew he could overreach. He was not yet ready, because an essential instrument for any aspirant to the monarchic power, which would enable him to reform the state and suit it to its new role as a world imperium, was an army. Pompey had one; Caesar had not, nor even anything like a serious military reputation. But since it was customary to give the outgoing Consul a proconsular command in the provinces, his opportunity was coming; for proconsular office meant command of garrison troops.

Caesar arranged (by making use of the Gabinio-Mamilian Law passed to secure Pompey a free hand in the East) for the Tribune of the People, Publius Vatinius, to propose that he be given the governship of Cisalpine Gaul and command of the legions stationed there. The commons granted the office to Caesar for a term of five years. The Senate, facing the fact that they could not undo what the commons had done, and anxious to seem to have a hand in so extraordinary an appointment, carried a motion put forward by Pompey that Caesar be allowed to add the territory of Transalpine Gaul to the more southerly provinces. 'As no troops could constitutionally be stationed in Italy proper, the commander of the Legions in Northern Italy and Gaul dominated at the same time Italy and Rome for the next five years; and he who was master for five years was master for life.'*

In short, the final destruction of the old oligarchic Republic by the new democratic monarchy was now clearly in sight. And the oligarchs knew it. One of them wrote: 'On all sides we are checkmated; we have already, through fear of death or banishment, despaired of freedom. Everyone sighs; no one ventures to speak.'

But the old right wing was not yet beaten. They still had

* Mommsen, op. cit.

Pompey, who, if Caesar grew too mighty, might be expected to change sides again.

During the nine years of his Gallic service, Caesar turned all Gaul – virtually modern France – into a province, Hellenized its culture, and made it worth an annual revenue of 400,000 gold pieces. He eliminated the German threat for at least two generations by inflicting such punishment on the Germans in their own country as left them cowed by the terror of Roman arms. He invaded Britain, reconnoitred it, defeated its people, and extracted tribute from them. And he created for himself a military force which could not be matched in the empire and which looked to him, not to the Senate or people, for orders; and a colossal reputation as a soldier and administrator.

Why did Pompey not only tolerate but actively forward Caesar's growth in political stature? The answer is that Pompey believed himself to be, beyond comparison, the greatest Roman of his times. Pompey, of course, overlooked one thing, that he was utterly incompetent to manage the Roman mob and the *Hetaeriae*; that only Caesar could, by bribes, threats, and cajolings, manage the mob, the clubs, the armed bands of anarchy. When he left Rome, Pompey was helpless to cope with the people; and the consequent disorders, exploited by demagogues and adventurers, led to a steady decline in his glamour. If a Gallup Poll had been taken at the beginning of Caesar's term of service in Gaul, Pompey's popularity rating would have been the highest in Rome, Caesar's among the lowest. By the end of Caesar's nine-year service the positions would have been reversed. Above all Caesar had, by making for himself a shining aura of glamour, fulfilled the last condition which makes it possible for one man to become the incarnation of a historical idea and so to bring about one of those great destructive-constructive changes which, from time to time, are necessary. By so doing, of course, he also made himself fit to become a scapegoat: such men as he had become tempt the enemies of the new idea to expose and ultimately destroy themselves under the illusion that, in destroying the man, they are destroying the idea. He had, finally, made himself fit to be one day offered the title Father of his Country, and, becoming

Father Surrogate (did he not both succour and chastise?) to all men, run the risk of provoking the parricidal impulse latent in all men and of which the rational mind, planning a political assassination, can make use of as of a weapon of destruction.

At last the very greatness of Caesar's stature frightened Pompey into the Senate's arms, the Senate into his. Pompey became the general of the Old Republicans, but also of many ordinary burgesses and squires who had been on the side of the democracy, of the people, but changed sides in their disgust at left-wing disorders and political crime.

The first attack on Caesar attempted by the new alliance was made in the Senate by the Consul M. Claudius Marcellus. His motion was to relieve Caesar of his command; deprive him of the privilege formerly granted him to stand for his second consular term *in absentia* (which was unconstitutional); and to recall him to give an account of himself to the Senate and People. At first Caesar was reasonable and offered generous concessions of several kinds in return for keeping part of his command and his right to a second term as Consul although still a soldier. So generous were these offers that he probably made them in the certainty that they would be rejected: with foolish confidence, while Pompey was busy raising an army and trying to turn farmers and city idlers into soldiers, the new anti-Caesar alliance remained implacable, and their refusal to negotiate led to that famous crossing of the Rubicon which entailed the next civil war. In that war Caesar, standing in theory for the people and democracy, and Pompey for the Senate, the Republic, and all the old establishment, fought it out first in Italy, then in Illyria, a campaign ending in Caesar's decisive victory at Pharsalus in Thessaly. The beaten Pompey fled to Egypt where, in Alexandria, King Ptolemy not only put him to death but is said to have declared his intention of doing the same to Caesar if he got the chance.

Caesar followed Pompey to Alexandria, defeated the Egyptian army, although handicapped by his own carelessness in the matter of supplies and situation, and had an affair with Cleopatra, whom he then married to her younger brother Ptolemy, crowning them joint monarchs of Egypt. In Alexandria news reached him that Pharnaces, son of Mithridates of Pontus, was exploiting Rome's internecine war to reassert Pontic independence. Caesar moved himself and his army into the Pontus, smashed Pharnaces at Zela within five days of his arrival, went thence to North Africa, where the Pompeyan-Republican party was trying to organize a fresh army, and destroyed that army which was commanded by Scipio for the Senate and King Juba for the natives. Finally he shipped his army to Spain and there broke the forces and the resistance which Pompey's two sons had raised in the province.

Caesar the effeminate; Caesar the profligate; Caesar the spendthrift; Caesar the homosexual debauchee whose soldiers, marching in his Triumph, sang of his affair with King Nicomedes of Bithynia:

> Gaul was brought to shame by Caesar;
> By King Nicomedes, he . . .

but also, of this man who was most things to all women as well as all to most men,

> Home we bring the bald whoremonger;
> Romans lock your wives away.
> All the bags of gold you lent him
> Went his Gallic tarts to pay.*

– this Caesar had, with consummate skill, tireless energy, flawless courage, and a will of steel, made himself master of the Roman world in a series of military manoeuvres and victories without precedent, as they are still without equal, in history.

*

When, following that extraordinary chain of victories, Caesar stood towering, already monarch *de facto* of all the western civilized world, he was fifty-six years of age. Neither his sexual indulgences, nor the great physical hardships of his campaigns, which he was famous for sharing with his men, nor his years of hard work, heavy responsibility, and strain, had in the least impaired his health and strength, nor much fatigued him. It is probable

* Suetonius, op. cit.

that he was spared the one attribute which, like a catalyst releasing destructive changes in the minds and bodies of ordinary men, causes that wear and tear which Caesar had not suffered: there is no noun for it, but it is implied in the phrase 'he did not care'; he could assume the appearance of *gravitas*, but he was not what the French call *sérieux*. Profoundly cynical, profoundly frivolous, involved in power politics as in a game worth playing well; despising men, unable, from what he had seen, to take their pretensions seriously, responsibility sat lightly on him. For much the same reason he could be dishonest, as he was, about money without suffering any crippling loss of self-esteem. Caesar was that very rare creature, a man who knew himself; but knowing other men he had little or no reason to feel that they deserved better than Caesar as their ruler. He could hardly help knowing that they would be very fortunate indeed to get a monarch as good as himself. For years he had considered how to remake the Roman state. He knew very well that no Roman living could do as good a job – and it had to be done – as he could.

Caesar was the one man 'modern' enough, at once enlightened and realistic to the point of cynicism, capable of forcing on the requisite changes. To the old aristocrats or oligarchs, of course, he appeared as the arch-enemy, the destroyer of their institutions and privileges which, as is usual in such cases, they called 'liberty'.

Because he was a creative statesman of genius, all that he proposed to do for Rome was good and necessary; but under all his good will, generosity, kindness, and courage, one senses the shrug of profound cynicism; and that shrug was offensive to lesser men. Mommsen says this of him: 'If in a nature so harmoniously organized there is any one trait to be singled out as characteristic it is this – that he stood aloof from all ideology and everything fanciful.'* True; and that kind of detachment, that very cool look at life which implies the littleness of men and the ineluctable absurdity of the human condition, is very hard to forgive. It is particularly hard to forgive in a father who is apt, unwittingly, to outrage the prejudices and the priggishness of his children and to shatter their illusions.

* Mommsen, op. cit.

Caesar refused the name of king. He accepted life-consulship; life-dictatorship; life-censorship; the title *Imperator* which, though it did not then mean what we mean by emperor, but, rather, commander-in-chief, was, according to Suetonius, unconstitutional; and the title 'Father of his Country' – and thereby, as I have suggested, placed at the service of his enemies who might want to assassinate him all the latent but powerful oedipal impulse to parricide. He allowed a statue of himself to be placed among those of the ancient kings of Rome; and as anthropology has taught us, the king, too, is a predestined victim of sacrifice. He allowed himself to be deified, accepting a cult, priesthood, altars, and images; are not gods, likewise, put to death for the people? When he reformed the calendar, he called the seventh month July, as if he were indeed a god. But above all, his crime was that he bore himself regally and in all he did made it clear that he was killing the old aristocratic Republic and creating a new, world-wide, popular monarchy. Moreover:

'. . . in the robe wholly purple which was reckoned in antiquity as the proper regal attire, he received, seated on the golden chair and without rising from it, the solemn procession of the Senate. . . . People felt, more clearly than was agreeable to Caesar himself, *that they no longer approached a fellow-citizen.* . . .'*

That feeling (my italics above) was surely the 'divinity which doth hedge a king'? It made him all the fitter for sacrifice that he had the aura of a royal scapegoat. But how deep must have been his silent laughter.

What Caesar saw clearly – that Rome could now be ruled only by a monarch who had courted and won the support of the people and whose outlook was to that extent democratic† – although surely true, was by no means admitted by the old patrician and die-hard Republicans who opposed the monarchy on ideological

---

* Suetonius, op. cit.

† There is an obvious parallel in the United States system: true, the monarch is elected and none has yet ruled more than twelve years; but it often happens that president and people are on one side, the Senate, representing the great industrial and commercial families and the new wealth, on the other.

grounds, or by the newly rich speculators and money-lenders and slave dealers who did not want their freedom to exploit controlled by law. But there was now less and less possibility of open and constitutional opposition; Caesar had no respect whatever for the constitution excepting when it suited him, and did not hesitate to exile or terrorize anyone who opposed him or his work, however constitutionally. He was not a killer; the sparing of enemy lives, in fact, cost him his own. But there were other ways to silence opposition. Consequently the opposition, nominally centred on Marcus Cato, 'went underground', and found expression only in political agitation and in plotting, all of it destructive, none of it positive. And this underground opposition to the dictator, although from time to time it flared up here and there in the empire as armed insurrection in the name of a party, a leader, or a principle, had really, and from the opposition party's point of view very properly, only one object: the assassination of Julius Caesar.

The old Republicans could not see, and their moneyed friends did not care, that Caesar had simply filled a political vacuum, and that if they killed him it would be filled by another man and never by a Senate or assembly, because it was the wrong shape. Many men have been assassinated because, as Ouspenski says, we believe when we kill a man that we kill his idea; but you cannot kill an idea, you can only kill an exponent of it. What the opposition did believe was that Caesar had taken away their old liberties and their old importance. They were wrong, it was the course of events, it was the Marxist goddess History, who had done them that wrong.

Not all of the anti-Caesarians were disingenuous; two, at least, of their leaders, and doubtless some of those who followed their lead, were genuine ideologues. It simply did not occur to the honest ones that their Republican Senate and People's Assembly, with their presidents-for-one-year, the Consuls, were incompetent to deal with a world-empire in the year 705 from the foundation of the city. It was not as if they were prepared to set to work themselves and create a new state machinery fit to do the work now to be done. Brutus and his friends were not interested in the present or in the future: like all conservative parties, they were crying for the past to come back.

*

Who were they, the men of the old Republican party and of the new rich, hostile enough and determined enough to destroy the dictator? Certainly they were many; there were twenty-three wounds in Caesar's body as he lay bleeding to death at the foot of Pompey's statue in the new Pompeian hall. And all the active ones were Senators, or they could not have entered the Senate where the assassination was done.

Caesar was well warned of their plot and in plenty of time, not only by the signs and portents of which he was contemptuous, but in so many words. Some say that, feeling his work was done, he was willing to die; I have offered two explanations of that state of mind. Others say that he was arrogantly incredulous of warnings. He was told that Brutus was plotting against him, but did not believe it; or, if he did, thought it fitting that the sacrifice of his life be made by a man he admired and loved as a son, and who may indeed have been his son – a case of Judas the favourite disciple. The motives of the assassins were those of their class; if Cassius hated Caesar, the others did not, and Marcus Brutus loved him; in a way; a filial way.

*

By some accounts, Gaius Cassius was the prime mover of the conspiracy; but Marcus Brutus was the best man among them, the man to whom those who hated the dictatorship looked both because of his name and because of his known principles. He was one of the richest men in the city, owning an army of slaves and lending money at interest. Yet by all accounts his assassination of Caesar was disinterested and contrary to his personal feelings, a noble outraging of his own nature. Among his ancestors on his mother's side was a famous tyrannicide, the assassin of Spurius Maelius who had aspired to the monarchy of Rome; and Marcus Brutus was the kind of man who knows and is influenced by his family history.

By marrying his cousin, Brutus became son-in-law as well as nephew of Marcus Cato, the shallow but honest prig who had long led the right in the Senate. But of more interest than this kinship is another: Brutus' mother Servilia, Marcus Cato's sister, had at one time been Caesar's mistress. Their affair* had been at its height and notorious during the two or three years before Marcus' birth; it is possible and even probable that Marcus was Caesar's son; and by no means impossible that he knew it.

If Marcus Brutus was at first far from whole-hearted in his wish to do anything to destroy Caesar's democratic monarchy, that may have been one of the reasons; for though a man may wish to kill his father he puts the wish from him, when he recognizes it, with fear and horror, until he can rationalize it. There were others: like so many men, he was under the influence of Caesar's charm; then, too, he hated Pompey who had put his legal father to death; moreover, according to Plutarch:

'. . . his zeal was blunted by the honours and favours he had received from Caesar. It was not only that at Pharsalus, after Pompey's flight, his own life had been spared and the lives of many of his friends at his request. He was also a person in whom Caesar had particular trust. He had been given the most important of the praetorships for this very year and was to be Consul three years later. For this post he had been preferred to Cassius who had been the rival candidate. Caesar is said to have admitted that Cassius had the better claim of the two to the office. "But," he added, "I cannot pass over Brutus." '†

As well as first Praetor, Caesar made Marcus Brutus governor-designate of Macedon.

Although he was not regarded by the Republicans as a leader of their cause, and had fought for Caesar against Pompey in the Civil War, Decimus Brutus, no kin, unless very remote, to Marcus, was the busiest of the conspirators, and but for him the plot would have failed and Caesar would not have died on the Ides of March.

---

* There was an amusing incident connected with this: during a debate in the Senate Caesar received a letter. Marcus Cato accused him of correspondence with the Senate's enemies. Caesar passed him the letter: it was a lewd love note from Cato's sister, Servilia.
† Plutarch, *Fall of the Roman Republic*, translated by Rex Warner, Penguin Books (Penguin Classics), Hamondsworth, 1958.

Plutarch says of him that the conspirators felt that they had to have him with them because – 'he bred so many gladiators', meaning, presumably, that he disposed of a large number of trained fighters who would be useful if Caesar's supporters among the city mobs rose against the assassins.

Decimus had been one of Caesar's most valuable officers in the Civil War, but also, what counted for more, in the Gallic War. In the difficult campaign against the then Bretons, that is the Veneti, the Romans had found themselves up against a seafaring people who had what they themselves had not – effective sailing-ships; it was Decimus Brutus who created and manned a fleet and destroyed the Veneti at sea in what was the first important naval battle ever to be fought on the Atlantic. In the Civil War Decimus Brutus again distinguished himself as an admiral. By way of reward for his services, Caesar had made Decimus Brutus a praetor and governor-designate of Cisalpine Gaul, Caesar's old province and recruiting ground. This was an extraordinary mark of confidence, for the officer who commanded the legions in that province (as Caesar had good reason to know) could effectively threaten Rome.

What, then, turned Decimus Brutus against Caesar? He was by birth a patrician and by trade a soldier and he does not seem to have had strong Republican sentiments. As a breeder and trainer of gladiators he should have favoured the party which made most use of demagogues and their tricks, such as shows for the mob of landless, jobless, and feckless parasites who were nevertheless citizens and therefore voters. Of the three or four leading conspirators he seems, unless we allow him to have had principles for which there is no evidence, to have been the least honourable and the most able.

'*It was said everywhere that whereas Marcus Brutus hated the imperial power, Cassius hated the emperor*' – thus Plutarch, who says, on the other hand, that even from boyhood Cassius had such '*a natural aversion to the whole race of tyrants*' that at school he once struck Sulla's son in the face for boasting of his father's unlimited power. We know too little of this man's antecedents, as of Decimus Brutus', to know whether it is necessary to invoke

a Freudian explanation – hatred of the father figure – for his part
in the assassination; but it seems probable that in the assassination
of such men as Caesar and Lincoln this motive usually lies deep
below the practical and manifest ones and informs them with its
power; and, again, there is the deep motive, as compared with the
conscious ones, of king-killing as a catharsis and a sacrifice which
is discussed at length in my concluding chapter.

At the time of that assassination, Gaius Cassius had received
from Caesar a praetorship, and the province of Syria. Like the
other leaders he came of an old patrician family, or rather from
the patrician branch of the family, for the plebeian branch was also
distinguished. His motives seem to have been the common,
historically justifiable, ignoble ones; in assassinating Julius Caesar
he was destroying a class enemy; yet to himself, no doubt, he
seemed noble and disinterested, a defender of his country and of
its ancient constitution.

The rest of the conspirators were Senators of so little character
that they were, for the most part, ignored by the annalists and
historians; they were, like 99 per cent of the Senators, Deputies,
Peers, and MP.s of our own time, ciphers. Casca, indeed, the man
who struck the first blow at the dictator, was apparently bought
rather than persuaded; that would seem to be the implication of
Plutarch's anecdote: '. . . a person came up to Casca . . . and taking
him by the hand said, "You concealed the thing from me but
Brutus has told me all," and when Casca expressed his surpise he
added, laughing, "How came you to be so rich all of a sudden as
to stand for the aedileship?"'*

*

Marcus Brutus was apparently brought to a decision by numerous
anonymous letters, usually left on the steps or the seat of his
praetorial chair, such as, 'Brutus, you sleep', or 'A fine Brutus you
are!' – a reference, of course, to his king-breaking ancestor; and
by Cassius' persuasive arguments. They and the other conspirators
discussed several plans – Caesar was to be attacked when super-
vising the polling station during the next consular elections; or

* Plutarch, op. cit.

maybe it would be better to catch him on the move during his next progress along the Sacred Way; or in the entrance to the Theatre. It is part of the very nature of a true assassination (as opposed to mere murder) that the ways and means of killing are thoroughly discussed in cold blood. And as has so often happened in such cases, Caesar himself unwittingly fixed the scene of the sacrifice by calling a meeting of the Senate in the Pompeian Chamber or Portico for the Ides (15th) of March: the conspirators decided that this would provide the opportunity they were seeking.

The accounts of the events which followed make much of the signs and portents which forewarned the people of some great event and Caesar of his death. Caesar was not, for his time, superstitious, and had often manipulated the omens to suit himself. I have suggested that deep and obscure guilt for the crimes entailed by leadership may explain an uneasiness ostensibly attributable to his wife, Calpurnia's, fears for his life, for she was a woman of sense and not given to fussing. Again, the victim elect is as subconsciously aware as the self-appointed sacrificial killer that the king must die; finally, Caesar knew a great deal about his men, knew that many of his closest associates were under immense obligations to him and that this is something few men can forgive and most men seek to avenge. There is no need to list the portents said to have forerun his death; superstitious people in terror bent on seeing into the future will always find omens in unusual meteorological phenomena and will believe wild tales of monsters born or stars misbehaving. Probably half the stories are invented after the event; or occurrences in themselves insignificant are given significance by that event in the minds of fearful men. More interesting than this nonsense is the case of the augur or fortune-teller Spurinna, who warned Caesar that he would be in danger of death on the Ides of March. Later, when Caesar was on his way to the Senate meeting, he saw Spurinna in the crowd and called out to him gibingly that the Ides of March were come, to which the augur replied, 'Aye, but not yet gone.'

It is said that what really upset Caesar was his wife's account of a dream which had greatly distressed her. Probably a dream of

hers was interpreted after the event as having forecast it. It is not
even clear exactly what she did dream: some say that she saw
herself holding her husband's stabbed and bleeding body in her
arms; others that she saw the ornament of honour erected on the
house gable by senatorial decree – an ancient practice revived to
honour Caesar – torn down. She is supposed to have been deeply
disturbed and implored the dictator not to go to the Senate.
Caesar was impressed, for this was not like the Calpurnia he knew
as a sensible and level-headed woman of education; as, moreover,
he was feeling unwell, he decided to send for the Consul Mark
Antony and cancel the Senate meeting.

'At this point Decimus Brutus, surnamed Albinus, intervened . . .
fearing that if Caesar escaped this day the whole plot would come to
light, he spoke derisively of the prophets and told Caesar that he ought
not to give the senate such a good opportunity for thinking that they
were being treated discourteously; they had met, he said, on Caesar's
instructions, and they were ready to vote unanimously that Caesar
should be declared King of all the provinces outside Italy with the
right of wearing a diadem in any other place except Italy, whether on
sea or land; but if, when they were already in session, someone were
to come and tell them that they must go away for the time being and
come back again when Calpurnia had better dreams, it would be easy
to imagine what Caesar's enemies would have to say themselves and
what sort of reception they would give to Caesar's friends when they
tried to prove that Caesar was not a slave-master or tyrant.'*

Caesar pulled himself together and went with Decimus Brutus.
They had, as usual, to make their way through the city crowd,
and many people were there who wanted to put petitions into
the dictator's hands. Also as usual, Caesar received them but did
not read them, passing them to a secretary for attention. One of
those papers might have saved his life: it contained an account of
the conspiracy written by a Greek teacher of philosophy, a
Cnidian named Artemidorus, who, being employed by Marcus
Brutus, a bookish man who always had some such teacher living
in his household, had learned of the plot.

Caesar entered the Chamber, the Senators rose in his honour,

---

* Plutarch, op. cit.

and he took his seat while some of Brutus' people sat down immediately behind him, and another group, led by Senator Tillius Cimber who pretended he wished to plead the cause of his brother whom Caesar had exiled, approached the dictator from the front. Cimber put his request, Caesar waved it aside, Cimber seized him by the gown as if to insist, and as Caesar protested against this discourtesy, Casca struck the first blow, stabbing Caesar from behind and just below the throat. The wound was not serious and Caesar struck back with his stylus. Because the compact among the assassins evidently called for a full sharing of the guilt for a tyrannicide which was felt as a parricide, all of them had to strike their blow so that no one man should be Caesar's sole assassin. Of the several accounts of the subsequent butchery, which do not differ on any point of substance, I prefer that of Suetonius:

'. . . he was leaping away when another dagger caught him in the breast. Confronted by a ring of drawn daggers, he drew the top of his gown over his face, and at the same time ungirded the lower part, letting it fall to his feet so that he would die with both his legs decently covered. Twenty-three dagger thrusts went home as he stood there. Caesar did not utter a sound after Casca's blow had drawn a groan from him; though some say that when he saw Marcus Brutus about to deliver a second blow, he reproached him in Greek with, "You, too, my son"!'*

*

I am not here concerned with the confusion which followed and the events which it entailed. From the subsequent civil war a man, a youth hitherto unknown, Caesar's adopted heir Octavius, later known as Augustus, emerged to put Caesar's political and social programme into execution, to destroy the Republic, and to create a People's monarchy. In short, to put the assassinated and soon to be deified Caesar's programme into practice.

This seems to mean that the killing of Gaius Julius Caesar accomplished nothing. It is true that it did not serve the purpose of the assassins and their party; but it did serve the people, for it

* Suetonius, op. cit.

revealed and exposed those who were the implacable enemies of the new monarchy; that is, of political and social progress, for the Caesarian-Augustan monarchy was well to the left of the old Republic; it forced them to fight and so made it possible for them to be destroyed and for the Roman Empire to enter upon its new phase.

The killing of Julius Caesar was an authentic and justifiable assassination; he did not die in vain. His assassination did more to ensure that his great work would be completed than another ten or fifteen years of active life could have done. It was a politically and socially valuable act. But since what his death accomplished was the establishment of that form of government which his opponents assassinated him to avoid, it should serve as a lesson to would-be assassins to consider carefully what, in fact, their crime is likely to entail.

Perhaps no other act could have so clearly and sharply marked, for the people, the end of an epoch and the beginning of another and different one as did Caesar's assassination. The empire could settle down, relieved, into its new arrangements, as a family grieving, yet relieved, can settle down to enjoy the estate of its just buried father.

4

ABRAHAM LINCOLN:
A VICTIM OF FACTION

It is one of history's greatest jokes that the assassination of Julius Caesar accomplished precisely what his assassins, justified in their deed by the interests of their party, were seeking by killing him to avoid: their own final destruction and the establishment of the new monarchy. To find a parallel case, but one in which the party of the assassins gained some, at least, of their ends (although their principal was disgraced and driven to suicide), it is necessary to move forward in time by nineteen centuries. Like Caesar, Abraham Lincoln had led one half of his countrymen into and through a terrible civil war fought against an old oligarchy by a new democratic 'monarchy';* like Caesar, he faced the task of rebuilding a badly shaken empire-sized nation by ridding it of old and inappropriate institutions; like Caesar, he was trying to unify an empire which was flying apart; like Caesar, he was a

* On the one hand President, whose powers are much greater than those of a constitutional monarch, and people; on the other the great southern planters and their followers. It is, no doubt, a simplification but a valid one. Lincoln, in his projected policy of magnaminity towards the South, would seriously have hampered the northern capitalists in their plans to exploit the South as colonial territory; cf. in, for example, Mommsen, *History of Rome*, op. cit., on Caesar's checking of capitalist excesses in the Roman empire. There are numerous other parallels which could be drawn.

liberal realist beset by ideologues among both enemies and supporters; like Caesar, he was a very great man among little ones; like Caesar, he was a father figure, beloved and bitterly, irrationally, hated; unlike Caesar, he had no Octavius.

If we were to consider Lincoln's killing as being no more than the work of a more or less mentally deranged popular actor, the John Wilkes Booth who fired the pistol, it would be mere murder or a case of murderous hooliganism like the murders of Unamuno or of Rosa Luxemburg, and beside the point of this book. To justify its inclusion here, and incidentally its value as evidence against the use of political assassination, it must be shown that it was indeed a party-political affair, and comparable with the assassination of Julius Caesar.

Four people were hanged for the murder of Abraham Lincoln, and several others were given terms of imprisonment as accessories. Of those hanged it seems quite clear that two were perfectly innocent; the explanation of their hanging which seems most plausible is that they were judicially murdered for a reason which will presently appear.

It is customary to deplore Lincoln's assassination as a particularly abominable crime because he was honest, upright, brave, generous, and kind, the antithesis of most of the politicians we are commonly obliged to put up with. There is no doubt that he was all those things, that he was a benevolent father when obeyed. But was he not also – look at his face and bearing – a stern father? Did he not, when half his 'sons' wanted their freedom from his rule, refuse it by force and so ruthlessly chastise them that their descendants suffer, in their economy, their minds, and their conduct, from his chastisement, until this day? One has only to read Faulkner to realize how great were the crimes of this very great man, the crimes a great leader is there to commit for the people. These truths are painful to many Americans; so painful that they resist, bitterly and fiercely, the duty to accept them as truths: and yet, they are self-evident. For that Lincoln was benevolent and magnanimous does not mean we should refrain from looking coldly at his record as a leader. The towering and noble figure of history and biography is in part a product of that glamour which creates legends. We can all forgive and love and admire the tyrant-father after he is safely dead. We would not have it otherwise, but it is right that we should face the fact that in his own times it is possible that Lincoln was hated and feared by as many people as loved him.

In his fight to remake American institutions to fit the realities of the times, to deny the right of secession to the millions of his fellow countrymen who desired and who lay down their lives fighting for it; and by so doing to enforce the emancipation of the slaves; and to abolish the plantation slavery which was an anachronism and a disgrace, Lincoln led tens of thousands of young men to their deaths. The war he led them in did free the slaves and created the problem of racialism, which, as I write, is producing robbery, arson, rape, and slaughter; it also enabled the great capitalists of the North to exploit and loot the South, which was for them the purpose of the war.

Lincoln has become a legend of nobility because, above other United States presidents, he is personally invested with all that is best in the American ideal; he cannot escape the duty of incarnating, also, the worst. Eighty letters threatening his life were found in his desk when he died; the first plot to kill him was uncovered in 1862; in 1863 a group of Southern land-owners and slave-owners offered a reward of $100,000 – say a million of our money – to any man who would assassinate the president; and published their offer. They were ordinary men, not monsters; they were not ashamed of their offer; they were proud of it.

*

The man who actually fired the pistol which killed Abraham Lincoln was an actor, John Wilkes Booth, member of a celebrated family of actors native to Maryland. His father was John Junius Booth, America's greatest actor until outclassed by his son Edwin Booth. John Junius was a drunkard who died insane. John Wilkes had none of his brother Edwin's great talent; it is quite clear from notices of his performances that he was a 'ham' actor of the worst kind, tearing his passions to tatters. Flamboyant,

acrobatic, and noisy on the stage, he was uncommonly handsome, a charmer, adored by women. By his early twenties he was
earning at the rate of $20,000 a year, say $100,000 in our depreci-
ated money, and there was not a theatre manager in the land but
was delighted to be able to bill him. From time to time he made
the mistake of appearing in a play with his brother Edwin and his
younger brother John Junius; it was then that he was apt to be
bitterly offended by and resentful of the unfavourable com-
parisons which were made by the critics. They drove him to
determine that he would do something totally to eclipse the fame
of his father and brothers. To a drunk who jeered at him, in a bar
near the theatre on the day of the assassination, that he would
never be the actor his father was, he replied, 'Possibly, sir, but
when I leave the stage I shall be the most famous man in America.'

By inclination as well as by birth John Wilkes Booth was a
Southerner. He did not join the Confederate army but he did use
his freedom as a celebrity to move where he pleased, to spy and
to carry contraband, for the Confederacy. And *outré* in all his
attitudes, a noisy actor off as well as on the stage, he was passionate and excitable in his declarations of loyalty to the South and of
his love for his country.

When, by 1864, it became clear to John Wilkes Booth, as to
most men, that though the war dragged on the Confederacy
could not now hope to win it, he conceived the mad yet perhaps
not utterly impracticable project of kidnapping President
Abraham Lincoln, carrying him off to Virginia, and handing him
over to the Confederate government. His idea was that that
government would then be able to dictate its own terms of peace;
or at least to exchange the president for 100,000 of the Confederate prisoners of war held by the Federal government, and so
enable the South to continue the war, which it was losing for
want of manpower, with renewed strength.

In order to execute this project, Booth recruited a number of
helpers.

George Andrew Atzerodt, thirty-three, was an immigrant from
Prussia. He never became an American citizen. He was a coachmaker
by trade. He lived and worked at Fort Tobacco on the Potomac

River, where Booth had come to know him during his journeys into and out of Maryland because Atzerodt was an experienced boatman who often ferried people, including Confederate spies, and goods, including Confederate contraband, over the river. Booth recruited the man because he would need a boatman to ferry the kidnapping party and their prisoner into Maryland. Atzerodt had neither the convictions, courage, nor resolution for the kind of work Booth had in hand.

Physically and morally the most formidable of Booth's recruits was a man named Lewis Thornton Powell, more commonly known as Payne or Paine, but who had also used the names of Moseby, and, in his guise of clergyman, of the Reverend Wood. He was born in 1845 in Alabama, son of a farmer turned Baptist minister, and he first met Booth, whom he greatly admired, when the actor was playing at Richmond, Virginia. Booth was flattered by the other's admiration, and himself admired Payne's enormous physical strength; moreover, he was fascinated by the man's aptitude for violence. Payne had joined the Confederate army at sixteen; he had had two brothers killed in the war; he was wounded at Gettysburg; he deserted in 1865 and thereafter drifted and starved, but he retained all his loyalty to the South and intense hatred of the North. He had a record of violence and had actually been run out of Baltimore by the police for a brutal assault on a Negro girl. He drifted back and was a penniless and starving vagrant when Booth picked him up outside Barnum's Hotel, fed him, and took him to Washington as a member of his band. At the conspiracy trial after the assassination, Payne's defender, W. E. Doster, suggested that he was ripe for Booth's plot because he wanted to: '. . . show the Northern Government that he is not a dog, the Southern Government that he is not a traitor, and give him but a chance and he will with one stroke pay off the scores he owes the Abolitionists, restore himself in the eyes of his comrades in arms, and throw himself into the arms of a pitiful Eternity.'*

* *The Assassination of President Lincoln and the Trial of the Conspirators*, the Courtroom Testimony as originally taken down by Benn Pitman (facsimile edition), Funk & Wagnalls, New York, 1954.

Perhaps; professional pleaders have a way of turning a homi-
cidal brute sullen from a run of bad luck into a figure of tragedy.
But Doster had also this impressive truth to say:

'He has been in four schools. Slavery has taught him to wink at
murder; the southern army has taught him to practice and justify
murder; cavalry warfare has taught him to love murder; necessity has
taught him resolution to commit murder. He needs no further education; his four terms are complete and he graduates as assassin. And
of this college we, the people of the United States have been the stern
tutors, guides and professors.'*

The assassin as well as his victim may be a scapegoat.

A third conspirator, John Harrison Surratt, was important
chiefly because through him his mother's boarding house was
used by the conspirators as a meeting-place. Involved in the first
kidnapping plan, he was not personally involved in the assassination. Surratt was a professional Confederate spy using his
mother's house as a *pied-à-terre* in Washington. According to
evidence given at the conspiracy trial by Louis J. Weichmann,†
who, as will appear, was to be the inadvertent means of identifying Lincoln's arch-assassin, Booth was introduced to Surratt by
a mutual acquaintance, Dr Samuel Mudd, to whose house in
Maryland Booth went for help when, with a broken ankle, he
was running from the Federal authorities after the killing, a fact
which was to cost Mudd his liberty when he was charged and
convicted as an accessory. It was Surratt who introduced Booth
into Mrs Surratt's boarding house where Weichmann, who had
been at school with John Surratt, was one of the lodgers.

Surratt's mother and the boarding-house keeper, Mrs Mary
Surratt, was the widow of a Maryland tavern keeper, a Catholic,
and possibly a Confederate sympathizer, but certainly innocent of
any part in Lincoln's assassination although she was hanged for it.

There were others in the conspiracy: David Herold, a drug
store assistant of twenty-three whose passion was shooting quail
down in Maryland and who, consequently, knew the country
really well; Samuel Arnold, twenty-eight, an ex-Confederate

* ibid.   † ibid.

soldier; and Michael O'Laughlin, another, and moreover a Knight of the Golden Circle, whose members had sworn a blood oath to kill the president.

These, excepting the woman, were the people Booth was to employ to kidnap Abraham Lincoln.

*

We have a brief and clear description of Booth's plan to abduct the president from a statement made by John Surratt some years later (1870):

'It was our intention to seize the carriage, which was drawn by a splendid pair of horses, and to have one of our men mount the box and drive straight for Southern Maryland via Bennings Bridge. We felt confident that all the cavalry in the city could never overhaul us. We were all mounted on swift horses, besides having a thorough knowledge of the country, it being determined to abandon the carriage after the city limits. Upon the suddeness of our blow and the celerity of our movements we depended for success. By the time the alarm could have been given and horses saddled, we would have been on our way through Southern Maryland towards the Potomac River. To our great disappointment, however, the President was not there but one of the government officials – Mr Chase if I mistake not. . . . It was our last attempt. . . .'*

Booth's first plan, however, had been to seize Lincoln at the theatre, which the President enjoyed and often attended. When it was announced that Lincoln would go to Ford's Theatre on 18 January to see a performance of *Jack Cade*, the plan was put into operation: Atzerodt was sent south to arrange for a ferry boat capable of carrying a carriage and fifteen horsemen over the river; Herold went to Maryland to arrange for relays of horses; and Booth had a carriage with blinds to cover the windows standing ready near the stage door at Ford's. But the weather was unpleasant, and the president changed his mind and stayed at home.

After this Booth was persuaded by his accomplices to abandon

* Otto Eisenschiml, *Why Was Lincoln Murdered?*, Little, Brown, Boston, 1937.

the theatre plan. It was then decided to waylay Lincoln's carriage when he went, as he had announced that he would, to visit the Soldiers' Home on 20 March. This was the attempt described by Surratt, made on Seventh Street at a lonely point beyond Florida Avenue. (Washington was laid out, but was not yet the city we know now.) Booth, Herold, Payne, Arnold, O'Laughlin, and Surratt were waiting, all mounted. But Lincoln had again changed his plans; he sent Chase to represent him and himself stayed at home to receive, from the 140th Indiana Regiment, a captured Confederate colour.

*

One member of Abraham Lincoln's cabinet, the Secretary of War, Stanton, the most important man in the country after the President, knew all about these plots in advance and did nothing whatever to prevent their execution.

Louis Weichman, who, as I have said, was a friend of John Surratt and lodged in his mother Mary Surratt's house, had become aware that something underhand was being plotted in the house; indeed he had overheard enough of the conspirators' talk to alarm him. He told a colleague at the War Department, where he worked, one Captain Gleason, that Surratt was a blockade runner and that he had heard Booth, Payne, and Herold discussing a plan to abduct President Lincoln and have him exchanged for 100,000 prisoners of war.*

Gleason undertook to inform Edwin Stanton, secretary for war, through an officer on General Augur's staff; meanwhile Weichmann also told another officer of his suspicions, one Lieutenant McDavitt, who likewise passed the information on to his superiors. It should be made clear that Stanton was complete and absolute master of the Army, that he was a man who had great difficulty in delegating authority and who attended to everything himself, that nothing was done without his knowledge, and that

---

* The source for this is the evidence which Weichmann gave at the trial of Mary Surratt as an accessory, after the assassination. A transcript of the whole conspiracy trial is available in *The Assassination of President Lincoln and the Trial of the Conspirators* by Benn Pitman, op. cit. Benn Pitman was the brother of Sir Issaac Pitman and a skilled reporter.

he had a particular taste for secret service, espionage, and police work.

The following points emerge: Edwin Stanton, Secretary for War, was informed of Booth's plot in advance; he took no steps to prevent its execution; the tribunal which tried the conspirators after the assassination was a military one, a court martial, which Stanton had insisted on in the teeth of an outcry and very stiff opposition, and of which he was master, the judges being his nominees; no evidence was ever called, though Gleason, for example, was available, to refute the extraordinary implications of Weichmann's testimony.

*

On 9 April 1865 General Robert E. Lee surrendered, on behalf of the Confederate government, to General Grant for the Federal government, at the Appomattox Courthouse in Virginia. The war was over; North and South were once more United States; Booth's plan of abduction had lost its purpose.

It must have been on receipt of this news that Booth, who demonstrated the most violent and passionate grief, exclaiming, 'O God, I no longer have a country!' made up his mind to assassinate not only Lincoln but two other members of the government, Secretary of State Seward, and Vice-President Andrew Johnson.

The plot to this end was again overheard by Weichmann and reported to the War Department.*

Booth was to shoot Lincoln at Ford's Theatre and escape by leaping from the presidential box on to the stage. Payne meanwhile was to go to Seward's house, where the Secretary of State was in bed badly hurt in a carriage accident, and shoot him. And Atzerodt was to shoot Johnson. It was virtually certain that Stanton knew of this plan, and that he had ample time to do something about it. A curious supplementary mystery must be dealt with here; on the day of the assassination Booth left a note implying that they were intimate friends, at Johnson's lodgings; this, together with evidence that he and Johnson had formerly

---

* See Pitman, op. cit.

been boon companions in drinking and whoring, was to lead
Stanton, later, to try to have Johnson impeached. What Booth
intended by this act has never become clear. For I am not going
to the length of suggesting that Booth was acting as Stanton's
creature, though that would, in fact, explain the mystery; only
that Stanton, aware of what was happening, did nothing; and so
ensured Lincoln's death.

If it be true that Stanton knew in advance of the plan to
assassinate (a) Lincoln, the principal obstacle in the way of
Stanton's policy and ambition (see below); (b) the Vice-President,
who stood between Stanton and the Presidency in the event of
Lincoln's death; and (c) the Secretary of State, who hated and was
opposed to Stanton in cabinet and would be president if both
Lincoln and Johnson died, with Stanton as next in succession – if
this be true, then Stanton's guilt must be assumed.

But is it credible that such a man would be guilty of such cold
villainy?

The question is misconceived; or, rather, deliberately mis-
stated. For it is morally and emotionally loaded. Stanton was a
fanatically dedicated Abolitionist; he was fighting the South with
every intention of humiliating and severely punishing the whole
Confederate land for the crimes of slavery and rebellion. He knew
that Lincoln, although an Abolitionist, was willing to save the
Southern face if he could, to ease and soften the process of
abolition of slavery, to protect the South from Northern wrath,
Northern self-righteousness, and Northern greed; Stanton was
contemptuous of such magnanimity; he was immensely ambitious,
he dreamed of empire and like other men who do so must doubtless have persuaded himself that in desiring to rule his country he
desired its good. Such a man does not seem to himself a villain for
contriving the death of a colleague, for him there is a special dispensation; and, as Secretary of War, Stanton had been sending
men to their deaths for years.

★

Edwin McMasters Stanton, Lincoln's Secretary for War since 20
January 1862, was a very singular man. He was small in stature,

he perfumed his handsome beard, which at that time was a very eccentric manifestation of vanity, he always arrived last at Cabinet meetings, making a theatrical entrance and never smiling or greeting any man. He worked tirelessly night and day, but was very secretive about the nature of his work, communicating only his decisions, and that very tersely, to his colleagues in Cabinet and refusing to discuss them. He was dictatorial, forcing through his ideas by bullying until challenged strongly, when he was apt to become apologetic, evasive, and fawning. He was distrusted by at least half his colleagues as being crafty, secretive, and totally unscrupulous. The opinions of his character left to us by, for example, Secretary of State Seward and by the Secretary of the Navy Gideon Welles, whose *Diary* is a valuable source for the events we are concerned with, could not be more unfavourable. He was, moreover, detested by several of his generals, and notably by General McClellan, who believed that Stanton was so managing the war as deliberately to prolong it.

This was true; he was, and had said so in so many words; it was deliberate policy.

There were two wings in Lincoln's government, a moderate wing and a radical wing. The moderates, of whom Abraham Lincoln was one, although with reservations about their tolerance of slavery,* subscribed wholeheartedly to the Congressional Resolution of 2 July 1861, which declared that:

'. . . the War is not waged in any spirit of oppression, or for any purpose of subjugation or conquest, *or the overthrowing or interfering with the rights or established institutions of those [Southern] States*, but to defend and maintain the supremacy of the Constitution, and to preserve the Union with all the dignity, *equality and rights of the several States unimpaired*. . . . As soon as these objects are accomplished the war ought to cease.'

The italics are mine and they make clear that the North, or at least the majority who were the moderates of the North, were not fighting to abolish slavery or to give the North dominion over the South; they were fighting simply to preserve the Union. It is wholly possible that General McClellan could have given the

---

* It is, of course, quite wrong to assume that the North and the Republican party was solidly Abolitionist. Only a small minority was so.

North a quick victory on those terms in the first few months, had
he not been prevented by Stanton, who, unfortunately, had
Lincoln's support.*

The radical wing, of which Stanton was a leader and which
got him his place, had very different ideas. They were a mixed
bunch; there were the passionate and dedicated Abolitionists who
objected violently to the implication that slavery (those 'established
institutions . . .' of the Congressional resolution) was to be
tolerated and even, perhaps, recognized; there were some
Northern capitalists who saw the South as a vast imperial domain,
the future economic empire which the Federal Army was
conquering for them – it would not suit them at all if the seceded
states were received back into the Union on equal terms; and
there were the Republican party professional politicians who
knew that if the Southern states returned to the Congress with
rights unimpaired, their voting strength would soon put an end to
the Republican domination and all the valuable perquisites which
went with it.

But Stanton himself went very much further than most of his
fellow radicals in his implacable attitude to the South. Basing
himself on a thesis put forward by Salmon Chase, Lincoln's
Secretary of the Treasury, and supported by a small number of
senators and congressmen, he aimed at depriving the seceded
states of their status as states; at reducing them to 'territories'
and so governing them from Washington. Later, with the end of
the war in sight, he went still further. He proposed that the
Southern states should be grouped in 'districts' – e.g. Virginia and
the Carolinas were to form one of them – to be ruled by military
governors; that is to say, simply as colonial territories. They
would lose their statehood and their legislature; the military
governors, virtually proconsuls, were to be appointed by and
responsible to Stanton himself; and he would take punitive
measures against these former 'rebels'.

In short, Stanton aimed at the dictatorship of a huge empire.

* McClellan was the idol of the Army and it has been suggested that Lincoln was jealous
of him, because McClellan wanted to use the Washington garrison troops as well as his
own 300,000 men for his projected *blitzkreig*. Lincoln accused him of being a traitor. See,
e.g., Otto Eisenschiml in, op. cit.

But there was even more in it than that: for him, the stake was colossal; it was entirely possible that the presidency, following the 1868 election, would be within his reach. Dictator of the South and president and commander-in-chief of the North, he would be an emperor indeed.

There were, of course, many difficulties in his way; but three of the obstacles were obvious and substantial. If the war were quickly over, and over before much bitterness had been engendered, the people of the North, being generous and anxious to maintain the Union in its constitutional form, would not allow Stanton to realize his plan for the South; and the real Abolitionists were in a very small minority. That could be overcome by prolonging the war until casualties and hardships had engendered a bitter and revengeful feeling which would enable Stanton to do as he wished. But even supposing he accomplished that much, two men stood in his way: Abraham Lincoln himself would never consent to such treatment of the South as Stanton had in mind: Seward, Secretary of State, would be equally opposed to a Stanton *imperium;* and he had a better chance of the presidency than Stanton.

'At the outbreak, the Radical party represented only a negligible percentage of the nation. Abolitionists were still regarded with abhorrence by the great majority. If the contest had come to a close within a year or two the Southern states would have been welcomed back into the fold as repentant "erring sisters". Therefore the war had to last long enough to embitter the Northern sections to the point where the populace, saturated with propaganda and embittered by the loss of relations and friends, would become as vindictive as the Radical leaders. Secretary of War Stanton was quite outspoken about this. When a commission from New York called on the President early in 1862 to urge upon him a more vigorous support of General McClellan, it found Stanton with the Executive. Stanton then stated:

". . . the great aim of the war was to abolish slavery. To end the war before the nation was ready for that would be a failure. The war must be prolonged and conducted so as to achieve that."*

Stanton's aim of prolonging the war to such a point that the

* George B. McClelland, *McClellan's Own Story*, C. L.Webster, New York, 1937.

conditions for realizing his policy were created, was accomplished partly by his successful hampering of General McClellan and partly by the chances of war, among them the military skill of Robert E. Lee. Thus by 1865 one of the obstacles in Stanton's way had been removed and the remaining ones were President Lincoln, and Secretary of State Seward.

It would be gross over-simplification to consider Stanton as acting as he did solely in the service of his personal ambition. A leader is bound to confuse his own desire for more and more power with the aims, more or less legitimate, of his particular crowd and the claims of a policy which he believes himself to have chosen on its merits and not because it serves his personal purpose. That the extreme Abolitionist cause served Stanton's ambition does not alter the fact that the cause was good. He may well have believed that only he had the strength to ensure his party's triumph; and only his triumph, and the punitive measures which would follow, could purge the South of the sin of slavery. He may well have believed that only through modern industrial exploitation by Northern capitalists could the South be made to yield the wealth to pay the huge price of abolition and of the war which, in his belief, had been fought to enforce it.

The ordinary, decent, moderately honest, moderately merciful, fairly intelligent and feeling man, who with all the kindnesses and all the timidities of his kind, puts himself in Stanton's shoes, as far as his imagination enables him to do so, will, judging by his own feelings and his own thoughts, be sure that even accepting all Stanton's arguments as I have supposed them to have been, it certainly does not follow that Stanton would have gone on to connive at the assassination of Lincoln, Seward, and Andrew Johnson, which is what I have accused him of doing. But, of course, Stanton was not such an ordinary, decent man. In all the ages of history men possessed by the taste for power more and more fully indulged; by a great cause which seems to them to enoble all they do; and by a towering ambition to be even greater, such men have always found the strength to break every law and every tabu and to commit great crimes. Perhaps we rather see such men in the transforming robes of nobility or majesty, or in armour, or in the outlandish garments of an alien civilization. But it would be a very simple-minded mistake to be misled by the fact that Stanton was a Victorian American and wore a collar and tie. The clothes and manners change but not the men.

*

On Good Friday, 14 April 1865, the Washington *Evening Star* carried an advertisement announcing that General and Mrs Grant, who were on their way from Richmond to Philadelphia, would visit Ford's Theatre in the company of President and Mrs Lincoln. The Grants had been invited by the president chiefly to give Washington a chance to see General Grant, hero of the North and arch-villain to the South, and by way of a compliment to the victor. Mr and Mrs Stanton had also been invited. The Grants did not keep that appointment; instead, they left Washington that evening, ostensibly in great haste to see their children; the only train they could catch was a slow one and would get them to their destination only about two or three hours before the morning express. But Grant had missed other and much easier chances to see his children; in short, the children were the only, and a very lame, excuse they could think of to rat on the President's theatre party.

What had happened was this: at three in the afternoon, while the general was at the White House, Mrs Grant had learned that the Stantons had refused the invitation to Ford's. She was unwilling to be in Mrs Lincoln's company without some other guests by way of buffer. She sent a note to the White House, and although we do not know what was in it, she was probably announcing her determination to leave the city as soon as possible, on some excuse or other, no doubt that of her children, in order to avoid the theatre party. She had a perfectly good reason – Mrs Lincoln's almost insane and quite uncontrollable jealousy. She had had two tastes of that and was not prepared for another. When, some weeks before, she had been the Lincolns' hostess at City Point, Mrs Lincoln had made a furious and very embarrassing scene at the beginning of a visit to the front lines because, while she and Mrs Grant were to be driven in an army ambulance, the only other woman present, a Mrs Griffin, was to ride horseback with the men. Mrs Lincoln had screamed at her hostess, 'Do you not know that I never allow the President to see any woman alone?' Mrs Grant, a woman of breeding and naturally sweet-natured, was upset. But her trials were not over, for on the following day Mrs Lincoln made another and worse scene of crazy jealousy when she accused the wife of General Ord of flirting with Lincoln, and called her some vile names. And when Mrs Grant intervened in an attempt to calm her rage, Mrs Lincoln accused her of having designs on the White House herself.

Grant did not immediately fall in with his wife's plan; he went over to the War Department to get the advice of his civilian superior, Stanton. Stanton strongly urged Grant to leave town with his wife and by all means to avoid the theatre party; Stanton told him that it was difficult enough to protect Lincoln against would-be assassins, let alone Grant as well.

In fact, of course, Grant's presence would have protected the President more effectively than almost anything else Stanton could have done. He would have had his guards, tough and vigilant soldiers; and at least a staff officer or two.

★

Abraham Lincoln was inclined to superstition and a sort of vague mysticism. His spirits and nerve were apt to be affected by his dreams. Lincoln was uneasy, perhaps because of the threats he had been receiving, although he usually laughed at them and declared that 'if they killed him they might get a worse man'; above all because of a dream in which he saw himself lying in state. It is not very satisfactory to say that there seems to have been tragedy in the very air of Washington that day, yet there is good evidence of a sort of underlying uneasiness and trouble before, and not merely after, the event. The reader is referred to the first pages of Chapter Six for some curious historical facts touching these kinds of 'premonitions' and their source in the most ancient layer of man's manifold spirit. The *New York Tribune* had contributed to this by printing a letter on 19 March about a conspiracy to kidnap the President. Lincoln's friend,

Provost Marshal Ward Lamour, had told Orville Browning that he believed Lincoln would be assassinated.* Another provost-marshal, David Dana, believed that the government had advance knowledge of the Booth conspiracy. William Crook, one of Lincoln's bodyguards, recorded that on 14 April Lincoln had said to him, 'Crook, do you know, I believe there are men who want to take my life? And I have no doubt they will do it.' Later he said, 'If it is to be done, it is impossible to prevent it.'

There is another possible contributory explanation of Lincoln's uneasiness: was he not beginning to feel the burden of guilt which he had taken on himself for the people? With the war won, the supporting tension of action was suddenly slackened. There would, of course, be heartfelt relief. But to win the war Lincoln had had to commit what, for a feeling man brought up in the Christian ethic and sufficiently imaginative to consider humanity under the aspect of eternity as well as under that of expediency, were great crimes implicit in the will of the embittered people, crimes troubling to the conscience of so good a man.

So disturbed was Lincoln that this brave man who had had to have a bodyguard forced on him and had laughed at threats against his life, whose courage was famous and who found the ordinary precautions taken to preserve a president most irksome, went himself to the War Department that afternoon and person-ally asked Stanton to give him a special guard at Ford's Theatre that night. The man he asked for was Stanton's chief *aide*, Major Thomas Eckert, an officer whom Lincoln had once seen break five iron pokers in succession over his arm and who was as remarkable for his discretion as for his physical strength.

Stanton, without hesitation, refused. He could not possibly spare Eckert, there was important work for him, he would be on duty in the War Department telegraph office. Lincoln then went to the outer office and asked Eckert himself if he would come, saying that surely his work could wait until the morning. In some embarrassment Eckert said that Stanton was his superior officer and left it to him; Stanton again refused. Lincoln left the office,

* Orville H. Browning, *Diary*, Trustees of Illinois State Historical Library, Springfield, Ill., 1933.

hurt and disappointed, saying, 'Then I shall take Major Rathbone along . . . but I should much rather have you, Major, since I know you can break a poker over your arm.'*

It may as well be said at once that Eckert was not required for any duty that night; that he had, as appeared in evidence at the trial of the conspirators, no work to do; and that Stanton dismissed him to his home at six o'clock.

*

This will be the place to consider what guard the President did have at Ford's that night. As for Major Rathbone, he was too much occupied with his betrothed, who was also of the party, to have been of much use as a watchdog.

But there was John F. Parker, who was detailed to accompany the President and sit on a chair outside the presidential box.

Parker was a constable in the Washington Metropolitan Police Force. He had joined the force in September 1861; in 1862 he was charged with conduct unbecoming an officer and with coarse and violent language and was reprimanded for it by the Police Board; in April 1863 he was charged with wilful violation of rules and conduct unbecoming an officer; in April 1863, charged with extortion of protection money from prostitutes, later in the same month with being drunk in a brothel. Twice more he had to appear before the Police Board in 1863, on one occasion for sleeping on duty.

One of the reasons why Parker was assigned to guarding the President on the night of the theatre party was that, improbable though it may seem, he had very recently been seconded to the White House as one of the four police officers permanently on duty there. If it be surprising that a man of such bad character was a member of the White House police guard, even that is less surprising than the way he attained that place of special trust: it was at Mrs Lincoln's special request. She had sent a note to James O'Beirne, provost-marshal for the District of Columbia, asking for John F. Parker to be detailed for duty at the 'Executive

* D. H. Bates, *Lincoln in the Telegraph Office*, The Century Co., New York, 1907. Bates witnessed the whole scene.

Mansion'.* No explanation of this behaviour has ever been offered, and no answer to questions which it gives rise to can be given.

*

On the afternoon of 14 April Booth was seen at Ford's Theatre: he had presumably gone there to make some simple preparations while management and cast were busy rehearsing the play, *Our American Cousin*. He probably used a gimlet to drill a hole in the door of the presidential box so that he could watch the president's movements from outside; and he may have tested the length of the piece of wood which he used to jam the door into the foyer leading to the boxes, so that it could not be opened from outside. It is possible that he made one other preparation; he may have used the fact that a full rehearsal was in progress to decide at what point in the play to shoot Lincoln; he chose a moment when a certain line in the play always produced a loud roar of laughter; a laugh from 1,700 people would cover the slight noise he might make in slipping into the president's box and even, perhaps, the sound of the shot from the small Derringer pistol which he proposed to use.

Booth was seen in various parts of the theatre that night; at his chosen moment he went into the foyer which gave access to the boxes. Whether by Booth's own management or by luck, the notoriously unreliable John F. Parker had left his post and gone for a drink. Booth shut the foyer door, jammed it with the length of wood which he had left in a corner, ready, that afternoon; verified, through his spy hole, that Lincoln was sitting where he expected to find him; he stepped into the box and shot the President through the back of the head. He then jumped from the box on to the stage – was he not famous for his acrobatic acting? – and despite a fractured ankle was able to reach his horse and gallop out of the city unhindered.

While Booth was shooting Lincoln and escaping into Maryland, Payne and Herold had gone to Secretary of State Seward's house where Seward lay in bed with a broken jaw, a consequence

* Eisenschiml, op. cit. Her note, on White House paper and in her own hand, was among the unpublished O'Beirne papers in Eisenschiml's possession.

of the carriage accident mentioned above. Payne carried a bottle of medicine; the plan was for him to say that he came from Seward's physician Dr Verdi and that his orders were not only to deliver the medicine but to see Seward take the first dose. Herold seems only to have accompanied him to see that he got to the house and understood his role, for having reached the door and seen Payne inside, he set off to rejoin Booth on their escape route, which he did, going into hiding with him after their call at Dr Mudd's house to have Booth's ankle attended to. As for Payne, here is a paragraph from Stanton's letter of 15 April to the U.S. Ambassador in London, Charles Francis Adams:

'About the same time this murder was being committed at the theater another assassin presented himself at the door of Mr Seward's residence, gained admission by pretending he had had a prescription from Mr Seward's physician, which he was to see administered, hurried up to the third-story chamber where Mr Seward was living. He here encountered Mr Frederick Seward, struck him over the head, inflicting several wounds and fracturing the skull in two places, inflicting, it is feared, mortal wounds. He then rushed into the room where Mr Seward was in bed, attended by a young daughter and a male nurse. The male attendant was stabbed through the lungs, and it is believed will die. The assassin then struck Mr Seward with a knife or dagger twice in the throat and twice in the face, inflicting terrible wounds. By this time Major Seward, the eldest son of the Secretary, and another attendant, reached the room, and rushed to the rescue of the Secretary. They were also wounded in the conflict, and the assassin escaped. No artery or important blood vessel was severed by any of the wounds inflicted upon him, but he was for a long time insensible from loss of blood. Some hopes of his possible recovery are entertained. . . .'*

Finally, there is Atzerodt. The wretched fellow, sent out with a pistol to find and shoot Johnson, the vice-president, did nothing. It transpired that he lost his nerve, got drunk, and threw away his weapon: that did not save him from the gallows.

*

If this was not, on Stanton's part, a case of assassination by refraining from, instead of by taking, action, then it is remarkable

* Quoted in Eisenschiml, op. cit. Seward recovered.

it should look so very like it. We hesitate to believe a man in great office capable of such a crime, though history is full of such crimes; it is the business of a war minister to send tens of thousands of men to their deaths, and in Stanton's case they were his countrymen on both sides; why, then, should such a man hesitate over expedient homicide? Supposing him guilty, Stanton had ensured the full triumph of the South's most implacable enemies in the North, of which he was the principal; he had rid himself and his party of the man who could and would have seen that the South was treated magnanimously and honourably by the North and not treated as a conquered country: and he had nearly succeeded in removing the three men who stood between himself and not merely the presidency but virtual dictatorship of his country. It was Stanton who so managed the pursuit of Booth and Herold, giving secret orders to one of the officers concerned, that Booth, instead of being taken alive to stand his trial, was unnecessarily shot dead; it was Stanton who delayed the despatch of the news of the assassination to the press outside Washington so that the danger of Booth being caught by any but his own officers was minimized; it was Stanton who alone was in a position to arrange for the cutting of all telegraph lines, but his own military one, out of Washington that night, an event that has never been explained; it was Stanton who, in the teeth of strong opposition and protest, insisted on the trial of the conspirators and accessories by a court martial, and so was able to nominate the judges; Stanton, therefore, who must be held responsible for the blunders and ambiguities of procedure, verdicts, and sentences; it was Stanton who so bungled the handling of the pardon which would have saved Mrs Surratt from the gallows, that she was hanged against the court's intention; it was to Stanton that the diary, taken from Booth's body and later found to have had eighteen pages covering the period before the assassination torn out, was delivered; it was Stanton who was responsible for the drafting of the indictment of the conspirators in such terms that Jefferson Davis and the whole South were likewise indicted and so by implication convicted of the crime; it was Stanton who tried to have Vice-President Andrew Johnson impeached.

Stanton died in mysterious circumstances in December 1869. President Johnson had proved uncontrollable; the attempt to impeach him had failed; the attempt of Stanton's party in Congress to treat the South as conquered territory had been only partly successful; Stanton's dream of empire had paled and, if he was indeed guilty of letting Lincoln be killed to serve his own ambition and his party's policy, he was left facing the hideous fact that, although his crime had given his party in Congress and government at least a measure of the power it sought to exploit the South as a conquered foreign country, it had failed to give him the empire he had dreamt of.

Those in a position to know said that he died by his own hand.

*

In 1960 a Mr Roy Neff of New Jersey, a research chemist by profession, bought a second-hand book for 50 cents at Leary's in Philadelphia, a bound volume of *Colburn's United Services Magazine* for the second half of 1864.* It was one of those casual purchases which one makes for no particular reason. A few months later Mr Neff was looking through the book and noticed numbers and letters pencilled in the margins of some pages. Their arrangement suggested a code; a professional cryptographer confirmed that they were – I know nothing of cyphers, but for those who do, this was a 'substitution cypher' of a sliding variety. Decoding of the pencilled entries on pages 181, 183, 185–211 yielded the following:

'I am constantly being followed. They are professionals. I cannot fool them. In new Rome there walked three men, a Judas, a Brutus and a spy. Each planned that he should be the king when Abraham should die. One trusted not the other but they went on for that day, waiting for that final moment when, with pistol in his hand, one of the sons of Brutus could sneak behind that cursed man and put a bullet in his brain and lay his clumsey [sic] corpse away. As the fallen man lay dying, Judas came and paid respects to one he hated, and when at last he saw him die, he said, "Now the ages have him and the nation now

* For a much fuller account of this curious affair, see John Cottrell, *Anatomy of an Assassination*, Muller, London, 1966.

have I. But, alas, fate would have it Judas slowly fell from grace, and with him went Brutus down to their proper place. But lest one is left to wonder what happened to the spy, I can safely tell you this, it was I."'*

This was signed, in code, 'Lafayette G. Baker'.

General Lafayette G. Baker was chief of Stanton's National Detective Police Force.

'The second message, running from pages 106 to 120, and continuing on pages 126, 127 and 245, could have been decoded by a child since it simply involved dots being placed under letters on the printed pages.'†

This message read:

'It was on the tenth of April, sixty-five, when I first knew that the plan was in action. Ecert had made all the contacts, the deed to be done on the fourteenth, I did not know the identity of the assassin, but I knew most all else when I approached E.S. about it. He at once acted surprised and disbelieving. Later he said: "You are a party to it too. Let us wait and see what comes of it and then we will know better how to act in the matter." I soon discovered what he meant that I was a party to it when the following day I was shown a document that I knew to be a forgery but a clever one, which made it appear that I had been in charge of a plot to kidnap the President, the Vice-President being the instigator. Then I became a party to that deed even though I did not care to.

'On the thirteenth he discovered that the President had ordered that the Legislature of Virginia be allowed to assemble to withdraw that state's troops from action against the U.S. He fermented immediately into an insane tyrade [sic]. Then for the first time I realized his mental disunity and his insane and fanatical hatred for the President. There are few in the War Department that respect the President or his strategy, but there are not many who would countermand an order that the President had given. However, during that insane moment, he sent a telegram to Gen. Weitzel countermanding the President's order of the twelfth. Then he laughed in a most spine chilling manner and said: "If he would to know who recinded [sic] his order we will let Lucifer

---

* Cottrell, op. cit. Mr Cottrell, an experienced journalist, satisfied himself that there could be no question of a hoax worked by Mr Neff.
† ibid.

tell him. Be off, Tom, and see to the arrangements. There can be no
mistakes." This is the first that I knew that he was the one responsible
for the assassination plot. Always before I thought that either he did not
trust me, for he really trusted no one, or he was protecting someone
until it was to his benefit to expose them. But now I know the truth
and it frightens me no end. I fear that somehow I may become the
sacrificial goat.

'There were at least eleven members of Congress involved in the
plot, no less than twelve Army officers, three Naval officers and at
least twenty-four civilians, of which one was a governor of a loyal
state. Five were bankers of great repute, three were nationally known
newspapermen and eleven were industrialists of great repute and
wealth. There were probably more that I know nothing of.

'The names of these known conspiraors is presented without com-
ment or notation in Vol. one of this series. Eighty-five thousand
dollars was contributed by the named persons to pay for the deed.
Only eight persons knew the details of the plot and the identity of the
others.

'I fear for my life, L.C.B.'

Mr Neff set out to try to discover whether his volume of
Colburn's *United Services Magazine* had belonged to General
Baker. Treatment of the pages with various reagents ultimately
developed a signature – 'L. C. Baker' – which was pronounced
genuine by a handwriting specialist; it was written with an
invisible ink with a ferro-cyanide base. Mr Neff then went on to
do some research into the last period of General Baker's life. To
cut short a story told in detail in Mr Cottrell's book, he succeeded
in proving that Baker's account was true and the conclusions to be
drawn are that Baker was trying to leave to posterity an account
of the plot to assassinate Lincoln so that colonial exploitation of
the South would be open to a syndicate of Republican radical
businessmen and politicians in which Edwin McMasters Stanton
was a leader; that Baker had accumulated a large fortune by
secret means; that Baker was poisoned to silence him.

This is not the kind of evidence which historians like; it is
suspect. And yet it does much, very much, to confirm all one's
other reasons for believing that Abraham Lincoln's assassination
was not the work of a crazy actor-patriot with an unslakeable

thirst for notoriety, but was a work of politics which, as I have said, because President Andrew Johnson turned liberal when ensconced in the White House, only partially answered the assassinating party's purpose, and, because Azerodt was not up to his task, failed entirely from the principal conspirator's point of view.

5

THE KING MUST DIE

A PROBABLE reason, in addition to the subjective ones already suggested, for the uneasiness of victim and people before the assassination of a great leader is that hints and rumours touching the preparatory conspiracy leak out despite secrecy. The sacrificial victim has been chosen and the choice is known. There is an analogous case: in that great and very curious study of the Old Religion (of all Eurasia), *The God of the Witches*,* Margaret Murray shows that the death of King William Rufus of England, of Thomas à Becket, of Joan of Arc, and of Gilles de Rais were not only announced a thousand miles away within two or three hours of the event, but that William Rufus and Thomas à Becket knew they were to die and prepared for it. Of course, there is an important difference: Dr Murray's argument is that William, incarnate god of the Old Religion, died as a ritual sacrifice; and that the other three died as sacred substitutes or surrogates for the god incarnate in the king.†

* Margaret Murray, *The God of the Witches*, Faber & Faber (new edition), 1952.
† To quote the arguments in support of this astonishing theory would mean reprinting *The God of the Witches*, to which the reader is referred, in its entirety.

Because the ancient practice of sacrificing the king, as god incarnate, may very well contribute, as I have already suggested, to the state of mind of the assassin in some of the cases which I deal with in this book, it will be worth spending a few pages on its history before coming to two cases of king-killing in Russia, at least one of which looks more like a 'ritual' sacrifice than a purely political assassination.

The peoples of Palaeolithic Europe, West Asia, and the southern littoral of the Mediterranean worshipped a god whom they depicted in the form of a horned beast; about 10,000 years ago, possibly more, a painted representation of this god, impersonated, and therefore incarnated by a man, was made on a cave wall in the Ariège. The painting shows a man in the skin of a stag, the antlered head on his head but with a tail longer than a deer's. In a similar painting in the Fourneau du Diable, Dordogne, the horns are those of a bull or antelope of some kind. The Abbé Henri Breuil* has argued that man's first attempt to give a figurative artistic expression to his feelings about religion was *dramatic:* he put on the skin of the divine animal whose sacrifice fed the people (quite literally, since it was a game animal), and so became the god for the time being; figuratively painting, such as those cave-wall representations of man-as-god, came later. Thus the religion was much older than the sacred paintings, perhaps as old as the species *Homo sapiens,* and conceivably even older. To sum up this point: the horned animal whose flesh fed the people is conceived of as god; so what we have, probably from more than 25,000 years ago, all over the western part of the Old World in Palaeolithic times, is a god who is worshipped, honoured, and, at a certain moment, killed and eaten.

This horned god is by far our oldest divinity and his worship by far our oldest surviving (for it survives still) social institution; feelings derived from the manner of worshipping and sacrificing this god, throughout all but the last couple of thousand years of our last 25,000 at least, lie deep in our spirits. Now three questions: How long did the horned god last into historical times? Can we

* Abbé Henri Breuil, 'L'Art Paléolithique', Chapter 4 of André Varagnac (ed.), *L'Homme avant l'écriture,* Librairie Armand Colin, Paris, 1968.

really exclude him, as a god still worshipped and sacrificed, from our last 2,000 years? Was the horned god also the King or Chief?

'The greatest of all the sacrifices was that of the god himself. . . . Frazer [in *The Golden Bough*] has shown that the Dying God was originally the ruler of the tribe, in other words the King. . . .'*

Doubtless the horned god of the Ariège and Dordogne caves was the ruler of his tribe and destined to die for the people.

'When the custom begins to die out in any country, the first change is the substitution of some person of high rank who suffers in the King's stead; for a few days before his death the substitute enjoys royal powers and honours as he is, for the time being, actually the King.'†

For dates later than the prehistoric ones to which Frazer's arguments are referred, there is much evidence that the horned and dying god was incarnate in the leader or king. The earliest Egyptian representations of the god (who in early avatars may be male or female) is on the very early (pre-Dynastic) slate-palette of King Narma. Here the horns are of the almost horizontal, goat-like, kind. Osiris is depicted with horizontal ram's horns; so is Isis. When the Pharoah was crowned it was with the horned diadem of Osiris and Isis: he became the god, and for a ritual dance which he performed as part of his sacring he was dressed not only in horns but wore a bull's tail fastened to his person. He was, in short, the horned god of Ariège still, as was the god Enkidu of Ur and Lagash and Eridu and cities not so ancient as these, Babylon herself even. In the proto-Hellenic world he appears as the Minotaur, begotten by a bull on the Cretan queen got up, like the Ariège figure, in the skin of a cow. Zeus himself has a taurine epiphany. Abraham has to sacrifice his son Isaac for the good of the people; he is allowed to substitute a ram; the ram becomes the prince. When Alexander the Great deified himself, he wore a horned diadem. The god is Pan in one later avatar. Consider, also, of course, John II: 50: 'It is expedient that one man die for the people.' The robber Barabbas in the rationalized and garbled crucifixion story is the *bar abbas*, a substitute for the

* Murray, op. cit.   † ibid.

divine king or incarnate god: there are many instances (cf. Frazer among others) of a criminal being chosen as a substitute for the divine king in the seven- or nine-year ritual sacrifice of the god. Robert Graves argues that Jesus was the rightful king of the Jews, and for the pagans (the majority) among them, he was no doubt the old horned god incarnate. God-eating, as old a practice as we can trace back into the remotest Palaeolithic, is still a part of the Mass.

The Christian clergy, in their very long and bitter struggle to impose the Iron Age Pauline religion on the Palaeolithic pagan one, and to wipe out the Old Religion entirely, chiefly by tireless abusive, 'newspeak' propaganda of the kind we were all too familiar with in the Nazi attacks on the Jews and their other crowd-enemies, and in Communist propaganda still, could and did transform the horned god into the devil in their mythology: what they failed to do was to make the millions of ordinary people – for a very long time indeed – accept their assertion that the old god was evil, the Evil One. For his faithful he remained the Good One; true, the faithful were fewer and fewer, but they still survive. They were, as Murray shows, the 'witches' and 'fairies' of the Middle Ages and into the eighteenth century; and she argues that the 'fairies' were Bronze Age Palaeolithic and Neolithic people driven into remote places by invading Iron Age people, and preserving the Old Religion, even reintroducing it among the newcomers.

As to the question, important in our context (for I am trying to show that deep in the spirit of some assassins can be found the originally holy (later stigmatized as diabolical) impulse to sacrifice the leader (god incarnate) for the good of the people), of how late into historical times the Old Religion endured, there is no difficulty in answering that. The God is Puck, Robin Goodfellow; he is also Robin Hood (Robin with a Hood), with his coven of twelve. How old are these 'Robin' names? I don't know, but, to quote Murray again:

'The earliest record of the masked and horned man in England is in the *Liber Poenitentialis* of Theodore, who was Archbishop of Canterbury from 668 to 690. . . . This was a time when – if we are to believe the ecclesiastical chroniclers – England was practically Christianized, yet Theodore fulminates against anyone who "goes about as a stag or a bull; that is, making himself into a wild animal [etc.] . . . because this is devilish".'*

Three centuries later King Edgar was having to urge his subjects to prefer Christianity to the Old Religion, to which a majority, according to his churchmen, still adhered. We have seen already that King William Rufus was almost certainly of the Old Religion and died for it as a sacrifice – god incarnate.† That, with a hundred other possible examples very well documented, gets us into the eleventh century. Skipping evidence from the twelfth century to the fifteenth century – extremely copious because the Church was waging its campaign against 'witches', i.e. against sectaries of the horned god (the Church's 'devil') – we come to the sixteenth century, and will take two instances by way of example:

'The cult of Robin Hood was widespread both geographically and in time, which suggests that he was more than a local hero in the places where his legend occurs. In Scotland as well as England Robin Hood was well known, and he belonged essentially to the people, not to the nobles. He was always accompanied by a band of twelve companions, very suggestive of a Grandmaster and his Coven. . . . Robin Hood and his band were a constituent part of the May-day ceremonies. . . . [In] 1580 Edmund Assheton wrote to William ffarington about suppressing "Robin Hoode and the May games as being Lewde sportes." . . . In all the stories and traditions of Robin Hood his animosity to the Church is invariably emphasized, an abbot or a prior was regarded as his legitimate prey. In one of the oldest Ballads of this popular hero, there is a description of how he went to be let blood by his cousin the prioress of a convent of nuns; she treacherously left the wound unbound and he bled to death. Part of the account shows, however, that his death was expected, for his route to the priory was lined with people, mourning and lamenting for his approaching death. The strong resemblance to the death-processions of Joan of Arc and Gilles de Rais cannot be overlooked, the weeping praying populace are alike in all three cases.'‡

In short, Robin with a Hood was a generic name for the god

---

* Margaret Murray, op. cit.
† For the fascinating details and argument, see ibid.   ‡ ibid.

and his sacrifice was to be expected as necessary. It is, by the way, pleasant that Robin's Day, May Day, is still the People's Day, Labour Day; the Day of the revolutionary political parties.

There is a much more recent piece of evidence. Within the lifetime of anyone over sixty the 'Dorset Ooser' was stolen, presumably for use, from its owners. The 'Dorset Ooser' is a mask to be worn over the head; it had a 'human', albeit terrifyingly fierce face, and bull's horns and frontal hair. It is quite obviously to be connected (through, as has been shown, an unbroken tradition) with the horned god of Ariège. Stag, bull, or great he-goat, it is all one. In France the god is a goat as often as not, in Germany he may even be a pig; he can be a cat, or even a dog, but nearly always he is horned. And what of America? In 1929, the Rev. J. R. Crosby, writing in *The Living Church*,* described how the rites of the Old Religion were still to be found very much alive in Pennsylvanian communities. The witch (i.e. sectary of the horned god):

'lives alone with the traditional black cat, in a small house filled with herbs, charms and the implements of her profession. Her compatriots have a firm conviction that she, together with her ancestors for untold generations, entered into a definite compact with the Devil who in his proper person is the father of all the children in the family. Certain other members of the Sect, the Elect Ones, are permeated with the Spirit of Good, and are regarded as incarnations of the Divine Essence. . . .'†

One final point before we come to the connexion between all this and our subject of assassination: 'Witches', that is to say, sectaries of the Old Religion, were accused of cannibalism, and especially of killing and eating Christian babies. There is an analogue here with the exactly similar accusation brought against the Jews, who were in some way connected, by Christian fanatics, with the pagans. But whereas there is no evidence that the Jews ever sacrificed children, there is some evidence that the worshippers of the horned god, while they did not kill babies, may have eaten some parts of already dead babies. There is a single

* 2 March 1929.   † Quoted in Margaret Murray, op. cit.

conviction on record (Scotland, 1658) for actually sacrificing a baby; and a number for eating a piece of the liver of a still-born child for the specific purpose of gaining the necessary power of 'tactiturnity' under torture. (This is very typical ritual canni- balism. The eater acquired the attributes of the eaten: new babies cannot talk.) However, the point here is that accusations of child- sacrifice against the Jews probably arose from confusion between Jews and pagans in the Christian mind: and they are relevant into modern times, as we shall see when we come to the assassination of Walther Rathenau, which was, at least in part, a ritual sacrifice.

What conclusions are we to draw from all this? First that up to 500 years ago, only twenty generations, a very large minority, possibly even a majority of Europeans, were wholly or partly loyal to the ancient, aboriginal religion of the horned god. That up to 300 years ago this religion still had so many sectaries that the Church, and the new Protestant sects as well, had to mount large, long-term, and cruel campaigns of persecution to keep it in hand. That it was primarily the religion of the people, although many patricians belonged to it. That it had, in its hold on very large numbers of people, the strength of its enormous antiquity. And that, central to it, was the belief that, from time to time (at seven-year intervals in England, nine-year intervals in France), a king, or a substitute king, in whom the god was incarnate, must die for the people.

I believe that some enlightenment may follow allowing our minds to be coloured by this knowledge, as well as by our know- ledge of the Freudian Oedipus complex, when considering the whole subject of assassination of leaders. The king's death saves the people; it puts an end to winter; a new spring can begin. Even if the gain is not such as can be counted by economists or recorded by sociologists, it may be very considerable, may usher in that renewal which comes with the grief – and relief – of the Father's death.

★

A king who was effectively sacrificed for the people was the Tsar Paul I of Russia.

The history of the Russian people begins in freedom but develops in slavery: perhaps no people was ever as forebearing with the leaders whom they allowed to impose themselves. The ordinary people of Russia were misled, abused, starved, enslaved, and butchered for many centuries before they themselves had recourse to the kind of violence which had for so long been used against them.

The part played by assassination in Russian history has been considerable, and its consequences often beneficial. The most interesting case which we come to later is that of Alexander II. But it is of interest because it demonstrated the futility of destroying a tyrant when there was another and much worse one ready to replace him. One of the social advantages of a republic is that the assassination of a president may lead to an entirely new policy; a hereditary, as distinct from an elective (e.g. that of the U.S.A.) monarchy, tends strongly towards continuity of policy. There is often less point in assassinating an emperor than a president. But emperors, even those who wish to confer liberty on their peoples (and the Tsar Alexander II was doing his best), cannot give from above what is only valid if taken from below – self-government.

It is far from surprising that the Russian revolutionary movements had to learn this truth by experience: for so excellent in its consequences had been the assassination of Alexander II's grandfather, the Tsar Paul, that liberals and reformers of all shades of opinion were entitled to believe that in the assassination of tsars they had found the means to improve the common Russian lot.

THE ORIGIN OF THE PROVOCATION

The hideous institution which disgraced the Russian past was serfdom. When first revealed by the, albeit dim, light of history, the Slavs who were to become Russians were free cultivators, farmers loosely organized into communes based on villages. Ownership of land was unknown among them; land was held in common and was inalienable.* It was out of groups of such free

* It is not sufficiently realized that until relatively recent times the idea of land being owned as alienable property by an individual would have been outrageous. Saint-Simon's dictum that 'property is theft' is strictly true in the case of real estate.

peasants that fighting princes of Scandinavian provenance, supported by a personal guard of warriors who were later to become
the Russian gentry, the *boyar* class, created small nations, like the
farming-fighting-trading principality of Kiev; the mercantile
republic of Novgorod; and the grand duchy of Moscow – the
nucleus of the enormous Russian empire. But the greatness of
states is too often founded on the misery of their citizens; the
greater Russia became, the more wretched were the majority of
her people.

The prince's bodyguard were given land, cattle, and slaves
taken from the communes. They, the *boyars*, became the first
individual landowners for whom land, and the beasts and men
living and working on it, were alienable property; or became so,
for at first they may simply have been held in trust.

Whatever its complex origins, the institution of serfdom spread
and grew until, in the seventeenth century, at least half the
population of all the Russias were serfs. Moreover, the institution
which had been merely customary rather than legal, and so had
left the peasants with some rights as human beings before the law,
was now given the force of law. From 1649 ownership of the
agricultural population by the landowning gentry was fixed by
government register; for the first time a child born to a serf was
automatically and inescapably a serf in law. Legally bound to the
estate where their fathers were registered were 'All who shall be
born after the census . . . because their fathers are written in the
census book'. In short, serfdom had become hereditary and the
whole Russian people was enslaved to the gentry by the state.*

The peasants were still not slaves in law; but this was a distinction without a difference since in practice they were chattels. For
example, if a landowner killed another's serf he was obliged to
give one of his own best serfs to replace the dead one. Serfs, in
short, were cattle. Still worse was to come: in the legal code
promulgated in 1754 the peasantry, that is the majority of the
Russian people, simply disappeared as a class of human beings and
became legally cattle: they were not legislated for because they no

---

* As far as I know, only one good thing ever came out of this monstrous injustice, i.e.
one of the greatest comic novels ever written, Gogol's *Dead Souls*.

longer had any rights whatever. They were mentioned in the code only under the heading of property of the gentry who had full power over them excepting to torture or to murder. From time to time the serfs, who by 1770 had been deprived of all human rights whatsoever and reduced to the status of cattle, rose and tried to assert their manhood; such risings were put down by armed force, often by the use of artillery.

When Catherine the Great came to the throne there seemed at first to be some hope of reforming this atrocious social system. But it is doubtful whether Catherine, a liberal by profession, would really have been able to accomplish much in that direction, opposed as she was by the entire aristocracy and gentry, with a few exceptions. In the event, she did not even get a chance to try: for when the peasants by scores of thousands joined to the forces of the rebel Cossack leader Pugachev, whose advances and victories for a while terrified the Russian ruling class and the Court, they condemned themselves. Pugachev was defeated, captured, and put to death by Suvorov in 1775; his movement collapsed; the gentry and the government, vengeful after their fright, made quite sure that the peasants were worse off than ever.

'In an edict punishing a cruel proprietor she used the ironical words, "Be so good as to call your peasants cattle": and she plainly predicted that the existing state of things was leading to a huge social cataclysm. . . . Yet the number of serfs was vastly increased under Catherine. The frequent and enormous grants of land . . . were grants of new-made serfs out of that diminishing section of the peasantry which still remained comparatively free. . . . Russian squires were now allowed to send serfs as convicts to Siberia without any restriction and to fetch them back when they pleased. . . . *All petitions, whether to the Empress or to government offices, were declared illegal and punished with knout and life exile.* . . . Public sale of serfs by auction were . . . allowed in 1773. . . .'*

★

The Russia-of-the-serfs thus completed by Catherine the Great was inherited by her son and successor the Tsar Paul I: he was an epileptic with a very bad digestion who bitterly hated his mother

---

* Bernard Pares, *A History of Russia*, op. cit.

and her (purely theoretical) liberalism. He was an insanely strict military martinet and very soon became a tyrant who believed his tyranny divinely decreed and justified. There was, of course, no question of the peasants' lot being improved under him; he even took to terrorizing the gentry, sent an enormous number of people of all classes to prison or Siberia, refused even his greatest subjects the right to travel abroad, and treated his best generals, including the great Suvorov, as if they were his personal slaves. It is probable that had he confined his brutalities to the wretched serfs, none of his gentry would have been found to oppose him, or at least the opposition of the few genuine liberals, the few enlightened landlords, would have been ineffective. The tsar's mistake lay in treating the upper, as well as the enslaved lower, classes like dirt. He behaved more like a Turkish sultan, the only free man in the Turkish empire, than like a European monarch. Such, in short, was his conduct that not only the handful of liberals among the Russian gentry and intelligentsia, but even many decent conservatives, began to look to the tsar's eldest son, Alexander, as a possible saviour. Margaret Murray might, perhaps, have argued that hearing of this prince's notorious anticlericalism, contempt for the church, and outspoken social radicalism, the pagans among his subjects, the 'witches' and their followers, took Alexander for the god incarnate who would at first live and at last die for the people.

Catherine the Great, a sardonic humourist if ever one such sat on a throne, had given her grandson, Paul's son Alexander, a French republican revolutionary named Laharpe by way of tutor and mentor and thereby ensured that the young prince who was heir to the Romanov tyranny would be reared on the most advanced leftist ideas of the times. More, she had personally drawn up for Laharpe's guidance a curriculum of education based on the French humanitarian, atheist philosophy which, as an honorary encyclopedist, she professed. By the time that Alexander was sixteen years old he was an avowed and enthusiastic liberal, all his friends were liberals, and he was openly proclaiming his admiration for the principles of the French Revolution. He condemned hereditary monarchy, advocated a liberal constitution for his country, and declared that the serfs should be free, land-owning farmers.

Such was the young man who, if the Tsar Paul could be put out of the way, would rule Russia. We have here, in fact, one of the few cases I have come across in which the assassination of the reigning chief-of-state was quite obviously and unquestionably the best move which his people could make if they wished – as ordinary people always do – to better their wretched condition. And this was realized even by men who were by no means in love with the young Alexander's ideas.

Count Pahlen, the military governor of St Petersburg, was the only man whom Paul trusted and confided in. When the tsar asked him if, as he began to suspect, there was a plot to depose or murder him, Pahlen replied that there was indeed, but that he had all the strings of it in his own hands. This was true since Pahlen was the prime mover in the plot. He even persuaded Paul to recall from exile a number of liberal aristocrats whom he wanted to involve in it.

The plan to get rid of Paul was then put to Alexander: the tsar was to be forcibly deposed; Alexander agreed to this, but for form's sake emphasized that his father's life was to be spared. It seems improbable that he had not understood the conspirators' real intention, which was assassination; as a brilliantly intelligent young man he must have realized that mere deposition would have been extremely foolish. A majority of the country squires were terrified of Alexander's liberalism. Unless their hopes for a reaction were to be entirely destroyed by Paul's death, there would always be the danger of a counter-revolution to replace the old tsar on his throne and restore the old régime. Alexander must have known that for 'deposition' he must understand 'assassination'; in some such terms must Alexander have rationalized his wish to see his crazy and hated father dead, and it is a fact that he did nothing, when on the throne, to punish his father's assassins.

What precisely happened in the event is not clear: but a group of the conspirators, including a Prince Yashvill and the extremist Nicholas Zubov, were smuggled into the vast new Mikhailobsky Fortress-Palace by Count Pahlen and into the tsar's bedroom at night. The 'delegation' asked the tsar to abdicate, he responded by violently assaulting the spokesman, whereupon he was knocked down and then strangled with a scarf. This assassination occurred on 23 March 1801 and few political acts in the history of mankind have had social and political consequences more immediately satisfactory.

Alexander's accession was hailed with joy. He formed a Privy Committee of Reform out of his circle of personal friends, all of whom were liberals, and he seemed, indeed was, bent on emancipating his enserfed people. Among other reforms, he promoted and financed a vast scheme for education entirely free from class distinction; he enabled peasants to buy their freedom and a plot of land on easy long terms; he stopped for ever the practice of granting away Crown land and peasants, thereby preventing the making of more serfs; he gave Poland a constitution which was liberal; in 1818 he emancipated the serfs of the Baltic provinces; and he had already called for projects and plans to do as much for the rest of his empire. It is, in short, quite impossible not to admit that the terrible sufferings and degradation of millions were somewhat relieved and a measure of hope restored by the assassination of his father Paul.

In our context, the case serves to prove that an assassination can have excellent consequences and that there is one way at least in which a ruler can usefully die for his people. And so clearly had this been demonstrated that when, in due course, Russian progressives and lovers of liberty again had reason to be dissatisfied with a tsar, they sacrificed him likewise. Unfortunately, whereas the circumstances favoured a happy outcome in the case of Paul I, in the case of Alexander II they did not. Quite the contrary. Nevertheless, the consequences of assassinating Alexander II taught the Russian people a lesson; they made use of what they had learned in October 1917.

In later years of his reign, under the influence of Metternich and of Sophie Krudener, the Tsar Alexander, who had accomplished great liberalizing reforms in the first years of his reign, fell a prey to that terror of revolution which was to hag-ride the European and American gentry and bourgeoisie for the next century, which still does, and which produced both the Korean and Vietnam wars. This change in the tsar, so bitterly disappointing to all those men of good will who had seen him make a fine start on the emancipation and modernization of their country, provoked the rehabilitation, and the new foundation, of political and Social Democratic secret societies more or less revolutionary in their aims. Some, of course, were for reform by peaceful means, by propaganda and education, by industrial and agricultural development. Others were for using violence, and they again were of two kinds: those whose activities, pre-figuring Marxism, were based on thought-out techniques of raising the people under the leadership of an intellectual, dedicated revolutionary élite; and those with an almost mystical faith in individual and self-sacrificing acts of tyrannicide.

Many of the reformers and revolutionaries were members of the Royal Guard, which had long been a maker of palace revolutions. The Guard made its last, and totally unsuccessful, attempt at such a revolution during the confusion which followed Alexander I's death in 1825.

This confusion was caused by the fact that Nicholas, Alexander's younger brother, had never been told that his elder brother, Constantine, Viceroy of Poland and a liberal, had abdicated his right to the throne; and that, consequently, he himself was the new tsar. While Nicholas, in St Petersburg, was proclaiming Constantine tsar, Constantine was doing as much for Nicholas in Warsaw. In this absurd state of affairs, and during the exchange of increasingly acrimonious letters which ended in Nicholas's accession, the Guard seized the occasion to make a bid for a liberal constitution: this was the famous Decembrist rising in which 2,000 soldiers beseiged the new Tsar Nicholas in his palace, calling for 'Constantine and Constitution!', many of the privates being, according to Klyuchevsky,* under the impression that 'Constitution' was the name of Constantine's wife.

Miloradovich, the Governor of St Petersburg whom Nicholas, unwilling to use force, sent to talk to the soldiers, was stabbed in the back and mortally wounded by a militant revolutionary

* In Pares's judgement, Russia's greatest historian.

named Kakhovsky who advocated the assassination of the entire royal family, a massacre which might just possibly have been justified in the results. The tsar thereupon cleared the square with a volley of grapeshot from a battery of artillery, a method of discouraging aspirations to liberty which he had learned from an ex-revolutionary called Bonaparte. Nothing could be more curious to a visiting Martian than the contrast between the complacency with which we read of a ruler massacring the ruled, and the horror we express when the roles are reversed.

Following an investigation and the turning of tsar's evidence by the leader Pestel, five leading Decembrists were hanged and others sent to Siberia. This significant act of 'firmness' and the subsequent rigorous police rule which Nicholas denied in speech as consistently as he used it in practice, had the inevitable result of provoking more conspiratorial revolutionary activity while discouraging open and peaceful reformism.

But it must also be said that the Tsar Nicholas's only attempt at a liberal reform, his effort to force a measure of emancipation of the serfs on his ruling class, was at least equally responsible for the growth of conspiratorial revolutionary movements dedicated to violence. For so slowly did the five royal commissions set up to deal with this question work, and so effectively were such reliefs as were granted blocked by bureaucratic caution or deliberate delay, that would-be liberals were driven into conspiratorial attitudes by sheer exasperation.

'In his measures for the welfare of the peasants Nicholas met with continuous resistance which even went so far as the omission from new editions of such statutes as established peasant rights. He himself, too, repeatedly reasserted the rights of the gentry, even declaring towards the end of his reign that all the land was their property. By then rumours of impending emancipation were frequent among the peasants, and in large areas in the south-east numbers of them made their way into the town declaring that they wished to join the militia for the Crimean War which was then in progress, and on the supposed authority of the Emperor claimed their freedom in return. The government used armed force to suppress the movement.'*

* Pares, op. cit.

It is unfortunately impossible to know how many Russians were made casualties in the Tsar Nicholas's war against his people's aspirations, but doubtless it was many thousands.

All of which availed the tsar nothing, but helped to ensure his defeat and humiliation in the Crimea and in Turkey. But he was an obstinate man, and his last recorded saying, before dying of a chill neglected in March 1855, was, 'I cannot change. My successor must do as he pleases.'

In the event, nothing which his successor could hasten to do was able to save him from that violent death which Nicholas's obstinate stupidity had condemned him to.

*

The accession of the Tsar Alexander II could, in itself, do nothing to cool the heads or soften the hearts of the men now dedicated in Russia to bringing about change by violent means including assassination. The new tsar had been devoted to his father and had been educated by that father in the business of ruling Russia; in a few instances he had shown himself even less liberal than Nicholas. But that was an evil effect of filial piety. For Alexander II proved almost as liberal in practice (though a conservative in principle) as the young Alexander I. But he was too late to convince the embittered opposition that evolution towards constitutional monarchy and parliamentary government were possible.

The principal object of the tsar's domestic policy became the same as that of the revolutionary movement, the emancipation of the serfs. But there continued, of course, to be bitter and persistent opposition to reforms and to proposals for emancipation. This drove the Tsar Alexander openly to lead the reformers against the reactionaries, even travelling in his Empire to propagate his ideas, seeking and appointing life-long emancipators to carry out the reforms and coming out unequivocally against the reactionaries among his gentry.

Why then was he, even at the very time, being condemned to death by the left? Partly because, with the whole emancipation question out in the open and agitating the entire country, such necessary concessions as the tsar was constrained to make to the right were there to be clearly seen and blamed; but chiefly because the idea of freedom being paternally given by the monarch instead of forcibly taken by the people had become extremely distasteful to the militant left, even – which is doubtful – if they believed in it as a possibility. Moreover, there was now a nation-wide impatience exasperated by rightist obstruction, bureaucratic delay, and ordinary administrative difficulties. Tensions had built up until they became intolerable; perhaps only a Father-King killing would be sacrifice enough to relax them and bring in that renewal which the country and the people so desperately needed. Even the tsar's own frantic and driving activity seems like a kind of desperation, the fierce effort of a man to placate the Furies; to say, as it were, I deserve to live and be loved. In short, we have here a perfect case of the assassinee as a scapegoat.

Count Rostovtsev, in charge of the great task, worked so hard that he died of exhaustion in 1860, but by then a workable scheme, which had only to be forced past the opposition, was ready.

On 17 March 1861 the Emancipating Edict was read aloud in all the churches of the Empire.

Then why, again, was the tsar assassinated? One might again answer – because by this time the people needed a victim, a scapegoat, a new incarnation of their god.

*

By abolishing serfdom, Alexander had destroyed the basis of his country's administrative system, and a flagging civil service was faced with the task of reconstructing it. The tsar himself, after years of tremendous strain, was compared to a man who with great effort reaches the top of a hill and is only too ready to slide down the other side.

'Meanwhile the new generation created in the universities, during the first years of the reign asked for . . . a new era of wholesale political experiment. . . . The question was only between Liberals and Revolutionaries, the choice between gradual and precipitate change.'*

                              * Pares, op. cit.

The tsar and his government, on the other hand, were under the impression that they had finished a piece of work. In fact they had only just started one; it was as if the monstrous, the colossal injustice of serfdom has masked all the lesser injustices inherent in any absolute monarchy. But what still remained to be done was work which they were unwilling and unable, socially, politically, psychologically, spiritually, and financially, to finish. So clear was it that the Liberals had no chance whatsoever of getting their programme of civil equality, trial by jury, reform of the police, responsibility of Ministers, public control of finance and legislation, freedom of conscience, press and trade, put into practice, that Liberalism could not attract the loyalty and energies of the less patient reformers. Even had there been a chance of the old liberal programme becoming law, it would have failed to interest the new generation of reformers, whose aim was to sweep away all authority of the old kind whatsoever and to substitute for it not, indeed, nothing, as the name given to them implies, but the new authority of Science.

THE NIHILISTS

It was Ivan Turgenev, in *Fathers and Children*, who called 'Nihilists' those intellectuals who followed the teachings of a brilliant twenty-year-old theorist named Pisarev whose writings began to appear in *Russkoe Slovo* in 1861. Pisarev envisaged the new science as a discipline sufficient in itself to be the basis of order in the community, almost as if it might become a religion. *A propos*, the bitter opposition offered to all scientific research and progress by the Churches and their associated royal and aristocratic establishments, and, on the other hand, the long alliance between left revolutionary political movements and science, may have an explanation different from that usually advanced. The early and not so early alchemists, fathers of the modern physical sciences, were for the most part 'witches', up to their eyes in ancient, magical lore, and making such useful discoveries as they did more or less accidentally, as by-products of their magical practices. In short, they were of the Old Religion (in Church parlance 'in league with the devil'). For Pisarev both political and artistic life were anachronisms and all authority but that of scientific thought anathema. He advocated their total destruction. His influence, despite, or perhaps because of, his early death, was surprisingly great; his readers all over the literate parts of Russia became sure that their proper course was to sweep all traditional authority, all religion, and the state itself into the dust-bin, by force, of course, and make a fresh start with science as god and tsar. The assassination of the tsar, and possibly of the entire royal family, would be unavoidable. And this conviction spread among young intellectuals as Alexander's government showed itself increasingly reluctant and unable to go forward, and more and more inclined to draw back.

As it became clear that the Liberals, now calling for a National Assembly, could accomplish nothing, the Nihilists, and other violent revolutionaries, including many Communists (as they later came to be called), began to call for acts of terrorism against the government; one of their fly-sheets addressed to 'Young Russia' in 1862 openly advocated the assassination of the tsar and in the same year revolutionary bands several times set fire to parts of St Petersburg with, apparently, every intention of destroying the whole city. The government rounded on both the Liberals, who had no hand whatever in this kind of thing, and the mili-tants, who did. Meanwhile in Poland agitation was more or less continuous and irrepressible; demonstrations were put down by the Cossacks. An attempt was made to assassinate the Viceroy Constantine, the tsar's brother. Students' meetings all over Russia developed into riots and were suppressed by the Cossacks. Every act of repression strengthened the convictions and in-creased the numbers of Social Democrats, Communists, and, above all, Nihilists. Thus Alexander and his government them-selves provoked the shift from the theory to the practice of violence by repressing every attempt by the students to argue and propagate their political ideas, nervously cutting down and going back on their own policy of advancement in the field of education. And the governmental terror of, and acts against, students became more intense after a Communist student, one Karakozov, who had been dismissed from his party and disowned by them as crazy, shot at the tsar in 1866. As a direct consequence of this attempt on Alexander's life,

'. . . the Liberal Golovin was replaced as Minister of Education by Count Dmitry Tolstoy, who had opposed even the emancipation. The *Contemporary* and the *Russian Word* were forbidden by an Imperial Rescript of 23 May. The kindly Governor-General of St Petersburg, Prince Suvurov, was replaced by a police martinet, General F. Trepov. . . .'*

Reforms were halted; those in hand were curtailed or suspended and the promise of freer institutions and more liberal education were not fulfilled; censorship, in a new and still more troublesome form, was reimposed; the government repeatedly interfered in the free working of its own new law courts. And meanwhile the results of the Emancipation Decree were proving very far from satisfactory, for the burden of direct taxation and of redemption dues placed on the peasants turned out to be a crushing one. Successive crop failures coinciding with swift development of industries manned by freed serfs, with a policy of balance or surplus budgetting, and with grain exporting to Britain (following Britain's Corn Law Repeal), appalling poverty and often mass starvation became general in the rural areas, that is to say in most of Russia.

The misery of the peasants became the chief concern of the revolutionary movements. Students and other intellectuals developed a keen sense of the huge debt they owed to the peasants, an awareness of obligation which Pares describes as 'almost crushing'.† To avenge the long misery of the people and improve its present and future lot became the aim of every revolutionary movement, every politically conscious group of enlightened intellectuals. Bakunin's Anarchism entailed armed insurrection; Nechayev's nation-wide conspiracy entailed the assassination of royal persons and other leaders. While the

---

* Pares, op. cit.
† Not only did the peasants create the greater part of the national wealth, they paid 267 million of the total of 280 million roubles of direct taxes and the whole of the 42 million in poll taxes.

followers of the gentle Prince Kropotkin sought amendment by non-violent means, by living themselves as peasants or workers in villages and factory communities, educating the people and propagating the liberal idea, those of Bakunin were urging the total and violent destruction of the state, and those of Karl Marx its violent capture by the people.

The war against Turkey suspended most revolutionary action while the country was in danger; Marx's lesson that the proper friends of the proletarians and peasants of one land are those of all others, had not, and has not, been learned. But violence broke out again after the war, and now its chief inspiration was Thachev, who again advocated unlimited terrorism as the right means to gain the people's end. The feeling of the country about this is clearly manifest in such events as the acquittal, by a jury, of Vera Zasulich, who was flagrantly and manifestly guilty of trying to assassinate General Trepov by shooting him; and in her rescue by the mob when the police tried to rearrest her outside the court.

In an imperial tyranny, the emperor *is* the government; it was therefore logical and right that Alexander himself should become the target of those revolutionaries who believed that the government must be forcibly destroyed; the whole hateful system was incarnate in the tsar's person and operated only by the tsar's will. In 1873 a militant named Solovyev fired five shots at the tsar; and although he failed to wound Alexander, his attempt was not a complete failure for it initiated an organized campaign to rid the country of the imperial incubus, to sacrifice the royal scapegoat and purify the state of its sins against the people. The government, aware of this open conspiracy, appointed six of its governor-generals to fight the conspirators, arrested the whole of the 'Kiev Group' of the Land and Liberty movement, and hanged their leader.

*

By this time the Land and Liberty movement was divided into two groups: the moderates, relying on non-violent means, and the militants, dedicated to the use of force. The two groups did not quarrel; they collaborated together, agreeing to differ about means. The moderates were led by Plekhanov, a Communist who did not believe in the efficacy of assassination. The militants were, at this time, led by a man named Zhelyabov, a militant Nihilist and a brilliant organizer, who did. In 1879 Land and Liberty convened its members to meet at Voronezh. On their way to that meeting the militants, summoned by Zhelyabov, held a preliminary meeting of their own at Lipetsk, decided on what their course should be at the big meeting, and there, calling themselves the Will of the People, deliberately and solemnly, and in opposition to the moderates, pronounced sentence of death on the tsar.

Three or four hundred in number, organized in cells, the Will of the People now adopted the bomb as their weapon. Their Voronezh resolution was an act of war against the government. It was as if the Russian people recognized and respected this, for in their struggle with the police and the special forces set up to destroy them, the conspirators had the support of the people, who fed and hid them whenever they needed such help, whenever the police were too close to their heels. These dedicated assassins made a number of attempts to blow up the tsar's train, and in 1880 one of them, a builder's worker named Halturin, used his access to the Winter Palace to introduce a quantity of dynamite and blew up the imperial dining-room; had the tsar's guest on that day, Prince Alexander von Battenburg, not been half an hour late, Alexander would have been killed.

Terrified, the government handed over all its powers to an emergency Supreme Commission under General Loris-Melikov. It is important to realize that this was victory for the terrorists: it proved that terrorism was being effective. For Loris-Melikov was a hard-working, able, conscientious, and liberal-minded man who was determined to give Russia a constitutional government: Alexander II and his friends had surrendered, and the moment had clearly come for the Nihilists to call off their campaign and leave it to the Liberals to negotiate with the Supreme Commissioners.

But such movements become obsessed with the purely symbolic, the, as it were, ritualistic value of assassinating a monarch; for them it is an act of purification. Loris-Melikov tried to buy off the tsar's life by making a whole series of very considerable concessions in all fields to liberalism – sufficiently successfully to bring a large number of people over to the government side. So successfully, indeed, that the Will of the People, fearful that if they did not act successfully soon they would lose their justification, the sympathy and support of the people, hastened anxiously to complete their plans. They had already, with remarkable forward planning for contingencies, mined a number of the St Petersburg streets which the tsar might be expected to use. Zhelyabov and his followers organized in groups of ten, free to co-opt new members and each under a group leader. Each group was instructed and drilled in the handling and use of bombs by a revolutionary firearms expert named Kibalchich. But the police were active and persistent and Zhelyabov was arrested before any fresh action could be taken.

But that contingency, too, had been foreseen and planned for. Zhelyabov had a very able lieutenant in Sophia Perovska, who for years, although of good upper class family, had lived and worked among the peasants and urban proletariat as one of themselves and had gone over to the militants probably at the time when the Will of the People minority separated itself from the body of Land and Liberty while continuing to co-operate with it. Perovska decided that there should be no more delays and failures. As it happened, she picked the very day, 13 March 1881, on which Alexander II signed Loris-Melikov's project for the beginnings of a constitution,* for the assassination; it was, indeed, the danger of that project being signed, and so cooling the temper of the nation, which had hastened her plans.

From the signature of the Melikov project the tsar drove to a military review, went thence to lunch with his aunt, the Grand Duchess Helen, and thence set out for home, driving alongside the Catherine Canal. The Will of the People was ready for him; the student Nihilists Rysakov and Grimevetsky were his executioners, with Sophia Perovska to signal the approach of the tsar's carriage and mounted escort. At a wave of Perovska's handkerchief

* It included a small measure of representation of the people, administrative and financial reforms.

Rysakov threw his bomb, which missed the carriage and exploded among the escort, wounding a number of Cossacks.
Alexander alighted from the carriage to speak to them whereupon Grimevetsky shouting, 'It is too soon to thank God!' threw
a second bomb between the tsar's feet, which exploded, shattering
his legs, tearing open his belly, and mutilating his face. He was
able to say, 'Home to the palace to die,' and die he did, an hour
and a half later. An ugly scene, is it not? Thousands of Alexander's
subjects had suffered that agony, at his word, during his reign.

*

The consequence of this assassination was reaction. Alexander III,
who succeeded the assassinated tsar, was a dim-witted and
narrow-minded giant ruled by his ex-tutor Pobedonostsev, an
honest ultra-reactionary who thought that all good was to be
found in Holy Mother Russia and that all Europe was wicked and
corrupt. Another influence on the tsar's policy was the German
Kaiser, likewise a man sunk in the gloomy *Urdumheit* of ultra-
reaction.

The lesson was clear: so long as there were heirs, so long as the
monarchy itself continued to exist, it was useless to assassinate
tsars unless you went on to seize, demolish, and replace the whole
social-political system from the ground upwards. Most reformers
failed to learn that lesson; only the Bolshevik section of the Social
Democratic movement took it to heart, and, in due course, acted
on it.

We are, it seems, no further forward. I suggest that, using only
the cases of Julius Caesar and Abraham Lincoln as criteria, we
should, on balance, decide against assassination as a social-
political instrument. Taking the cases of the Tsars Paul I and
Alexander II as criteria, we should probably decide, again on
balance, in favour. We had better examine some cases of a very
different kind, cases in which sacrificial victims died, not with
their own consent, for the people.

Part Two

6

GAVRILO PRINCIP AND FRANZ FERDINAND

THE four assassinees we have now to consider were scapegoats, that is, they were assassinated not so much, even not at all, as themselves, but as representatives of alien crowds or alien principles or both. They were killed, as Mount Everest was climbed, because they were there.

Not all in the same measure: the Archduke Franz Ferdinand of Austria was assassinated because he incarnated and personified the Habsburg Empire which denied freedom, denied autonomy, and denied union to the South Slavs; a case, then, of one crowd making war on the leader and personification of the enemy crowd. But even so, his assassination is not quite a pure case of sacrifice for he had shown himself the personal, as well as the political, representative enemy of the South Slavs, so that they could and did condemn him to death on two counts. Mr Burke and Lord Frederick Cavendish, on the other hand, were pure, unsullied scapegoats: the Irish Invincibles would have assassinated, or tried to assassinate, any man who occupied their places and, as it happened, as a man Cavendish was guiltless towards Ireland. Walther Rathenau is a very special and especially interesting case.

A political enemy of the crowd whose assassins killed him, and in that sense a representative or scapegoat victim, he was a particularly suitable – although in my sense 'impure' – victim because he was personally responsible for, and not merely carrying out, the policy which offended the party of his assassins. But an extra dimension is added in his case; his assassins were Germans of the *Völkischer* persuasion, that is to say, the only remaining men of the west who, although they accept and use twentieth-century technology, are moved by very ancient superstitions. Thus it was of great importance to his assassins that the man they had to kill for political reasons was a Jew, particularly suitable as a sacrifice to their old German gods. As a consequence Rathenau was killed, on a religiously significant date, as an offering to the Teutonic gods, as well as to political expediency. Finally, there is the case of Lord Moyne, another pure scapegoat.

Although the Irish case among these four comes first in time, I am giving precedence to the Bosnian case here because, following the 'impure' case of the Tsar Alexander II, it is a natural link between the category of the assassination of politically offensive *persons*, and that of the assassination of 'representatives'. For, as I have said, Franz Ferdinand was not assassinated 'purely' because he represented the hated Habsburg Empire, but also because he was a personal enemy of the South Slavs.

The tale of nationalist revolutionaries and social revolutionaries who employed terrorist assassination against the Habsburgs is a long one. The Swiss were the first in the field; the ultimately successful revolt of the peasants of Uri and Schwyz against their Habsburg masters was fired by William Tell's assassination of their bailif, Gessler. We have already noted that Giuseppe Mazzini repeatedly urged his followers, the Italian Nationalists, to use assassination against the Austrian tyranny. In 1853, the Hungarian Janos Libenyi knifed, but just failed to kill, the Emperor Franz Josef. *Die Freiheit*, a journal published in London by an ex-Reichstag radical member, Johann Most, openly advocated assassination as a means to political freedom and social progress, and later, in New York, Most published a handbook for aspiring assassins, *Revolutionare Kriegswissenschaft* (*Revolutionary*

War Tactics) dealing, among other things, with 'the making and use of bombs, burglary and arson for the good of a cause, and certain aspects of toxicology already known to the Borgias'.*

In 1884 there was such a campaign of both nationalist and socialist-revolutionary terrorism in Vienna that a state of siege was declared.† Some actual and some would-be assassins were caught and hanged but, fearless and implacable, the revolutionaries were not to be deterred by counter-terrorism (i.e. application of the laws) and they demonstrated their ruthlessness by assassinating the Empress Elizabeth in 1898.

I repeat that such methods were by no means universally condemned even by respectable liberals. The gentlest of revolutionaries, the Anarchist Prince Kropotkin, wrote:

'We hate murder with a hatred which may seem absurdly exaggerated to apologists for Matabele massacres, to callous acquiescers in hanging and bombardments, but we decline, in such cases of homicide or attempted cases of homicide as those of which we are treating, to be guilty of the cruel injustice of flinging the whole responsibility for the deed upon the immediate perpetrator. The guilt of homicide lies upon every man or woman who intentionally or by cold indifference helps to keep up social conditions which drive human beings to despair.'‡

*

The complaint of the peoples of the many small nationalities within the Habsburg Empire was twofold: they were denied national self-determination; and their social conditions were vile. It was therefore inevitable that some of them should have recourse to terrorism and assassination against their tyrants. The South Slavs within the Empire looked longingly across the frontier to the Kingdom of Serbia and dreamed of unity with their fellow nationals in some sort of Serbo-Croat federation. There were thus numerous small secret societies of South Slavs in Dalmatia, Bosnia-Hercegovina, Slovenia, and Croatia, linked

---

* See George Woodcock, *Anarchism*, Penguin Books, Harmondsworth, 1963.
† *Annual Register*, 1884.
‡ P. Kropotkin, 'Anarchism and Outrage', *Freedom*(December 1893).

with others in Serbia itself and in Montenegro. All of which were more or less associated together in an unplanned, unorganized, and spontaneous movement of revolt which became known as the Young Bosnians after the title of an article, 'Young Bosnia', by one of their leaders, published in 1911 in the almanac of a Serb welfare society promoting education for young Serbs in the empire, *Prosvjeta*.

A common aim, the destruction of the Habsburg Empire, united secret societies which were purely nationalist in their aspirations with others which were revolutionary Socialist and dedicated to the emancipation of their countries from the shackles of an outworn and tyrannical political, social, religious, literary, and artistic 'establishment'. But revolutionary violence was not the only method they depended on for the emancipation and advancement of subject peoples. For example, there was education: *Prosvjeta* gave scholarships to poor but clever boys from the erstwhile Turkish and very backward provinces of Bosnia and Hercegovina to take them to high school. So did the Serbian government. Some of these youths went on to university in Vienna, Prague, Zagreb, or Belgrade, where they were brought into touch with all the new political, economic, and literary ideas which were agitating Europe. They read all the great revolutionary writers, studied the *Risorgimento*, and made heroes of Garibaldi and Mazzini. Then, in the long vacation, they returned to their primitive villages and again shared the misery and degradation of the peasantry they came from.*

When, in 1908, Bosnia and Hercegovina were finally absorbed into the Habsburg Empire and lost all their local autonomy, the South Slav students at Vienna University transformed their particular cultural society, *Rad*, into a secret revolutionary society to wage war on the Austrian tyrant. Members travelled their country and set up branches in Bosnia, Hercegovina, and the district of Sarajevo. A number of student members went to Serbia to receive from Narodna Odbrana (National Defence) some training in military and revolutionary action. Links were formed with the Viennese Social Democrats, and members went

---

* See Dedijer, in *The Road to Sarajevo*, op. cit.

to Russia to meet revolutionaries there and study their methods, including terrorism. One of the most active and influential members after 1910 was Vladimir Gacinović, who went to Switzerland to gather revolutionary ideas and learn the new economics from the Russian Socialist exiles, studied at Lausanne University, was much influenced by such men as the Communist Nathanson, and, later, in Paris, Trotsky; and who, in his turn, fed the Young Bosnians with ideas and inspiration.

Gacinović's principal link with these young people was a writer and school-teacher named Danilo Ilić, whose home was in Sarajevo. The son of a cobbler, he had sold newspapers as a child, had worked as a prompter and handyman in a theatre, had taken jobs in various parts of the country as a labourer, railway porter, quarryman, longshoreman, anything that offered. He knew the people and their sufferings and aspirations. Ill health forced him to take to a more sedentary occupation; he graduated as a teacher in 1912, but in 1913 he was off again, first to Switzerland, to visit Gacinović and meet the Russian Social Democrats chiefly of the Menshevik group, thence to Serbia to serve as a volunteer in the Second Balkan War. Thereafter he returned to Sarajevo to teach again, and his teaching was not confined to school subjects.

Whenever Danilo Ilić was in Sarajevo, he lived in his mother's house; it was a lodging-house for schoolboys of country families who were studying at the famous Merchants' School there. One day in 1907, during one of his periods of living and working in Sarajevo, Ilić's mother told him that he would have to share his room with a new lodger, a thirteen-year-old peasant boy who had just enrolled at the Merchants' School.

The boy's name was Gavrilo Princip.

★

Gavrilo Princip came of a family of Serbian *kmets*, peasant-serfs, living in a remote valley of a thinly populated region of West Bosnia, a region of rugged mountains in which only the valleys, with their deep deposits of aluvium, were fertile. From 1463 their country had been Turkish, and some of its inhabitants, especially in the upper class, were Moslems; the Serb *kmets* were Eastern Orthodox Christians, and the Croats Roman Catholics.

When the Turks conquered Bosnia and Hercegovina they left the established pattern of life unchanged, simply taking tribute from the conquered people; but their authorities would not tolerate any changes. Consequently, while the rest of Europe was changing rapidly, in Bosnia a very ancient way of life was preserved into the late nineteenth century. This way of life was based on the *zadruga*.

' "The *zadruga*", a familial community, was the basis of Bosnian patriarchal society. It was both an economic and a social institution. The means of production were owned communally. Relations within each *zadruga* were regulated on the basis of old custom which contained elements of patriarchal democracy and mutual aid. The joint family's decisions were reached through communal discussion. Complete equality prevailed among the male members.'*

This *zadruga* belonged to the Jovicević clan, whose feudal overlords, to whom the Princips were still paying tribute when Gavrilo was a lad, were the Sijercici. The burden of tribute to this noble family and of the taxes payable direct to the central Ottoman government, and collected by detachments of the Turkish army, kept the *kmets* miserably poor, and in 1875 the West Bosnians, shortly followed by the *kmets* throughout the province and in Hercegovina, rose in armed revolt against the Turks. At that time Jovo Princip, Gavrilo's grandfather, was serving the Turkish authorities as a policeman (*zaptije*). Nevertheless, he and the other adult men of the *zadruga* joined the rebellion, while the women and children sought sanctuary by crossing the frontier into Austria-Hungary.

The Turkish army was held in check by the Bosnians for more than two years. Meanwhile Serbia and Montenegro had declared war on the Ottoman Empire in defence of their fellow South Slavs within that empire, and when Russia did likewise, and made a swift advance on Istanbul, which the Turks could not contain, Bosnia and Hercegovina suddenly became of international

* Dedijer, op. cit.

importance. In fear of Russian ambitions in the Mediterranean, Britain sent her fleet to Istanbul; and in fear of Russian ambitions in the Balkans, the Austro-Hungarians mobilized their army. This dangerous state of affairs resulted in the convening of the Congress of Berlin.

The extraordinary result of the conflicting interests and shrewd horse-trading between Russia, Austria, Britain, and Turkey at the Congress of Berlin was, briefly, that while the sultan retained sovereign rights over Bosnia and Hercegovina, the Habsburg Empire was to occupy and administer those provinces. For the Princips and their like, this meant exchanging King Log for King Stork, and the national enemy of the South Slavs ceased to be Turkey and became Austria-Hungary.

Required to serve in the Habsburg army, the Bosnians began resistance again. A sort of sporadic half-war was waged between the *kmets* and the Austrian authorities. Jovo Princip, shot down while out duck shooting, was one of its casualties. Another was the *zadruga:* true, it survived into Gavrilo's childhood, but when Petar Princip, Gavrilo's father, succeeded to the headmanship it was decaying fast.

Petar did not marry until after his father's death, and his wife was fourteen years younger than himself. She had a firm and masculine character, whereas he was remarkable for gentleness, goodness, and piety. Of their nine children, all five girls and one boy died in infancy, leaving three boys alive. At that time and in that place, this was about the usual proportion of deaths to survivals among infants. Vladimir Dedijer describes Gavrilo's birth as follows:

'. . . when Gavrilo Princip was born on 13 July 1894 his mother did not believe he would live long. It was a very hot day even at such a high altitude as Grahovo Polje. The mother had been working all day long in the meadow, gathering grass which had just been cut. She had to make big bundles of hay, each of them weighing sixty pounds. When this work was over she went back home and washed linen in the brook. After milking a cow, she felt labour pains and ran towards the house. She was not allowed to make any sign that she was going to have a baby, not to cry or shout. She had only enough strength to enter the low door. She fell on the earth by the open hearth, and in a very short time the boy was born, falling on the stones formed around the fireplace. Nana's mother-in-law rushed into the house, bit the cord, and washed the newly born child in a wooden bowl and wrapped him in a coarse, hemp cloth. She built up the fire, brought in a bale of barley straw for the mother, and soon the house was filled with relatives, who were served with plum brandy. . . .'*

When the old parish priest, a greatly respected veteran of the *kmet* war, registered the boy's birth, he made a slip which saved Gavrilo's life twenty years later. Although he dated the entry in the Parish Register correctly as 13 June, he misdated it 13 July in the Civil Register which he also had to keep. Under Austro-Hungarian law a criminal could not be condemned to death for a crime committed when he was under twenty years of age; that month was to make the difference between life and death for Gavrilo.

As there was no living to be got at Grahovo, the Princip boys would have to go elsewhere to earn a livelihood as soon as they were old enough. Jovo, Gavrilo's elder brother, left home when he was fifteen and was soon doing well, so well that in due course he was able to send money home to help his parents, and later to make himself responsible for the education of his brothers.

Gavrilo resembled his mother, in looks and character, rather than his father. His father did not want him to go to school, needing him as a shepherd; but his mother overruled her husband and Gavrilo went to the primary school in Grahovo when he was nine. Gavrilo was vaguely ambitious, he resented his father's attempts to bind him to the land, and despised his father's gentleness, piety, and resignation. It was to his mother that he gave his affection and from her that he expected support for his ambition to study and to become an army officer. It is likely enough that a psychological analysis would have revealed a parricidal impulse nearer the surface than is usual even in so clearly oedipal a situation; which, of course, does not mean that the boy would have been anything but horrified at the idea of laying a finger on his father. But this is one element in the making of some assassins. He became a great reader and he was reserved and silent, but

* Dedijer, op. cit.

when he did play with the other boys he was aggressive and rough and he resented any slight with a violence which earned him respect even from the older and bigger boys. His marks were good and he was given a prize, a book of heroic Serbo-Croat poetry which he used to read aloud to the *kmets* who gathered round the fire of his father's house at evening.

At thirteen Gavrilo went to Sarajevo, where his brother Jovo proposed to send him to the Military School as a cadet; he would be an officer in the Habsburg army. He was glad to leave the village; it depressed him. Yet in his heart and mind he was never to be free of it; it is not too much to say that Gavrilo's memory of the kind of life his people had to lead cost the Archduke Franz Ferdinand his life.

On their way into Sarajevo from the outlying village where Jovo Princip had his small business, the brothers called at the shop of one Pesut to buy the boy clothes. Pesut was one of Jovo's most respected friends and he now begged Jovo not to send his young brother into an institution which would make of him 'an executioner of his own people'. Let the boy, instead, be sent to the Merchants' School. Jovo was impressed: better for Gavrilo to be a rich trader than a Habsburg officer. We do not know what the boy himself thought of this. It seems to have been his own idea to become a soldier; perhaps it was an instinctive rationalization of his aggressiveness. He accepted the change of plan. So, in August 1907, Gavrilo was enrolled at the Merchants' School and went to lodge with the widow Ilić and her revolutionary of a son, Danilo.

*

For three years the boy worked steadily and read everything he could lay hands on. He was still reserved and still apt to resent slights, especially on his small size, with violence. His holidays were spent at home in the village. His school friends were among the romantic and idealistic boys, rather than the sober and practical ones, so that after three years he became very ashamed of being at a school which would make a merchant of him. In those days literary and idealistic boys held business in contempt as the basest of occupations. And as he began to be interested in politics and to mix with juvenile revolutionaries, there was added to this contempt that hatred of the burgess class which is proper to a burgeoning democrat. Moreover, and finally, to an aspiring intellectual of peasant origin, the petty trader was what the gombeen-man was to the Irish peasantry. At all events, at the end of his third year Gavrilo, after a battle with Jovo in which again he had his mother's support against the substitute-father which this elder brother had become, and who was hurt since he himself was a small businessman, transferred to the Classical High School in Tuzla after passing a difficult entrance examination in Latin and Greek.

At his new school he sought his friends among the older boys, was awkward, restless, reserved, read voraciously and broke rules with deliberate ostentation of defiance. After a term or two he transferred to the High School in Sarajevo and passed the examination at seventeen which left him with two more forms to work through before he could be regarded as matriculating. His one absorbing interest was literature and now his single ambition was to be a poet; he had the makings, for he was a sensitive observer and he entered almost excessively into the feelings and sufferings of others, even of people he did not know. It was this, as much as anything else, that led him to join one or more of the Young Bosnia secret societies, to become politically conscious, and finally to take part in demonstrations of nationalist and Socialist students against the Austrian authorities. As a result, he was expelled from school in 1912 and lost the small allowance or grant he had been getting from *Prosvjeta*. Without a word to anyone, even to his brother, in whose house he was then living, he set out to walk into Serbia and to Belgrade and there, with other Bosnian students, he led a life of miserable poverty, sleeping in doorways and getting occasional meals to relieve starvation from the monks of the neighbouring monastery; but still he talked revolutionary politics; and still he read and wrote.

When Serbia went to war against Turkey in 1912, Gavrilo tried hard to join the army; he was turned down as being too small and weak; he took that as an insult and it rankled for the rest of his short life. He returned to his brother's house in Hadzici and went back to High School to complete the last two forms or grades, brooding darkly on his failure to play a part in the heroic Serbian victories over the Turks, and determined to do something for his country, something more dangerous and braver than anyone else.

*

The Serbian and Croatian nationalist struggle against first the Turks and then the Austrians was not the only struggle of the first decade of this century in Yugoslavia. There was also a social struggle by the industrial workers and the peasants against the authors of their misery. The man who came to personify both the oppression of South Slav nationalists and of the workers was the Archduke Franz Ferdinand von Österreich-Este, heir to the imperial throne.

Franz Ferdinand was not born to the purple. The Emperor Franz Joseph had come to the throne in 1848; at the time he had no son and his heir was his brother Maximilian von Habsburg, who, involved by Napoleon III in his crazy Mexican adventure, was captured and shot by Juárez. By then Franz Joseph had a son, Rudolf, who was Crown Prince until he shot himself at Meyerling. Next in line was the ultra-pious, Jesuit-ruled Archduke Karl Ludwig, who insisted on drinking Jordan water for the good of his soul while on a pilgrimage to Jerusalem, whereupon and predictably he died of typhoid and his son Franz Ferdinand became heir-apparent.

He was ultra-pious like his father, had been overstuffed with 'education' by four tutors so that he knew nothing properly but everything very earnestly. At fourteen he was commissioned second-lieutenant in the army and by his twenty-eighth year was a major-general.

He travelled widely, making a tour of the world and writing a book about it. But his health broke down; he was so ill with pulmonary tuberculosis that his early death was looked for; his lifelong aversion to the Magyar element in the empire may well have originated in a Hungarian newspaper article which declared him to be at death's door. He recovered from this lung trouble but was subject to fits of temper so violent that some observers suspected insanity.

He had fallen in love with a Countess Sophie Chotek von Chotkova. She was not within that degree of nobility which made her a suitable wife for the heir and the Emperor Franz Joseph forbade him to marry her. Very much under her influence, Franz Ferdinand persisted and was finally allowed to marry her morganatically. His wife was excessively religious, under Jesuit influence, vain, clever, and ambitious; she had every intention of behaving like an archduchess and of being empress. Her influence on her husband was such as to discourage the least vestige of any but the most illiberal ideas and policies.

He found his political policy and philosophy in a form of ultra-right 'Christian' Socialism which was neither Christian nor Socialist but was the forerunner of Adolf Hitler's National Socialism. In about 1880 the Vatican, much of its power and influence eroded by the union of Italy, revived anti-Semitism as a means of reviving ultra-Catholicism and striking at its Jewish competitors in the money and industrial markets. Anti-Semitism made a strong appeal to a section of the Austrian aristocracy, though not to all of it and never to the old emperor. But the Ultras attributed the rise of the finance-capitalism so damaging to landed toryism, the rise of *laissez faire* capitalist liberalism, and the rise of Socialism to the Jews. They took the fantasy of a world conspiracy of Jewry to buy all political power, the fantasy which was to find expression in the forged *Protocols of the Elders of Zion*, seriously. They found their ideal politician in the founder and leader of the fiercely anti-Semitic Christian Socialist form of proto-Fascism, Doctor Karl Lueger. The heir-apparent became Lueger's most powerful patron and supporter.

Franz Ferdinand's attitude to the Serbo-Croat component of the empire was at first a liberal one; he played with the idea of giving them the same measure of autonomy as Hungary, with their own parliament, so making the empire triune. At one time he even wanted to make the whole empire a federated state, as Yugoslavia is today. But when, in their 1903–5 nationalist struggle against the Magyars, the Croats turned out to be as anti-Vienna

as they were anti-Budapest, and when the Bosnian, Hercegovinian, and other Serbs supported the Croats, and themselves
continued irreconcilable, the archduke changed his mind. He
visited the Serbian provinces of the empire in 1906 and was
received with silent hostility, and even, in Dubrovnik, with
insults. As his policy hardened it became clear that he would be an
arch-centralist, hostile to local autonomies, bent on forcing the
total absorption into the empire of Magyar, Serb, Croat, Czech,
and Polish elements, with the Austrian-German element pre-
dominant in all things. When Franz Ferdinand emerged from his
formative period he did so as an arch-imperialist and anti-
nationalist; an extreme social reactionary; an extreme economic
conservative; a rabid anti-Semite. The Italian diplomat, Daniele
Varè, who knew him, says that he was a heavy, gloomy, and
unbending man: '. . . there was something menacing about the
personality of this prince. . . . He sought neither sympathy nor
affection. On the day when an assassin's bullet laid him low at
Sarajevo, the stock on the Vienna bourse rose, as if a public danger
had passed with his passing, and American newspapers welcomed
the tragedy, as making for a surer peace in Europe. . . .'* It would
not be unjust to label him as Europe's proto-Nazi.

*

Early in 1906 there was a general strike of industrial workers
throughout Bosnia-Hercegovina; soon, the peasants joined the
proletariat in this strife. The workers were demanding a nine-
hour day; and that their wages be paid them when they were due
and not when it happened to suit the boss; the *kmets* wanted their
freedom; and the free peasants a reasonable livelihood. The
Bosnian and Hercegovinian landowners and industrialists received
orders from Vienna to concede nothing; and the strike was put
down by military force with some loss of life. This was the
beginning of a long struggle in which the Archduke Franz
Ferdinand took the extreme reactionary side with such obstinacy
that, in the end, those Serbs and Croats in the revolutionary secret
societies who had not yet come under the influence of the more

* Daniele Varè, *Laughing Diplomat*, John Murray, London, 1938.

sophisticated revolutionary theorists who rejected the old way of individual terrorist action as ineffectual, concluded that the slavery and misery of their people would not be relieved until the archduke was out of the way.

There was nothing sensational in that decision; the Young Bosnians had been making numerous assassination attempts. Increased police action against high-school boys and students, including closure of schools, led merely to the terrorist militants in the South Slav political societies getting the upper hand of the moderates. Hundreds of students became marked men and any kind of movement inside the country or over the frontiers was almost paralysed by police controls and checks. That resulted in the secret societies taking pains to provide members with the right passes and passports.

A leader and model for the Young Bosnians was a law student named Luka Jucić, and when, in 1912, he organized demonstrations which led to battles with the police, in support of the Croat struggle in Hungary, Gavrilo Princip was one of the leaders. In the first big demonstration he was wounded by a mounted policeman's sabre. He thereupon organized a second demonstration coincident with a general strike of all the high-school and university students. In a schoolmate's diary he is described as going '. . . from class to class threatening with a knuckle-duster all those boys who wavered'. Princip then became the leader of one of the groups which were bent on assassinating Habsburgs and Habsburg officials. Their activity was suspended during the First Balkan War in 1912 when many South Slav schoolboys and students crossed the frontier and fought in the Serbian army as *komite*. But it was resumed in 1913 when the new Governor of Bosnia-Hercegovina, General Potiorek, used the excuse of war tension between Serbia and the empire to declare a state of emergency and suppress all Serbian and Croatian cultural organizations, all trades unions and all left-wing political parties.

*

Early in 1914 the old emperor ordered his heir to represent him at the military manoeuvres which were to be held in Bosnia in June.

Tension between Serbia and the empire was still high and the civil war between students and police still raging. The Austrian government thought that a visit by the heir to Sarajevo and his presence at military manoeuvres would be a clear warning to Serbia not to let her victories in the two Balkan Wars go to her head. The archduke himself was in two minds: he wanted a chance to wipe out the disgrace of his insulting reception in 1912; and according to A. J. P. Taylor* his wife, still known only as the Duchess of Hohenberg, wanted a chance to appear publicly on an official occasion as his consort. At all events, in March 1914 it was announced by the newspapers that Franz Ferdinand would visit Sarajevo in June. Young Bosnian groups at once decided that this was the chance they had been waiting for.

Princip, and his friend Cabrinović, were in Belgrade, attending high school and working on a plan to assassinate the archduke in Vienna, for which purpose they had been trying to procure weapons. Their friends in Sarajevo sent them a newspaper cutting announcing the archduke's visit to Sarajevo. Princip then asked Cabrinović if he would help him to assassinate Franz Ferdinand in the course of that visit, and Cabrinović agreed to do so. They recruited a third assassin, Grabez, Princip's room-mate. As for weapons, they next approached a young man, Milan Ciganović, who had won a gold medal for bravery in the Second Balkan War and was believed to have brought weapons home with him. Ciganović asked them to wait a few days as he had to see 'a gentleman' about this.† In due course he provided them with six bombs and four revolvers, and it is very probable that he got them from Colonel Apis, head of the Serbian Secret Service.

In most of what he did in his twenty years of life, Princip seems to have been amateurish; he dropped and resumed his schooling in a restless way, he seems to have found sustained effort difficult, and he never applied himself to the study of revolutionary or social and economic theory. But as an assassin he was thorough. For example, he now went to the Kosutujak Park, which was usually empty and, with three other conspirators, practised shooting with

---

* *Observer*, 16 November 1958.   † Dedijer, op. cit.

a revolver until he was tolerably sure of hitting his target from a standing position or while he was running. He kept up this day-long practice for a week. Meanwhile, he and his two team-mates needed money to get from Belgrade to Sarajevo. How they got it has never been made clear; the few dinars Princip got by pawning his winter coat would not have got them far. They claimed later that they borrowed the money against an I.O.U. or several I.O.U.s; on another occasion they said that they begged it from some Bosnian merchants settled in Belgrade. In all probability the invaluable Colonel Apis was really their banker. Was it he, also, who provided the cyanide pills they were to swallow when their work was done? If so, they seem to have been of inferior quality.

To get from Belgrade to Sarajevo the three youths had to cross Serbia, and the Bosnian frontier, and then cross a part of Bosnia; they had to do this in a country under such rigid police control that they were likely to be challenged, made to account for themselves, and searched. They would have to carry their weapons. In the event they only carried them part of the way: as far as one can discover now, a sort of underground or smuggling organization of pan-Serb police officers in both the Serbian and Austrian services, subverted frontier guards, and revolutionary peasants was used, with the help and connivance of Colonel Apis, if not of his department, to get them to their destination. The organizer seems to have been the secret society Ujedinjenge ili Smrt, of which Colonel Apis was some sort of associate if not an actual member.

In this, as in so many other of the cases we have dealt with, there was an element of foreboding. The archduke had once been told by a gipsy that he was 'destined to unleash a world war'. He seems to have taken this half-seriously; there was war tension between Austria and Serbia. Many friends urged Franz Ferdinand not to leave Vienna. He knew himself hated in Bosnia-Herce-govina, as well he might be, and jokingly (but not altogether jokingly) said that he expected bombs to be thrown at him there. There is no doubt that he was uneasy, talked morbidly of the visit, and would perhaps have avoided it if he could.

He and the Duchess of Hohenberg travelled separately to Ildize Spa, a few miles south of Sarajevo, arriving there on 25 June. General Potiorek, the Governor, met them there. Army manoeuvres were to start the next day.

Princip, meanwhile, had been to see Danilo Ilić, chief organizer of the assassination, paid a visit to his brother at Hadzici, and returned to his old lodgings in the widow Ilić's house. As chief-of-staff of the assassination project, Ilić had set up a second team of three assassins in case the first should fail; their leader was a Moslem, Mehmed Mehmedbasić, initiator of a plan to assassinate Governor Potoriek, which had been dropped. The other two were schoolboys, members of a secret society which worked for union of all the South Slavs and the overthrow of the Habsburg Empire, to begin with the assassination of the archduke. It was also Ilić who collected the weapons left with Jovanović at Tuzla, a dangerous operation because of the numerous police checks which had to be avoided, and hid them under Princip's bed. Cabrinović went to stay with his parents in the town and Grabez at a village about fifteen miles from Sarajevo.

The period of waiting which followed was trying for all but Princip, who remained cool and determined; he took a job to earn his bed and board and in the evenings '. . . I went around with chaps who liked to drink, but this was only so as to arouse no suspicion. They were people incapable of a great idea.'* Ilić, though at no time did he consider ratting on his friends, was having troublesome doubts about the efficacy of acts of individual terrorism unless they could be used to detonate a mass rising and unless there was a political party in readiness to make use of that rising. He busied himself in organizing such a party and he started publishing a magazine of left-wing politics and letters, *Zvono*. But he could not put his doubts out of his mind, he voiced them to Grabez and Princip, and for hours at a time he and Princip argued over the question of whether the assassination was necessary and would be effective. The sense and feeling of these arguments were clearly reflected in Ilić's long *Zvono* article on the

---

* Nachlass Erzherzog Franz-Ferdinand, *Prozess in Sarajevo*, Haus-Hof Staats-archiv, Vienna. Quoted by Dedijer in op. cit.

work of the Russian writer Leonid Andreyev: it was as well that the official censor, like official censors in general, was a man of no penetration.

Ilić was soon trying to persuade Princip that they should drop the project and he still did his best to make Grabez give it up; what is more a directive was received from Colonel Apis ordering the conspirators to drop the assassination plan. Only Princip remained implacably firm and presently began to swing the other conspirators back on to his side of the question: the archduke must die; only so could the evil power of the Habsburgs be destroyed and the nation of Yugoslavia be created. This firmness on Princip's part is of particular interest. It seems perfectly clear that without it the plan would have come to nothing. It is equally clear that Princip had neither the reading nor the wit to support, by convincing arguments, his opinion against the arguments of his associates which, based on reading and experience, ranged from the subtle Marxist ones to the expedient ones of Colonel Apis. What Princip did have was a deep, intuitive, irresistible desire to kill the Austrian Empire in the person of its archduke; and an implacable will. In short, and oddly enough, he had the qualities which make a 'king', a leader – conviction and will. His life suggests to me that certain assassins are, in fact, leaders *ratés*; and that just as very successful policemen have many of the impulses and attributes of the criminal, and the best gamekeeper is an ex-poacher, so the successful assassin is a man who, in other circumstances, would have made a great national leader, a Bonaparte or a Hitler.

Princip's firmness had its reward. Ilić was persuaded to go on with their plans and Mehmedbasić was summoned to Sarajevo; he got a movement pass from the police by saying that he had to see a dentist. Ilić decided to place himself and all six of the other assassins in the street alongside the river, the Appel Quay, because the royal procession would pass through it twice. He disposed his men along a 300-yard stretch which gave them the best chance. First, Mehmedbasić, with a pan-Yugoslav student named Vaso Cubrilović; then Cabrinović, Popović, a schoolboy member of the pan-Yugoslav movement, with Ilić himself to back him up;

Princip was posted near the Lateimer Bridge, and Grabez still further along the quay.

The seven would-be assassins were all ready to take up their posts early in the morning of 28 June; and all were in place when the procession of six cars appeared.

Mehmedbasić did not throw his bomb. Because a policeman happened to be standing behind him, he hesitated, and lost his chance, for the cars were being driven fairly fast. Cubrilović did not shoot because, as he said later at his trial, the duchess sat beside her husband and he had pity on her. Cabrinović not only threw his bomb, but, with almost incredible coolness, he first asked a policeman to point out which of the cars carried the archduke. The policeman obliged, Cabrinović knocked the pin out of his grenade against a lamp-post and then found he had not time to wait the recommended number of seconds before throwing the grenade because the car was passing him. He threw the bomb, it fell on the folded hood behind Franz Ferdinand's head, rolled off under the next car, and exploded, partly wrecking the car and wounding a number of the royal escort. Cabrinović meanwhile had swallowed poison, dashed for the parapet and jumped over it into the River Miljacka. Seconds later he was dragged out by security men and asked who he was, to which he answered, 'A Serbian hero.' The poison failed to kill him.

The archduke's chauffeur had driven on fast. But seeing that the next car was not following, Franz Ferdinand ordered the man to stop, and sent an *aide* back to see what had happened. He returned in a few minutes to say that three of the escorting officers were wounded, one badly, and about twenty bystanders. Meanwhile the leading car, carrying the mayor and the chief of police, had gone on to the Town Hall, keeping to the official programme. The archduke ordered his chauffeur to follow. When they reached the Town Hall the archduke and the duchess alighted and the mayor (surely this is history's greatest comic scene?) immediately began his speech of welcome. Its phrases of fulsome loyalty were hardly appropriate and the enfuriated archduke interrupted him: 'Herr Bürgomeister, what is the good of your speeches? I come to Sarajevo on a friendly visit and someone throws a bomb at me. This is outrageous.' However, on the quiet intervention of the duchess, who, fortunately, had no sense of humour, the mayor was allowed to continue his speech and the programme was gone through in due order. While the duchess was visiting the wives of Moslem notables upstairs, Franz Ferdinand made a grim joke about expecting more bullets later, and then asked Potiorek whether he thought there was, in fact, any danger of a second attempt on his life. The governor replied that he did not and that all danger was over.*

Franz Ferdinand had decided to change the programme. The next item had been to visit the Museum, going by way of Franz Josef Street; he decided instead to drive straight along the now cleared Appel Quay to visit his wounded officers in the Military Hospital. The procession of cars set out again, led by the mayor's. There had either been a failure to transmit the new order, or there was treachery. The mayor's car turned into Franz Josef Street and the archduke's chauffeur, a Czech, followed. Governor Potiorek called out to him to stop; they should be going along the Appel Quay. The man braked and prepared to back down. This gave Princip his second and much better chance to kill the heir-apparent.

When the archduke's car had been driven on after the bomb throwing it passed Princip and Grabez, but neither had taken action: Grabez did not even try to throw his bomb; there are various explanations, but the true one seems to be that he could not bring himself to use that undiscriminating weapon in a crowd. When the archduke's car passed Princip, he did not shoot; he had not known which car Franz Ferdinand was in and had failed to recognize him in time. By the time the car had passed him the police were clearing the Appel Quay as a result of Cabrinović's attempt, and Princip had to move. He crossed from the embankment side and stood at the corner of the Appel Quay and Franz Josef Street. As it happened he could not have done better. He was still hanging about that corner when the procession of cars reappeared and when Potiorek stopped the archduke's car and

* There are other versions of his reply, but this is the best vouched for.

ordered the chauffeur to go along the Appel Quay. Here, in Princip's own words, is what then happened:

'. . . I recognized the Heir Apparent. But as I saw that a lady was sitting next to him I reflected for a moment whether I should shoot or not. At the same moment I was filled with a peculiar feeling and I aimed at the Heir Apparent from the pavement – which was made easier because the car was proceeding slower at the moment. Where I aimed I do not know. But I know that I aimed at the Heir Apparent. I believe I fired twice, perhaps more, because I was so excited. Whether I hit the victims or not, I cannot tell, because instantly people started to hit me.'*

Princip would not have succeeded had not two bystanders unmentioned in this statement come to his aid. A security policeman saw Princip raise the revolver and was close enough to run in and knock up his arm; but as he moved to do so an out-of-work actor named Pusara shoved into him, deliberately giving Princip time to fire. Moreover a second young man, Ferdinand Behr, gave Princip a chance, which the assassin did not take, to escape, by punching the policeman in the stomach. On the other hand a third, Velić by name, knocked the revolver out of Princip's hand as he raised it to his head with the object of shooting himself.

*

Gavrilo Princip had, of course, no idea of how mightily he had wrought, that the shots he had fired had put an end not only to the Habsburgs and their empire, but to three other dynasties and theirs. But that he had done well, that his life had been worthily staked, he had no doubt. Dr Leo Pfeffer, the examining magistrate charged with the 'instruction' of the case within an hour of the assassination, wrote of the young assassin:

'It was difficult to imagine that so frail-looking an individual should have committed so serious a deed. Even his clear blue eyes, burning and piercing but serene, had nothing cruel or criminal in their expression. They spoke of innate intelligence, of steady and harmonious energy. When I told him I was the investigating judge and asked if he had

* *Prozess in Sarajevo*. This statement was made within an hour of the assassination.

strength to speak, he answered my questions with perfect clearness and in a voice which grew steadily stronger and more assured.'

When, later that day, Princip was formally charged following the deaths of his two victims, he said, 'I acknowledge it and do not complain but I am sorry I have killed the Duchess of Hohenberg, for I had no intention of killing her.' At a later point in the investigation he said that he hated all representatives of the constitutional system (what we should now call the Establishment), not as persons but as bearers of the power which oppresses the people. And later, again, 'I aimed specifically at the Archduke because he . . . is an enemy of the Slavs in general but especially of the Serbs.'

Princip instructed the counsel appointed to defend the assassins not to bother with his case but to concentrate on defending the others: for it was he who had killed the archduke and the duchess. And in the course of the trial he replied to a question:

'I do not feel like a criminal because I put away the one who was doing evil. Austria as it is represents evil for our people and therefore should not exist.'

No general commanding an army has a better reason than that for putting to death his tens of thousands. And to his principal reason Princip added others which have long been universally accepted as respectable ones for waging war:

'The political union of the Yugoslavs was always before my eyes, and that was my basic idea. Therefore it was necessary in the first place to free the Yugoslavs from the *sväbe* and from Austria. This . . . moved me to carry out the assassination of the Heir Apparent, for I considered him as very dangerous for Yugoslavia.'

Princip believed all along that he was giving his life for his country. But the doubt which Dr Feldbauer was able to introduce touching his age, whether he was or was not twenty at the time of the assassination, led the Court, satisfied with having offered up three other lives, including that of Danilo Ilić, on the Habsburg altars, to sentence him to twenty years' hard labour, a monthly fast of twenty-four hours, and a hard bed in an unlit cell. Because of the atrocious prison conditions Princip was liberated long before term by a creature as merciless as man: on 28 April 1918, with the empire he had destroyed falling in ruins all about him, one arm destroyed, and the rest of his meagre body decayed by tuber-culosis which had been eating him away since 1916, he died. In his cell they found these lines scratched on a wall:

> Our ghosts will walk through Vienna,
> And roam the Palace frightening the lords.

7

PHOENIX PARK: MR BURKE
AND THE INVINCIBLES

THE struggle between Great Britain and Ireland was a war which lasted nearly 1,000 years. It did not, despite the vulgarly accepted Saxon-Celt antithesis, begin with the Saxons. The noble and gentle Saxons of the pre-Conquest years were generally on good terms with those kings of Dublin with whom Harold Godwinson and other Saxon grandees often found refuge, and even allies in their wars. It was the ferocious Normans and the Norman-Welsh of the twelfth century who began the long strife which did not end until the twentieth.

The British conquest of Ireland, or that pacification which completes conquest, was never accomplished. At times the war was hot; in the intervals there was no real peace but a cold war. In the periods of cold war when the Irish either held their own Parliament under a viceroy in Dublin, or when they sat with the English, Scots, and Welsh at Westminster, there was never an Irish 'consensus' for real union with England; and the most Irish of the Irish remained totally irreconcilable. This, of course, is a very great pity: the two peoples are in a measure mutually complementary, and if, today, Great Britain and Ireland were one country, the problems of space, of economy, and of strength in the world would be halved for both countries. Nationalism is a curse, perhaps the worst we labour under; but it is an extremely recalcitrant fact. Julian Benda's vision of mankind as a single crowd against God as the enemy is a grand one (did not Milton first have a glimpse of it?). But it is not for today. I published a novel many years ago, *The Astrologer*, a sort of joke, in which all mankind is linked in brotherhood by a faked threat from Mars. For Mars read Benda's God. It is perhaps the only way, given the conflict which Koestler makes so much of, between the old and the new parts of our brain.

At all events, the terrible evil of nationalism can be overcome, if at all, only by an act of renunciation on both sides, certainly not by the conquest of one country by the other. And for eight centuries the Irish gave bloody proof that they would not submit to English rule even when their own representatives sat in the British Parliament and helped to make laws for both countries.

Unhappily, the English too often behaved as conquerors in Ireland, not as partners in a condominium. And every social and political difference was aggravated by the savagely un-Christian quarrel between Catholic, Anglican and Protestant churches; there are no fouler fighters than priests whose temporalities or whose area of power is at stake.

It is of importance to make this point because in the epoch, the late nineteenth century, with which I have to deal here, whereas the English regarded the Irish nationalists as rebels and traitors and heretics, the Irish nationalists regarded themselves as soldiers of Ireland at holy war with a foreign and heretical occupying power. Thus acts which, for the English, were stigmatized as common murder, were, for the Irish who did them, heroic acts of war.

The bitterness of this struggle was much aggravated by a class struggle. The class war is never so keen as where the belligerents are also of opposing national or racial groups: for example, in South Africa, and to a lesser extent in parts of the United States, the master class is white, the proletariat black. In Ireland the master class was Anglo-Irish and Protestant, the proletariat and peasantry (but there was hardly any proletariat) Irish and Catholic.

I have already said that the religious difference was the gravest of aggravations between the two sides. Even Catholic emancipation could not alter this. In 1735 the heavy burden of tithe collected to support the always rather greedy and grasping Anglican clergy, no worse than other clergies but here in a position to squeeze and extort, was shifted wholly on to the backs of the poor, of the Catholic, anti-Anglican, peasant majority. The Protestant nobility and gentry, their agents and hangers-on, whose Established church it was, paid no tithe. And even in cases of flagrant extortion of tithe or tax, which were common, the peasant had no hope from the law; defrauded of £10, an appeal would cost him £60. Here is what Arthur Young (1741-1820), that great English agronomist who studied farming and peasant conditions all over the British Isles and France, and whose genius transformed European agriculture, wrote of what he saw in Ireland:

'The domineering aristocracy of five hundred thousand Protestants feel the sweets of having two million slaves. . . .'

And, bearing this out:

'The landlord of an Irish estate inhabited by Roman Catholics is a sort of despot who yields obedience in whatever concerns the poor to no law but his own will. A landlord in Ireland can scarcely invent an order which a servant, labourer or cottier dares refuse to execute. Nothing satisfies him but an unlimited submission. Disrespect or anything tending towards sauciness he may punish with his cane or a horse-whip with the most perfect security; a poor man would have his bones broke if he dared lift his hand in his own defence. Landlords of consequence have assured me that many of these cottiers would think themselves honoured by having their wives and daughters sent for to the bed of their master; a mark of slavery which proves the oppression under which such people must live. Nay, I have heard anecdotes of the lives of people being made free with without any apprehension of the justice of a jury.'

In short the landlords enjoyed all rights, including those of the *droit du seigneur* and life-and-death, over tenants who were serfs in all but name. That was published in 1820, the year of Young's death. One trouble seems to have been – it is even apparent in the novels of Maria Edgeworth – that the men of the ascendancy had as much difficulty in recognizing the Irish as human beings as today's white South Africans have in believing that the Bantu are quite human. Young says elsewhere, and he knew from observation and experience what he was talking about, that the Irish peasantry were the most miserable and degraded in Europe, and that their occasional acts of violence in protest or revenge were often punished with hanging without trial.

As they had tried to do in their American colonies, the English had very shrewdly made as sure as they could that the Irish were no match for them in economic or military strength; but this unhappily meant that the Irish were left with the one resource of the weak at war with the strong – secret terrorist societies.* Of these Richard Piggott, in his account of some eighteenth-century examples, says that their revolt, supported by the peasantry, was '... a rising of a people almost literally for leave to live'.†

The earliest society of which we have some record – 1772 – was the Peep O'Day Boys. This was a Protestant society which sprang up in Ulster with the openly avowed object of exterminating the Catholic settlers. The Ulster landlords, following an example set by the Earl of Donegal, were forcing up rents by playing Catholic against Protestant tenants – the connexion between Protestantism and successful capitalism is here nicely demonstrated, the Protestant Europeans and those of America having been quicker than the Catholics to realize that when it came to a matter of money, God was either dead or had the morals of a money-lender. The Protestant farmers, recruited by the Peep O'Day Boys, responded by murdering those Catholics who were so foolhardy or so pressed by need as to take farms in Ulster.

A number of Catholic secret societies were formed to enforce refusal of the tithe which supported the hated alien Church: typical of these were the 'Carders', who tortured farmers who

* But was this to be regretted? Supposing the Irish to have been capable of mounting conventional military resistance, how many more lives would have been lost?
† Richard Piggott, 'Irish Murder Societies', *Contemporary Review*, XLIII (April 1883).

were cowardly, complaisant, or terrified enough to pay the tithe, with steel carding-combs; the 'Threshers', who used flails; and the 'Oak Boys', who might even resort to hanging the recalcitrantly law-abiding. All aimed to enforce resistance to coercive laws and to starve out the clergy of the occupying power; all occasionally made use of punitive assassination; all justified their violence by reference to the ugly injustice of the Act of 1735 and to the oppression of the peasants by landlords favoured by a vicious system of land tenure.

Not all the Irish nationalist movements, the properly political as distinct from the merely social, secret societies, used assassination as a matter of course. The Irish Republican Brotherhood, or Fenians, founded by the Irish in New York in 1857, did not normally use assassination against the national enemy, although they used punitive assassination against traitors, informers, and delators in their own ranks. This necessary disciplinary rigour, precisely comparable with the shooting of deserters in the face of the enemy, or of spies, by national armies all over the civilized world, was particularly necessary in the Irish case, for informers have been the bane of Irish terrorist societies, and even of political secret societies eschewing terrorism. The reason for this is obscure, but may perhaps be sought in the early practice of confession to lighten the heart of guilt, to the notorious Celtic tendency to quarrel with the leadership, and to divided loyalties, since naturally not all the British or Anglo-Irish were villains. As a general rule the United Irishmen, founded as a union of Catholic and Protestant Irishmen in 1790 to further Irish independence, did not, despite some excesses following the excitement of a victory over British troops in 1798,* use assassination.

The 'rebellion' of 1798 was the only occasion, until 1914 and 1916, when, because of Wolfe Tone's temporary and personal triumph over the religious difference, the Irish were in a position to use the ordinary and conventional methods of warfare, rather than the methods of the Old Men of the Mountains, against the British enemy. If Lord Lake had not won his victory at Vinegar Hill and taken Wexford from the Irish army in June, if the Irish

* Before the defeat of their forces by Lord Lake at Vinegar Hill.

had been able to put off the decisive battle until their French allies landed in August, Ireland's sovereign independence might have come sooner, the struggle between Britain and Bonaparte might have been fought out in Ireland – and the casualties in the long Anglo-Irish strife been multiplied by a thousand. As it is, the Anglo-Irish war of 1798 serves to prove very clearly the point I have been at pains to insist on: that the struggle between the two peoples was indeed, on the Irish side at least, a state of war and not of civil strife.

*

The landlord's privilege of plundering his tenants, of confiscating the fruits of their labour, and in general of treating them as serfs, remained, despite some minor legal mitigations of the cotters' lot, virtually intact until Gladstone's Land Bill of 1881. But that Act of Parliament was, as I shall show, a case of too little done much too late. The Irish had become, even if they had not always been, irreconcilable.

Following the famine of 1847 and its atrocious consequences, and before the American foundation of the Fenians, there arose a new and formidable secret society, the 'Ribbon Society'. A word about that famine, perhaps the only word which has not yet been clearly said among all the hypocritical blather of verbiage which has been spewed over it. That government or that social class which, to spare its own pocket, puts its community at the mercy of a one-crop economy, subsistence, or cash, puts the lives of that community at risk: potatoes were favoured in Ireland as bread-fruit was imported into the West Indies, as cheap food for slaves. If the Irish agonizing and dying in the famine, and the embittered survivors who emigrated to America, blamed their fate on the Ascendancy, they were entitled to do so, and the Ribbon Society was only one of the movements which sought to avenge the past and ensure a better future. The society used terrorism, including assassination, against landlords and their agents until about 1871, when its activity declined. By then its American offspring, the Irish Republican Brotherhood, had also declined, but unlike the Ribbon Society it was soon to enjoy a revival. It made a spectacular reappearance in the activities of the 'Skirmishing Fund', a loosely organized body with nationalist as well as social aims and strong connexions in America among former emigrants. In fact the 'Skirmishing Fund' was largely financed by Irish Americans who had fostered the bitter hatred of Britain carried overseas by their wretched fathers or grandfathers. The 'Skirmishing Fund' declared war on Britain on all fronts, civilian and military; and its sectaries consciously aimed at national sovereignty for Ireland and a republican constitution. And when, in 1878, they assassinated the Earl of Leitrim, they chose him not simply as a particularly vicious specimen of the rack-renting landlord kind, but as a symbol of the Anglo-Irish Ascendancy: thus Lord Leitrim was, in our sense, a true scapegoat victim.

Then, in 1878, came the Land League, a much more 'constitutional' movement than those we have been glancing at, with a clear programme of reform of land tenure by parliamentary means: the league was not overtly nationalist, but every such movement in Ireland had nationalist tendencies if only because the enemy, the landlord, looked to Britain as his patron and protector. Parnell, its president, spoke for the league in the British House of Commons; and Parnell never countenanced the use of violence. Yet was he not to some extent in league with the violent, like it or not? The case is not unlike that of Haganah and Lohmey Heruth Israel, as described in Chapter Eight. Fenianism, like Land Leagueism, had two sides: a respectable, parliamentary, and conventional warfare side; and a terrorist offshoot side. And though the pacific and parliamentary might repudiate the violent with all its heart, it could not but suffer for its mistakes and benefit from its successes.

*

Because of the romantic prejudices which are still so often cherished by the English, it is now necessary to make a point about the Irish attitude to the law. Otherwise, the terrorism used by the latter-day Fenians, by Sinn Fein and by the Irish Republican army, can be too easily dismissed as 'typical' Irish lawlessness; there is nothing typical about it. Setting aside the case of politics and of social protest, were the late nineteenth-century Irish really such wild, lawless, and ungovernable men?

The contrary is true. At the time in question Ireland's crime record was very much less disgraceful than England's. (It still is.) Tighe Hopkins, who had studied the subject, and who, by the way, was very hostile to Irish nationalism, writing in the *Windsor Magazine* (1896) had this to say:

'It is, in truth, a grateful and refreshing thing to pass from the casual study of crime and criminals in England to the casual study of crime and criminals in Ireland. There are no penal institutions in Ireland to compare with the superb prison at Wormwood Scrubs or with the great convict establishment at Portland; but the fact in explanation is that while we cannot do without these places in England they are not wanted in Ireland. . . . In a word, so far as habitual and professional crime is concerned, there is not as decent a country in Europe.'*

In a typical year of this period more than 82 per cent of persons convicted in Irish courts were drunks and petty larcenists who received sentences of less than one month in prison and who, for the same offences, would today have been put on probation or lightly fined. In 1895, for example, only 107 convicted persons received penal servitude and most of them got the minimum three-year sentence. At least the figures show that the Irish, for whatever reason, were exceptionally law abiding.

And the fact is that only the most severe provocation could bring them to commit acts of violence against the officers and beneficiaries and parasites of the alien who oppressed them. If you doubt whether the Irish terrorists and assassins, and in general the Irish nationalists at odds with Britain, still, despite their defeat in 1798, felt and thought not as villains but as soldiers, here is the form of oath taken by those who joined the Irish Republican Brotherhood, the Fenians: it is taken from the evidence of the informer Robert Farrel, one of the Invincibles, who (see below) assassinated Mr Burke and Lord Frederick Cavendish in Phoenix Park:

'I, Robert Farrel, do hereby swear that I will serve the Irish Republic

* Tighe Hopkins, 'Kilmainham Memories', *Windsor Magazine* (April 1896).

now established, that I will take up arms at a moment's notice and will obey all lawful orders of my superiors. And I take oath in the true spirit of a soldier.'

*

In the year 1880 Great Britain and Ireland had a general election. The liberals were returned with a large majority and Mr Gladstone became Prime Minister for the second time. He appointed Earl Cowper Lord-Lieutenant of Ireland, that is Viceroy; and Mr W. E. Forster, M.P., Chief Secretary of State for Ireland. The new House included a small but exceptionally able Irish party, led by Charles Stewart Parnell.

Gladstone hoped to answer the Irish Question by a measure of land tenure reform embodied in a Land Bill. But the Land Leaguers were very suspicious of British good will; to no man is it as obvious as to the nationalist in a land ruled by an imperial power that the good is the enemy of the best; he wants no gifts from the Greeks, thank you. During the vacation before the 1881 session of Parliament when the Bill was to be introduced, Parnell made a speech at Ennis which implied that the quality and value of the coming Bill would depend on the militancy of the people:

'Depend upon it that the measure of the Land Bill next session will be the measure of your activity and energy this winter. It will be the measure of your determination not to bid for farms from which others have been evicted and to use the strong force of public opinion to deter any unjust man among yourselves – and there are many such – from bidding for such farms. Now what are you to do to a tenant who bids for a farm from which his neighbour has been evicted? . . .'*

The speaker was answered by a tumult of cries of 'Kill him!' and 'Shoot him!' This was by no means just noisy rhetoric. Although the majority did not approve going to such lengths, there were doubtless a few bolder spirits among Parnell's hearers. Parnell went on to deprecate killing the recalcitrant neighbours and to advocate boycotting instead. The word was new then, derived

---

* John Adye Curran, K.C., *Reminiscences*, Edward Arnold, London, 1915. As a junior counsel, Curran helped to defend Parnell at his trial on charges of conspiracy to incite tenants not to pay rents and to practise boycotting.

from one Captain Boycott, the notoriously cruel agent of the Erne estate against whom the method was first used.

When Gladstone's Bill became law it pleased nobody. It was an advance, certainly, setting up Land Courts to hear appeals and ensure fair rents, security of tenure, and free sale of leases. But the Irish were no longer in a mood to be placated by this, and the Land League issued orders that farmers were not to apply to the new Land Courts until the League had tested their efficacy and the government's good faith by bringing two test cases before them. Meanwhile 'agrarian crime' and agitation continued as before; in fact they got worse: in the twenty-four months of 1880 and 1881 there were twenty-five 'agrarian murders', that is, punitive assassinations of landlords or their agents; whereas in the twelve months of 1882 there were twenty-seven such killings. The Land Bill could not restore the peace for at least four reasons: that the Irish were not willing to trust or even try it fairly; that there was a new Coercion Bill to put down the violence it had failed to allay; the Phoenix Park assassinations in 1882; and the oppressive and vicious reaction of the government and the courts to those assassinations.

Forster, the chief secretary, had little faith in the policy of conciliation expressed in such measures as the Land Bill; and with the rising incidence of boycotting and 'agrarian crimes' Gladstone agreed to give him the 'Coercion' Bill which the Secretary of State for Ireland wanted. More, according to Dillon Cosgrave, Forster, '. . . exercising a free hand in Irish affairs, which Gladstone allowed him, proceeded with his chief's concurrence to most despotic measures'.*

These included the arrest and incarceration in Kilmainham Prison of the whole Irish parliamentary leadership, including Parnell, and about 200 other Irish nationalists of all ranks and degrees of fervour. The predictable consequence of this idiotic 'firmness' was a sharp increase in Fenian and Land League activity, including violence, including assassination. It was soon obvious that Forster and his 'firm' policy had made bad much worse.

* Dillon Cosgrave, 'The True History of the Phoenix Park Murders', *New Ireland Review* (1906). Cosgrave was mildly pro-British and strongly against Irish political violence.

Gladstone, and a majority of his party, repenting of their repudiation of liberal principles, turned again to a policy of conciliation.
Mr Forster refusing to give up the use of force, he was obliged to
resign; and Cowper, his nominal chief, resigned with him.

Parnell and his friends were released from prison on giving an
undertaking to help the government to dissuade the Irish from
boycotting and 'crime', and persuade them to use the Land Bill
instead. They gave the undertaking in good faith, no doubt, but
it was one which no Irish leader could possibly have made good.
The Fenians had never been social reformers; they made use of
social discontents to further political ends – the ends of Irish
nationalism. Conversely, the Land League, whose purpose was
reform of land-tenure laws, i.e. a social one, was being driven to
violence, 'the politics of despair', and therefore, inevitably, given
the place and the time, into nationalism.

Earl Spencer was appointed Lord-Lieutenant of Ireland in
Cowper's place, and Lord Frederick Cavendish Chief Secretary
of State in Mr Forster's place. Since civil servants, unlike politicians, do not resign, they were to find as their guide, philospher,
and friend, and, I suspect, the real policy-maker at Dublin Castle,
the Irish and Catholic Permanent Secretary, Mr Thomas Henry
Burke.

★

Although the Irish Republican Brotherhood countenanced the use
of assassination against cruel and oppressive landlords and their
agents, as a protest against vicious rackrenting and evictions,
assassination of enemy, i.e. British and Anglo-Irish, politicians and
government servants, was not a part of its policy, in the sense that
it was, for example, part of the declared policy of Mazzini, of the
Young Bosnians, or of the Lohmey Heruth Israel discussed in
Chapter Eight. We have this on the very high, and anti-Irish
Republican, authority of John Adye Curran, K.C., who was to be
examining magistrate, under the Prevention of Crimes (Ireland)
Act, conducting the 'instruction' of the Phoenix Park case.

But at some time after mid 1881 a group of Dublin Fenians
formed a separate and break-away society, a society which went

beyond Irish Republican Brotherhood aims and rules, and openly declared a policy of assassination against British government officers in London and in Dublin. These militant Fenians called themselves the Invincibles, and it should be said that the things they were to do were not of the kind the Brotherhood would have approved of, and they were to be more or less repudiated by orthodox Fenians. Yet there is no doubt that to the idealists among the Invincibles their attempted and their successful assassinations were acts of war and, as such, justifiable: they were 'furthering by force civil policies which could not be furthered by other means'; and they were particularly merciless in their attitude to Irishmen who had made themselves allies or servants of the British and whom, logically enough, they looked upon as traitors.

To their own bane the Invincibles were amateurish and ill-organized. There is some evidence that they were being directed from the United States and it may be that this long-distance control was part of the trouble. As I have written elsewhere, secret political societies, and especially terrorist societies, are best organized in small cells whose component members remain unknown to those of other cells. The method of organization, used successfully by Communist parties in their early, clandestine phase, and doubtless still used by them in countries where the party is illegal, is probably as old as the Holy Vehm. In principle the Invincibles seem to have recognized this; for example, recruiting was done only by the four leaders, the members of the central committee; and the other ranks, as it were, may not have been intended to know each other. But organization was sloppy and casual, and in practice far too many of the Invincibles were known to each other, an inevitable consequence of their policy of behaving as a fraternity and holding, on some occasions, special meetings. Because of their poor organization, their want of professionalism, the Invincibles were all in a position to betray each other; or, at least, many of them were.

Now it is true that the last quarter of the nineteenth century and up to 1914 was probably the only period in western history when physical torture of political prisoners was not used. It has been restored to general use in our own time, first by such proto-

Fascist, para-military forces as the British 'Black-and-Tans' and the Italian Fascisti, in the 1920s; then by the degenerate National Communists or Stalinists in the U.S.S.R.; next by the Nazis, and by them on an unprecedented scale; and finally by the political police and military intelligence officers of the western democracies. It is now established practice, although universally illegal, protested against only by a few elderly radicals and juvenile idealists. But in the 1880s and 1890s there was no danger of any Invincible who fell into the hands of the Dublin police being systematically tortured or beaten up. Still, torture is not the only way of making men talk, and as it happened Dublin had, in Superintendent John Mallon, a police officer of something like genius, a man who would have had nothing to learn from modern police psychologists and brainwashers. Mallon had no need of such gross crudenesses as physical torture in his work; and, as a consequence, the slack organization of the Invincibles was to be their undoing.

The Invincibles were not even, as a rule, competent assassins. Those members appointed to carry out their sentences of execution seem too often to have suffered a failure of nerve, a softening of the heart, or a semi-collapse of the will at the critical moment. Moreover, they appear to have been uncommonly unlucky, and if some of their several attempts to assassinate Ireland's worst enemy, Mr Forster, the Secretary of State for Ireland, failed because the would-be assassins were not up to their work, their well-planned and well-mounted final attempt was defeated by an unforseeable and whimsical change of plans on the victim's part, a change of the kind which several times frustrated attempts to kidnap or kill Abraham Lincoln.

Mr Forster having got out of Ireland with a whole skin, the Invincibles turned their attention to a man whom they had probably already condemned to death, the Permanent Secretary, Thomas Henry Burke. From their point of view Burke was fair game, probably the fairest, for he was what, in Fenian circles, was called a 'Castle Rat'. Castle Rats were Irishmen, and especially Catholic Irishmen, in the pay of and completely loyal to the British administration at Dublin Castle, the national enemy within the Pale. The final executive decision to assassinate Burke

was taken at a meeting of the Invincibles' central committee of
four on 3 May 1882.*

Tighe Hopkins, who wrote an excellent if insufficiently critical
account of the Phoenix Park assassinations, based on what
Detective Superintendent Mallon told him about the case,
provides proof, if it were still needed, that the Invincibles were
pure-hearted assassins and not common murderers:

> ' "These men," he writes, intending to impress the reader with
> particular horror. "These men, it is to be remarked, had nothing in the
> nature of a private wrong to avenge. Not a man among them had ever
> in his lifetime suffered directly or indirectly the very smallest injustice
> at the hands of Mr Burke. To one and all of them he was a name and
> nothing more." '†

This is all but literally true; to all bar one Invincible Mr
Burke was not even a face; just as they have no faces or even
names who lie burning to death as I write, under napalm bombs
in Vietnam; just as the men whom a gunner blows to pieces as
they advance to kill him in battle have never suffered the smallest
injustice at their hands nor he at theirs. The Invincibles, planning
to kill Mr Burke, identified themselves with Ireland's wrongs and
were fighting a national, not a personal, enemy. The deed they
plotted was horrible, exactly as horrible as the deed any general
officer plots before giving battle – the killing of unknown men.

*

The Invincibles probably numbered about forty at the beginning
of 1882, but only a few of them are of interest in our context. A
number of them were known to John Mallon; and he suspected
that they might have been responsible for one or two mysterious
killings and disappearances. He also knew, through his informers,

* Those who collect and rejoice in really good examples of English snobbery should give
some attention to this case. It has become notorious as the assassination of Lord Frederick
Cavendish, with Mr Burke as an incidental victim. The reverse was true. Burke's com-
panion was killed because he went to Burke's aid, and his assassins had no idea who he was
until afterwards. But for the English press and people the assassination of a lord is more
interesting than that of a commoner.

† Hopkins, in op. cit.

of whom he had a network, that they were plotting a number of assassinations. The reader who is interested in the work and character of a policeman of genius should try to read Frederick Moir Bussy's *Irish Conspiracies*,* but it is now a rare book and even the British Museum has no copy. Mallon had a knowledge of Dublin's political underground and its chief personalities which was almost uncanny; but most of what he knew he could not prove in court, so that it did not enable him to make arrests before more damage was done. Moreover, knowing his fellow-country-men, he was in another difficulty: he might hear through his net-work of a plan to assassinate Mr Gladstone or blow up Dublin Castle; he then had to judge whether to discount this as mere romantic bombast, or to take it seriously.

Take an example: Mallon knew that the Invincibles had threatened to kill Mr Clifford Lloyd, one of Dublin's resident magistrates who was particularly severe and not perfectly impartial in political or 'agrarian crime' cases. And sure enough Mr Lloyd was twice shot at. Nor is that all: Lady Julia Roundell recorded in her Diary that, '. . . several attempts were made to blow up Mr Lloyd's rooms, and after a package containing dynamite was found just inside the front door, his landlady requested him to take lodgings elsewhere'.

Mallon, at all events, was uneasy at what he was hearing, and he sent a warning to Scotland Yard touching some bomb out-rages planned for London, and possible attempts to assassinate members of the government. And so good were his sources that he was able to send Mr Burke an almost verbatim account of a meeting of the Invincibles at which plans to assassinate him had been discussed. Unfortunately Burke had a contempt for all such conspirators and he wrote across Mallon's report: 'These men may talk this and that but they have not the courage of their words.'

Despite this discouragement, Mallon applied for warrants to arrest a number of conspirators, for he was becoming more and more convinced that the Invincibles meant business. This was partly because he now had reliable information that weapons had

* Frederick M. Bussy, *Irish Conspiracies*, Everett, London, 1910.

been bought in London and that they had been successfully smuggled across the sea and into Dublin by a woman, presumably a fanatical nationalist but possibly simply for pay, since the Invincibles were well provided with money. There were firearms among the weapons; but also a number of large surgical knives, a detail unknown to Mallon. His request for warrants was refused.

Over all that is on record touching the Phoenix Park case, unless there is more in the secret archives of the Irish Republican movements, there hangs an uneasy feeling that the prime movers, the men of determination and will who forced brave words to be followed by appropriate actions, were never identified; or, if identified, remained out of reach and danger. Names crop up – Flood, Tynan – attached to shadowy figures, and drop out of the case. Tighe Hopkins, who had, as I have said, all his information directly from John Mallon, says that while some of the Invincibles were indeed sincere nationalists, moved by the ideal of a free, republican Ireland with justice for the people, others were activated by greed. The ugly implication of what he has to say in that context is as follows: the men who wanted deeds of terrible violence done to the British were the American Fenians, the parent organization; and that in return for promise of such deeds they could be made to pay over very considerable sums of money; and that some of the moving spirits of the Dublin Invincibles were misappropriating the money to their own uses. Thus, for example, Mallon did not believe that James Carey, a member of the central committee of four, could have afforded the very smart turn-out he was driving out of his ordinary sources of income. That the Invincibles were financed by Irish-American Fenians is certain; that at least two American representatives of the Brotherhood were in Dublin to help direct an assassination is probable; that they fled back to America as soon as the assassination was done is also likely; that Carey, if none of the others, misappropriated American funds to his own use is quite possible and does not necessarily make him no better than a hired assassin.

The central committee of four who, helped or not by the American Fenians, planned the assassination and helped to execute it, were James Carey, Daniel Curley (chairman), Tom

Caffrey, and James Mullet. James Carey was a small businessman and he had recently been elected a town councillor of Dublin; a respectable burgess. Patriot he may have been, and sincerely a Fenian even though slightly dishonest in the manner of his class; but when he took to plotting assassination he really was acting above his intellectual and moral station; a little man assuming a great and terrible task, he was certain to come to grief. He had been a member of the Irish Republican Brotherhood until about 1879, but had opted out of it and been politically inactive, excepting for his municipal candidacy, until, by his own account, he was invited to join the Invincibles in November 1881 by a man whose identity remains obscure.

Daniel Curley, believed by Curran to have been the chairman of the committee, was a respectable carpenter by trade, reasonably prosperous, twenty-five, very good-looking, a staunch Fenian, an idealist fervently dedicated to winning freedom for his country: he was to make a good and moving impression even on the jury and judge who tried him. Thomas Caffrey was a small shopkeeper concerning whom singularly little is on record.

James Mullet was an interesting case of the politico-religious fanatic. He seems to have regarded Protestants as in league with or creatures of the devil. A publican by trade, with a good and prosperous house and an excellent name both in the trade and, as a licensee, with the police, he was deeply religious and went daily to mass. Completely convinced that right and justice were on the Fenian side, he had no hesitation in praying to Jesus, Mary, and Joseph, and no doubt his patron saint as well, for their help in assassinating Thomas Henry Burke.

With a single exception, not one of these men of the twenty-six Invincibles who were eventually arrested, and for that matter of the forty whom Mallon knew to be Invincibles, were, in the cant phrase, 'known to' the police. The exception was one of the rank and file who had served a six months' sentence for a political 'crime'. In short the Invincibles were respectable men dedicated to a cause.

The decision to assassinate Burke having been taken at the committee meeting on 3 May, a general meeting was called at a tavern in Dame Street – again, we have that lamentable amateur-ishness – and there eleven Invincibles were chosen to carry out the work. There was no discussion necessary of a suitable place for the assassination: Mr Burke was in the habit of taking a 'car' (a car was an open trap drawn by a pony and many were licensed as hackney carriages in Dublin) from Dublin Castle to a gate of Phoenix Park and then walking across the park to the Viceregal Lodge. It would be easy to waylay him as he took this almost daily exercise. It is remarkable that the danger, indeed the near certainty that the deed would be witnessed by one or more passers-by, was not even considered as important. Ordinary Dubliners going about their business knew better than to interfere with or inform on Fenians going about *their* business.

Of the eleven Invincibles chosen to be on the spot and lend a hand if it were needed, four were selected by lot to be Burke's executioners. The fact that one of them happened to be Joseph Brady, a man of gigantic physical strength and iron will, was used by Tighe Hopkins to suggest that the lot was fraudulently forced on him, as being particularly well equipped for the work, by the committee. But there is no evidence whatsoever that Brady was reluctant to perform the terrible service required of him. Brady was twenty-five years old, burly and square in build, bull-necked, and in some measure a leader, for if he was not very intelligent he did have determination and the will to act. He was a good and re-spectable workman, a labourer, in regular employment, as also was Tim Kelly, a lad of nineteen and completely under the influence of Brady, whom he looked up to as a hero. Both men were official alms collectors for their respective chapels; presumably, therefore, strictly honest; and both were Irish patriots convinced that Burke's death would be Ireland's gain. The other two chosen as the actual assassins were Patrick Delaney and Thomas Caffrey. None of the contemporary accounts have anything interesting to say about them, but Delaney was to be the inadvertent cause of the Invincibles' downfall by bungling an attempt to intimidate or assassinate Judge Lawson some months later.

A key man in the plan was a Dublin Castle maintenance work-man, Smith by name, one of the eleven, a Fenian. He was the only one of the forty Invincibles who knew Mr Burke by sight and so could identify him. He was needed to point out their victim to the assassins, further proof, if it were needed, of the 'purity' of this case.

Tighe Hopkins makes much of the fact that 6 May was chosen as the day for the assassination because it was the day on which Lord Spencer and Lord Frederick Cavendish were to arrive in Dublin, and Spencer to be sworn in as Lord-Lieutenant. But statements made by several Invincibles after their arrest and after Mallon had broken down the three whom he judged to be weak sisters, make it quite clear that the committee had had no such idea. The first two attempts on Burke's life were, in fact, made on the morning and in the evening of 5 May, and a third was mounted for the morning of 6 May. The one which succeeded was the fourth, the others being defeated by the fact that Burke's habits were disturbed by his preparations to receive Spencer and Cavendish, so that he was not where he was expected to be in Phoenix Park at his usual times.

*

On 6 May Spencer and Cavendish arrived in Dublin from London and went to Dublin Castle for the swearing-in. After the ceremony and the reception were over, Lord Spencer drove to the Viceregal Lodge. Lord Frederick set out alone to walk to the lodge; Burke left later in a car as usual, overtook the new chief secretary, dismissed the car, and got out to walk with him. So that it was Burke's friendly decision which condemned his new colleague to death. It was at the park gates that Burke caught up with Cavendish; it was seven in the evening when they set out to walk the mile to the lodge.*

The eleven Invincibles were waiting for them, or rather for Burke. Carey, and Smith the 'finger', were sitting on one of the park seats. Brady, Kelly, Delaney, and Caffrey were riding up and down in a car driven by a cabby named Kavanagh, who was not an Invincible, was a feeble-minded drunk, and whom, for some reason, the Invincibles trusted. Four other Invincibles,

* Cosgrave in op. cit. Mentioned also in Lady Julia Roundell's Diary.

whose services were not, in the event, required, were waiting in a closed cab driven by a man with the singular nickname of 'Skin-the-Goat'; all four carried loaded revolvers. The other three of the chosen eleven lay concealed in the long grass, in case they should be needed or, perhaps, so that all should be equally involved.

When Burke and Lord Frederick were near enough to Carey and Smith to be distinguished, Smith identified Burke as the one in the grey suit, whereupon Carey signalled to Kavanagh by waving his handkerchief. Kavanagh drove up and the four assassins dropped down from the car. As they did so Carey murmured to Brady, 'Mind the man in grey.'

Brady, Curley, Delaney, and Caffrey walked abreast along the broad path towards Mr Burke and the Chief Secretary, who were in close conversation and hardly noticed them, Brady, who was left-handed, being immediately opposite Burke. From what transpired later it seems that the park was by no means deserted and that there must have been at least one eye-witness of what followed, a witness who doubtless turned and hurried away as soon as the 'scuffle' started.* Just before the two parties drew level Brady halted and stooped as if to tie a bootlace, but as Burke and Lord Frederick came level with him, he rose, gripped Burke with his right hand, swung him round, and drove the long surgical knife which he held in his left hand into Burke's back. Burke uttered a single groan, which Carey was to imitate at the trial, and died. Lord Frederick tried to beat Brady off with his umbrella, Delaney cried out, 'Ah, you villain . . .', Brady dropped Burke and started driving his knife into Cavendish while Kelly stooped over the fallen Burke and, also using a surgical knife, cut his throat.

Brady, who may or may not have realized that he had killed Lord Frederick with his first blow, stabbed him repeatedly in a kind of berserker rage before he dropped him to the ground.

The closed cab driven by 'Skin-the-Goat' had driven off as soon as the victims were seen to be dead, followed by the car with the

---

* This sort of thing was, of course, Mallon's greatest difficulty. When the Fenians were at work the ordinary passer-by was wise to see and hear nothing. Witnesses might lay information, often anonymously, but they could not be induced to give evidence in court.

four assassins, of whom two only, Brady and Kelly, had struck blows. The committee had probably insisted on four assassins in order to have enough men to mask what was really happening, as a minor brawl. Kavanagh went a roundabout way so as to enter Dublin from the opposite direction to Phoenix Park. The car was noticed by numerous witnesses from whom Mallon later learned that during the first part of the drive its occupants were silent and gloomy, but that during the second part of it they were talking and laughing so excitedly that a witness took them for a party returning, drunk, from a day's outing. Success may have intoxicated them; but more likely they had had with them – what could be more natural? – a drop of the hard stuff. All the Invincibles involved scattered to their homes, but later that night they foregathered to report to Carey, who had made off when his part was done; and perhaps to the mysterious and vanishing Mr Tynan. That was not all the work done that night: for even before news of the assassinations had got about the city, which it did with astonishing swiftness, plain white, black-edged cards had been dropped into the letter-boxes of Dublin's three principal newspapers, bearing, in what later turned out to be Dan Curley's hand, the words: 'This deed was done by the Invincibles.'

Those who are firmly convinced that assassination is not an admissible means of furthering by force a political or social policy which cannot be furthered otherwise, will seize upon this matter of the mourning cards to argue that terrorists are immature romantics, retarded juvenile delinquents. It may be so. Yet one cannot help remarking that it is customary for soldiers to boast of their victories; we have all, for our sins, heard the verbose and vainglorious orations of politicians who have happened to find themselves at the head of a nation in a moment of victory; or we have read, doubtless for want of a better book, the tedious memoirs of commanding generals who were, by chance, at the head of a victorious army; that is an army whose casualties were a few thousand fewer than the enemy's. At least the Invincibles got their memoir of victory down to seven words, six of them monosyllabic.

*

Almost as soon as the assassinations were known, Superintendent Mallon had his first clue towards finding the assassins: the fact that they had driven to their work in licensed Dublin cabs. Very soon, he had from informers, who were never, of course, to appear in any court of law, the names of several of the Invincibles involved in the assassination. He gave orders that all Dublin's cab-drivers were to be interviewed – there were 4,000 – until the police found the men whose account of their time between five and eight on the evening of 6 May was unsatisfactory and unsupported. 'Skin-the-Goat' got through this net; Kavanagh did not: a heavy drinker, and almost an idiot, he seems to have given answers which put Mallon quickly on the right track. But whatever Kavanagh may have said, and whatever Mallon knew from his under-cover men, he had little or nothing he could act on.

*

The horror and anger which followed this double assassination had some remarkable results. In London Parnell immediately repudiated and denounced the act in the strongest possible language; he also went to call on Gladstone and offered to withdraw at once from public life, an offer which Gladstone refused. The Land League in Ireland also repudiated and denounced the crime.

The government offered a reward of £10,000 – say, £100,000 of our debased money – for information leading to convictions. Whether this was ever paid, or even claimed, is not clear; if so the transaction was kept a secret, and this may well have been the case since the recipient of the money, if known, would hardly have lived very long. 'Coercion' was at once resorted to again, and now it was not only used to deny mercy and even sense, it was deliberately used as an instrument of reprisal; the half-starved peasant, his wife and children, evicted to make way for one who would pay more rent, were being punished for what the Invincibles had done. This, of course, had the effect of hardening all Irish hearts against the British and making more and more Irishmen look to Fenianism as the only hope of earthly salvation; thus, from the Republican Nationalist point of view, the assassinations scored a very important success.* Finally, the government rushed a Prevention of Crimes (Ireland) Act through Parliament, an Act which suspended the ordinary juridical system in Ireland and substituted one which gave the police and the magistracy far greater powers, at the expense of liberty.

The difficulty of punishing 'agrarian crime' and 'political crime' in Ireland had long been a problem without a solution unless the laws were changed. The problem was the impossibility of getting convictions where the people were either too sympathetic to, or too terrified of, the Fenians, or of other nationalist societies, or even of small sharked-up gangs of killers avenging the victims of vicious landlordism, to bear witness in court. The Crimes Act, as it was called for short, enabled the police to hold arrested men for months without bringing specific charges; and it legalized a procedure rather like that of the criminal section of the *Code Napoléon*: an examining magistrate was given power to call and question witnesses, and to arrest them if necessary, in order to investigate a crime and provide the material for a prosecution. The Gladstone government's Crimes Act was at once denounced in Britain as well as Ireland as a reversion to Star Chamber methods; Parnell and the Irish fought it angrily in the House and a large number of Liberals were made very uneasy by it. So obnoxious was it considered to be by English lawyers that the Lord Chief Justice called a meeting of the judges and publicly denounced the Act as 'unconstitutional' (whatever that may mean in Britain), and contrary to the spirit of justice. None of which protests made an effective impression on the government.

Dublin was in something like a state of siege, for one of the security measures taken by Dublin Castle was to borrow hundreds of marines from the Fleet, put them into civilian clothes, and keep them walking about the city in case of a rising. Lady Julia Roundell describes how every Dublin Castle official, visiting M.P.s, and other government servants, not only went armed but were followed by police guards. Driving into the city with the

---

* 'It was strange that many Englishmen believed Forster and his policy to have been vindicated by the great crime that had been committed, although it afterwards appeared that it was the outcome of that policy' – Cosgrave in op. cit.

new Permanent Secretary, Mr Trevelyan, months after the
assassinations, to attend the first day of the trial of the Invincibles,
she noted that: '. . . savage looking men lounged at every corner.
They scowled at us as we passed, and every time we passed one
of these groups I felt Mr Trevelyan's arm stiffen as he grasped his
revolver.'

Mallon was soon in a position, by means of his informers and
some reasoning based on many years' knowledge and study of the
political underground, to arrest Carey, Curley, Mullet, two
brothers named Hanlon, and another Invincible, McCaffrey by
name, not to be confused with Caffrey. The arrests were made
under the Crimes Act; but even under that Act he had to be able
to produce witnesses, or at least confessions, and his witnesses
were not such as he could produce; if subpoenaed they would
turn mum on him. In September he was forced to release the
prisoners. He could have held them for six months, under the
Act; he preferred to let them go and, as he hoped, make some
mistake which would enable him to take effective action against
them.

★

There are two similar but not identical accounts of how, in the
end, the Invincibles were brought to trial and the assassins to
conviction and sentence. One is in Curran's *Reminiscences*,★ and in
it, while he gives rather condescending words of praise to Mallon,
he attributes all the credit to himself, whom he presents as being
as cunning as he is brave. The other account appears in Moir
Bussy's biography of the detective, *Irish Conspiracies*,† and it is
based on many long conversations with Mallon. Curran seems to
have been a vain and self-important man and on balance I conclude that the brainwork and knowledge of the world they were
plunging into was supplied by Mallon, who had the tact to use
Curran, his superior in the business, to get the results he saw were
possible. Other, minor, sources, such as a curious series of pamph-
lets published by Nugent of Dublin in 1882 and 1883, tend to
bear out this conclusion.

★ op. cit.   † op. cit.

When Mallon released the men he had been unable to bring into court, he had them watched and shadowed. His difficulty was still the same; no witnesses. Fortunately for him, the Invincibles were not resting on their laurels and their new activity was to be the death of them. They made an attempt to assassinate a grand juror named Field who had shown hostility to the Irish cause; and they tried either actually to kill, or perhaps only to intimidate by threats, Judge Lawson, whose bias against political 'criminals' was notorious. In both these cases the man with the knife was Delaney. He badly wounded but failed to kill Field on the man's own doorstep; evidently Mallon's men had relaxed their watch on him or had blundered; but they were right behind him when he attacked, or maybe only feigned to attack the judge; and he was instantly arrested. He was held under the Crimes Act; and under the same Act the special Minister for Crimes, one Jenkinson, and the Attorney-General, appointed John Adye Curran, K.C., to investigate the Field case.

Field recovered from his wounds and Curran was able to call him as a witness. The procedure, for the benefit of those who are familiar with French practice, was that of a *Juge d'Instruction*. Field told Curran and Mallon, who had been appointed to work with the examining magistrate, that his assailant had cried 'Ah, you villain!' as he struck at his throat with the knife. Curran claims that it was he who recalled that one of those non-appearing secret witnesses of the 'scuffle' in Phoenix Park had heard one of the men involved shout 'Ah, you villain!'; and that this was a clue worth following up. It is much more likely to have been Mallon who made this connexion. At all events, on this very slender thread the magistrate hung an argument which he put before the authorities at Dublin Castle, and a request to be allowed to extend his investigation beyond the Field case to the assassination of Mr Burke and Lord Frederick Cavendish. The Secretary of State was only too pleased to agree; the government had begun to consider the case as hopeless.

Thus it was that Mallon at last had the apparatus he required to bring the Invincibles into court; but the work was only just begun.

Curran had power to summon the witnesses he needed and to apply for warrants to arrest those who refused the summons. By this means all the men whom Mallon suspected could be submitted to an ordeal of relentless questioning, and they had, under the Crimes Act, no recourse to legal dodging, could not, for example, plead that they could not be made to incriminate themselves. Tighe Hopkins sums up Mallon's method, which Curran applied, in a score of words: '. . . by word and deed they were made to feel that they had been betrayed on all sides.'*

What did he mean by 'deed'? That will be clear when we come to the breaking down of James Carey. But the rot started with Robert Farrel. Curran, in his own account of the investigation, says:

'I next called before me a man against whom I had evidence proving that at all events he was a leading Fenian: his name was Robert Farrel. In the course of my examination in the presence of Mr Mallon I put certain questions assuming all my suspected facts to have been proved. Farrel appeared to be very much surprised and a few days later on 3 January 1883 he went to Inspector Kavanagh and told him, from his interview with myself and Mr Mallon, he was sure that someone had turned traitor and given information which had led to my questions. He further said that he did not intend to be left in when others were turning informers and then made a statement which he signed giving full details of the conspiracy and the names of those engaged from time to time in carrying out its objects.'†

Mallon knew that Farrel's statement was not enough to hang the assassins. And since he could still not get any outside witness to come into court and talk, he knew that he would have to persuade others of the Invincibles to turn infomer; to that end he needed some of them under his hand in Kilmainham prison. He favoured Kilmainham because it adjoined the courthouse, which meant that his prisoners could be moved in and out of court without any passage through the streets of the city, which would have entailed the danger of a determined attempt at rescue by the mob. He urged Curran to apply for warrants to arrest the twenty-

* Hopkins, in op. cit.   † Curran, op. cit.

seven men named by Farrel. Curran did so: the Attorney-General was willing to agree, but Jenkinson, the Crimes Minister, was not; he thought he had a super-informer of his own whose evidence would be conclusive. (In the event the informer turned out to be useless.) Curran went over the Minister's head by taking Mallon to see Lord Spencer and Mr Trevelyan; they were so impressed by Mallon and what he told them that Spencer used his viceregal power to order the warrants to be issued. For some reason one of the twenty-seven was not to be found, but twenty-six arrests were made by Mallon's men, all on the same day.

The evidence which Mallon wanted was either Curley's or Carey's; he soon realized that Curley was not a man whom he could persuade to betray his friends and his cause, but that Carey could be driven to turn informer, although only with difficulty. Mallon's method was brilliant, worthy of the protagonist or antagonist of an Edgar Alan Poe story. Day after day, night after night, he walked down the corridor of the prison, past Carey's cell, accompanied by a clerk carrying writing materials and a desk, and into the cell next door or beyond. Sometimes he brought other men with him; there were snatches of talk for Carey to brood over, lights and movements and loud voices at night, long murmurings from the next cell punctuated by sudden exclamations, intervals of silence, then a bustle as men were moved from cell to cell, or some high official, treated with deference, paused in brief talk with Mallon just outside Carey's cell. Carey was made to believe that others were saving their necks by turning Queen's Evidence.

The twenty-six Invincibles were brought into court and charged, and the preliminaries of the trial began. The prisoners asked themselves and each other why Farrel was not among them; had he escaped Mallon's net? Or had he turned informer? Carey broke at that and asked to see Mallon so that he could make a statement; Mallon pretended that he no longer needed Carey's information; and he so played on the man's nerves with his coolness, his almost solicitous kindness of manner, that Carey was driven to plead the special value of the information he could give. Mallon agreed to take his statement, and what he then got from

Carey was enough. He could now hang the assassins at the cost of letting Carey go free. Meanwhile similar methods had been used to break the cab-driver Kavanagh, who was the third of the accused to turn informer, and the last.

*

Whenever the accused Invincibles filed into court they always counted their own number anxiously. When the day came on which they saw that James Carey was no longer with them, a groan and mutter of rage and fear went up from the dock. They knew that Carey, their leader, had turned informer.

But as he had not done so easily, so now he found it a hideous ordeal to appear and display his treachery before his friends, the friends he was hanging. That he broke at all is a remarkable tribute to Mallon's skill, for Carey was known to have a particular horror and loathing of informing, that vice of a people brought up from childhood to find comfort in confession. Perhaps he hated informers so bitterly because he had always known that he had some flaw in him, the makings of an informer. So appalled was he at the prospect of having to appear in court and give his evidence, that he collapsed, and could not appear until he had been got on his feet with half a tumbler of brandy. And when he did appear, and the part he had now to play became apparent, it was a nightmare, for his old friends threatened, cursed, and damned him to hell from the dock; Brady made a savage attempt to get at him and had to be held down by the police, and others wailed aloud.

On Carey's evidence, confirmed by Farrel's and Kavanagh's and by some outside witnesses, Brady, Curley, Kelly, Fagan, and Caffrey were condemned to death. Such was the impression which Daniel Curley had made on the court that the judge was seen to weep as he passed sentence on the young man. The rest of those accused were sentenced to varying but long terms of penal servitude. None of the condemned confessed before they were hanged: and only Curley prayed, in Irish, as he stood on the trap.

As for the informers, Farrel was shipped for his own safety to Australia, where the colonists refused him permission to land; his end is obscure. Kavanagh died of alcoholism in a lunatic asylum. Carey was smuggled out of Dublin by the police and put on board a ship for Cape Town. Very shortly after landing there he was shot dead by a member of the Irish Republican Brotherhood, O'Donnel by name.

★

In this case it is as beside the point to ask whether the deaths of Burke and Cavendish on the one hand, and of the five Invincibles on the other, served a useful purpose, as to ask whether those who fall in war die usefully or in vain. War, whether waged by assassins or by armies, is to further a political or social policy which cannot be otherwise furthered. So one can only ask whether the assassinations furthered the purpose of the Fenians by bringing Irish independence nearer. The answer is that it probably did. Imperial governments take a lot of convincing that their dominion is very unwelcome to the natives; terrorist acts help to change the governmental mind. Their immediate consequences may often be terrible for the people who are meant to benefit from them; in that case these people are rendered as irreconcilable as their more militant fellows always were. From all this it follows that, however we may dislike the idea, and if we accept the nationalist case for sovereign independence of small nations, the assassinations of Thomas Henry Burke and Lord Frederick Cavendish are justified by the existence of the Irish Republic today.

8

LOHMEY HERUTH ISRAEL:
THE SACRIFICE OF LORD MOYNE

THE long campaign of terrorist war waged by the Irish nationalists against England, and the ultimate victory implicit in the
attainment of independence and establishment of the Republic,
were an example and encouragement to other peoples who, ruled
by a foreign power, aspired to independence and national sovereignty. The young men who yearned and fought to bring the
state of Israel into existence sometimes encouraged each other by
pointing out what the Irish had accomplished by the one means of
warfare open to a weak people fighting a greater power: terrorism. But this word is unfairly loaded; for terrorism is, in
practice, no more than ordinary warfare in which the objectives
are the enemy's highest officers and principal buildings and the
maximum use is made of surprise. It is an infinitely cleaner kind of
warfare, than, for example, the pattern bombing of enemy cities
in which, as in terrorist warfare, civilians are as often the objectives as soldiers; and it is far more discriminating. The only serious
question in the context of war is – is terrorism effective?

It is customary and expedient to pretend that established
governments do not surrender to terrorism. This is untrue: if the

Russian government yielded nothing to the terrorism which culminated in the assassination of the Tsar Alexander II it was because there was nobody and nothing – the Nihilists – to yield anything to. But it was the long practice of terrorism in Ireland, of which we have seen a single aspect in Chapter Seven, that forced the English government to concede Ireland her freedom. Britain, until 1945 the greatest imperial power since Rome, was repeatedly forced to modify, or radically to change, her policy by successful, sustained terrorism, that warfare of the very weak against the mighty: terrorism using, moreover, assassination as well as sabotage. The Irish, the Israelis, and the Aden Arabs were all successful in their terrorist war against Britain. The Algerians forced the French to surrender by terrorism. This may or may not be cause for rejoicing but it is certainly a fact.

In the case of the Israeli terrorism practised by the Stern group and its derivative, the Lohmey Heruth Israel (the Fighters for the Freedom of Israel – we shall call the movement F.F.I. for short), which gave the Israelis, most of whom feared, hated, and even fought against it, the chance to create the modern Israeli nation, it had a special justification over and above nationalism. The British, by refusing to allow Jewish refugees from the Nazi campaign of genocide to land in Israel, were condemning thousands of Jews to a horrible death; even seemed guilty, in some cases, of doing Hitler's work for him. Not content with the offence, as Jewish nationalists naturally thought of it, of occupying the land of Israel by armed force, the British were using that force in such a way that thousands of Jews who might have lived were dying in misery and degradation.

*

For the European Jews in the 1930s there were two alternatives: to die horribly in the Nazi death chambers; or to find a national home. The problem had existed for centuries: it was the policy of Russian governments, for example, to follow any attack on their absolute sovereignity by a pogrom by way of *catharsis*: a slaughter of scapegoats. In 1881, when the Tsar Alexander II was assassinated, there was the usual pogrom and it was followed by the first

great *aliya* ('coming-up'), that is, a wave of migration, of Russian
Jews into Palestine; there was another such *aliya* after the pogroms
of 1904; another in the 1920s following the Balfour Declaration.
But until the 1930s there had always been alternative refuges for
such Jews as did not have strong nationalistic feelings, who were
not, that is, Zionists: many could go to the United States, to
Britain, to France and Germany. But by the mid 1930s, when the
Nazis began their twelve-year pogrom of total extermination, no
country was left willing to receive large numbers of penniless
immigrants; the famous invocation engraved on the Statue of
Liberty, although not covered by a black veil, had become null
and void of meaning. Zionism remained – the only hope, the only
alternative to a role which some writers have thought that the
Jews accepted too readily, the role of Europe's scapegoat, Europe's
manifold assassinee, as it were. Such writers have felt that the
Jews of Germany and East Europe would have done better, less
ignobly, to die fighting even with their bare hands, or to take
their own lives *en masse*, as their fore-runners did at York in the
eleventh century, than do as they did – go naked and meek like a
sacrificial herd to the slaughter, serving by their resignation the
sadistic lust of the Nazis. One can see this history of mass slaughter
in many lights: as the sacrifice, on the altars of Germany's ancient
crowd-gods, of an alien and in some sort sacred human herd; as
the sacrificial massacre of Christianity's Father-People; as the
final consequence of the ideology of the Archduke Franz Joseph
and his friends. When I come to deal with the assassination of
Walther Rathenau I shall have to discuss the anti-Semitic state of
mind in detail and I propose to leave it until then.

It is not here necessary to repeat the whole history of Zionism:
but, it will be remembered that in return for Jewish support during
the First World War the British had promised the Zionist leader,
Dr Chaim Weizmann, a Jewish National Home in the Palestine
they were liberating, with both Arab and Jewish help, from the
Turks. At the same time they promised the country to the Arabs.
From 1918 and for a quarter of a century thereafter they were in
Palestine, first on their own account and later as League of
Nations Mandate administrators, trying in vain to fulfil these two

totally incompatible promises by persuading the Jews and Arabs to share the land in peace. Not only was there a clash between the rival nationalist aspirations of both Jews and Arabs, but the Arabs were driven by their rising fear of Jewish immigration, of the higher Jewish infant survival rate, by their inability to compete with Jewish efficiency in agriculture, industry, trade, and education, into a campaign of terrorism against both Jews and British.

The situation in the country was made much worse, of course, by the Nazi persecution of European Jewry. A few rich Jews with money in Britain or America or Switzerland might escape torture, degradation, and death in those countries, and a few others, whose services in science, learning, or the arts would enrich the country which welcomed them. For the rest, the vast majority, the only possible refuge was Palestine. The Jews already in that country hoped and expected that their persecuted fellow Jews would come to them and were ready to share what little they had: American Jewry was ready with huge sums of money to finance the operation. But Britain, anxious to placate Arab nationalism, which had asserted itself by terrorism, and to stand well with the Arabs not only of Palestine but of the whole Dar-al-Islam, would allow only a tiny minority of these helpless and hopeless refugees to enter their only possible refuge, the land which their religion taught had been given to them by God and which they regarded as their own.

*

The majority, the easily dominant political party among the Palestine Jews at the time in question here, was Mapai, the Labour party led by David Ben-Gurion. Its origins, traditions, and principles were pacifist-Socialist, a complex reflection of Chaim Weizmann's gradualism: immigrant Jews were to buy land from the Arabs, to drain swamps, irrigate desert, clear scrub; they were to live communally in settlements, *kibbutzim*; and any wealth they created by their work was to belong to the collective and not to the individual; they were to be makers, working slowly, carefully, thoroughly, and above all pacifically.

To the Arabs they must, when stricken, turn the other cheek;
or, at the utmost limit of what was permissible, defend their lives
when they were threatened. There is no doubt that an astonish-
ingly large number of Israelis did succeed in carrying out this
policy even when the pressures set up by the atrocious German
persecutions made such pacifism well-nigh intolerable. These
Jews were, in fact, among the very few people who have ever
tried to practise 'Christian' quietism, and nothing in modern
history is more curious than the fact, as lamentable as it is un-
deniable, that their 'Christian' conduct earned them an extra
measure of impatient contempt in the great Christian and
Moslem countries; and that this contempt endured despite lip-
service to social progress in Israel until the Jews, forsaking the
quietism which was deeply rooted in Jewish mysticism, showed
themselves to be very successful soldiers (that is, as ferocious,
cruel, and 'un-Christian' as any other people); whereupon they
were regarded with a new and surprised respect.

This military and militant ferocity was, until the three Israel-
Arab wars, confined to the small minority which rejected the
gradualist way and was attracted to the near-Fascist ideas of a
remarkable man called Vladimir Jabotinsky. He was a Russian
Jew of powerful character and fiery spirit who believed that the
Jews should take up arms and conquer their country and not rest
until its frontiers were those of all ancient Israel – that is, Palestine
with Transjordan. It was Jabotinsky who founded the Jewish
Legion to fight shoulder to shoulder with Britain against the
Turks in Palestine in 1914–18; it was he who initiated the foundation of Haganah, of which more below; it was he who, moreover, inspired and in some cases led the various small militant
Israeli movements, and above all the 'underground' military
organization which emerged from the militant wing of Haganah,
Irgun Zwei Leumi; and its extremist terrorist offshoot founded
and commanded by the Fascist poet-patriot Abraham Stern; and
its derivative the F.F.I.

★

Abraham Stern had reached Israel from Poland, by way of half a dozen countries torn by war and revolution through which he made his way alone, at the age of fifteen; that was in 1922. An excellent Latinist and Hellenist, he enrolled in the Hebrew University and supported himself by tutoring less advanced students. He joined Haganah and did some gun-running for them. Haganah was the semi-secret homeguard formed to give the *kibbutzim* that protection which the British could not or would not give against Arab raiders; as it was not allowed arms legally, it obtained them illegally; but it rigorously practised *havlagah* ('self-restraint') and would not countenance reprisals. When Stern was twenty-one he won a scholarship which took him to Florence, where, as well as learning Italian, he became passionately absorbed in the history of the *Risorgimento* and Garibaldi; and an admirer of Benito Mussolini. On his return to Israel he found, within Haganah, a faction inspired by Jabotinsky and known as the Revisionists.* The Revisionists were demanding not merely defensive action against the Arabs, but reprisals, offensive action, an eye for an eye. In 1937 a minority of these Revisionists, led by David Raziel, one of Jabotinsky's lieutenants, separated themselves from the Haganah on this issue, though without entirely breaking with the parent body. This new movement was called the National Military Organization (Irgun Zwei Leumi), was inspired by Sinn Fein, and had, among its first officers, Abraham Stern.

Irgun struck blow for blow against the Arabs; and if the Arabs were protected by the British, then against the British; it used sabotage, bombing, and assassination, and it roused in the ordinary Jews a horror and protest which it ignored as weakness. Stern, by this time a man of thirty-two of considerable physical beauty and personal charm, found its methods, its ruthless militancy, much more to his taste than the careful defensiveness, the only slightly modified *havlagah* of the Haganah majority. But although Irgun moved over to the offensive, it did so in a way which Stern treated with contempt in his poetry, prose, and actions. He did not approve of its military conventions, its command hierarchy, nor

---

* The Revisionist cadet movement was called 'Betar' and was a sort of training school for terrorists.

its chivalry: for example, when the Irgun decided to blow up some British institution, it first sent warning so that staff could be evacuated. This, said Stern, was not real war. By this time he believed that he had a mission not only to liberate his country from the alien oppressor but to make it the nucleus of a great Middle East empire stretching from the Nile to the Euphrates.

Stern's belief in and urging of total war against the British was strongly reinforced by the Chamberlain government's White Paper on Palestine, published early in 1939. At the very moment when European Jewry stood in the most acute and terrible need of the National Home promised them by Balfour, the White Paper reversed the Balfour Declaration. With twelve million Jews in danger of death at Nazi hands (the Chamberlain government cannot be blamed for trying not to believe in this monstrous truth at that time), Jews were to be allowed into Palestine at the rate of 15,000 a year for five years, and then no more, ever, without Arab consent; in ten years Palestine was to become an Arab Sovereign State.

Britain stood revealed as the national enemy, as distinct from Germany, the 'racial' enemy. Israel was a sovereign nation whose land was occupied by an alien army, and clearly that army was the enemy and the British must be driven out of the land whatever was happening to men abroad who might be Jewish by religion and 'race' but were not Israeli nationalists. Some extremist theorists who, without always approving Stern's methods, approved his fiery patriotism, went further: they held that the whole business of racial and religious Jewishness was confusing the issue; the real Israelis were aboriginal Cannaanites who had been conquered by the Egyptians but had reconquered their country in 1200 B.C. These people actually called themselves Canaanites and repudiated the name of Jew. They were, in short, ultra-nationalists.

Nothing could better reveal the sort of man Stern was than the extraordinary plan which he put to the Polish government when, early in the year 1939, he went to Warsaw to arrange for supplies of arms to Irgun, and for the training, by the Polish army, of Irgun officers. His official Irgun mission successfully accomplished, he went on to urge the Polish government to help him recruit 40,000 young Jews throughout Europe, train them, move them to Italy and from there launch a one-day invasion of Palestine during October, an invasion which would seize the country and proclaim a sovereign state of Israel.

While Stern was in Warsaw, however, the British Palestine Police had swooped on Irgun. Helped by the ordinary Jewish people, who detested Irgun methods, and even by the Haganah, they were able to round up and impound almost the entire leadership, including David Raziel. Abraham Stern returned to Israel, took command of the movement, and published a death 'sentence' on Assistant Superintendent Ralph Cairns of the C.I.D., who had become notorious for torturing Jewish prisoners. This sentence was, in due course, carried out at the cost of several Irgun lives. Stern then launched full-scale terrorist war on both Arabs and British.

The break between Stern and Raziel came after the outbreak of war. Raziel, backed by Jabotinsky from the United States, insisted that Irgun must ally itself with the British against Germany until the end of the war; Stern, followed by a small minority of the rank and file, demanded continuous terrorist activity against the nearest of the nation's enemies, Britain. Once again, we have the Irish pattern repeated, but with this difference, that the Germans were by far the most convinced and determined Jew-haters whereas they had been friendly to the Irish. Stern took his followers out of Irgun and set up his Lohmey Heruth Israel. His recruiting methods and his rules of conduct are as revealing as that invasion plan he had urged in Warsaw. New members, usually in their late teens, were recruited by actual members only after long and careful observation and probing; their initiation was calculated to impress the kind of romantic lad he preferred; it took place, including a solemn oath of loyalty and obedience, in an empty room lit only by a candle and with a voice which spoke to the recruit from behind a curtain. The recruit to the F.F.I. placed his life at the organization's disposal and its cause above family and all other loyalties.

Nor, after Abraham Stern was shot by a British police officer while trying to escape arrest, did the F.F.I. change its nature or tactics; the new leaders, and notably the new leader Friedman-Yellin, famous for his stirring writings in the F.F.I. journal *Hazit* and for his successful leading of the great gaol-break of F.F.I. prisoners from Latrun Camp, had much the same ideas as Stern, who, dead, and in the eyes of his young followers a martyr, still exercised all the power of glamour over those who had followed him.

*

One of the differences separating the Irgun and the Sternist (later F.F.I.) group, was about tactics. Irgun was organized and tried to operate as an army. Stern and his colleagues thought it ridiculous for a force of about a thousand men to operate against a great power by conventional military methods. The only kind of war the weak could wage against the strong, as the Irish and the Palestine Arabs had demonstrated, was terrorism; and the proper targets for terrorist soldiers were the highest officers of the enemy. The policy of attacking high government officials, of trying to assassinate the High Commissioner, and, in due course, the Resident British Minister in Egypt, his master, was not crystallized until after Stern's death, but he would have approved it.

But although the F.F.I. under Friedman-Yellin set out to kill Sir Harold MacMichael and Lord Moyne, they realized that it was important to make it clear to all the Israelis that there was no question of mere revenge against individuals who had done harm to the Jews. Articles in the movement's widely read illicit journal, *Hazit*, must emphasize that Britain's representative was the national enemy whatever his personal behaviour, whether he was merciless, like the High Commissioner, or magnanimous. It was of the first importance to make this clear in the case of Sir Harold MacMichael, should they succeed in assassinating him, because he was hated by all Jews, in and out of Israel; so aware was the F.F.I. command of the exact nature of the war they were waging, that one of the Central Committee, Itzhak Yizernitsky, wrote: 'A man who goes forth to take the life of another he does not know must believe one thing only – that by his act he will change the course of history.'*

Sir Harold MacMichael was an able and unimaginative official who had earned Jewish hatred by what they regarded as a consistently pro-Arab policy; in this he was simply the scapegoat for his government, who found it expedient to placate the Arabs even though the most influential Arab militant leader was a Nazi ally. But there was some justification for hating Sir Harold as a man, personally, when from 1940 onwards he rigorously applied his government's policy of turning back shiploads of fugitives from the Nazi death camps, a policy which it might have cost him his career but would have earned him world-wide applause to reverse. He sent 1,700 Jews of the refugee ship *Patria* to their death, later the 231 of the *Salvatore*, and the 800 of the *Struma*. From the Jewish, and above all from the F.F.I. point of view, Sir Harold MacMichael was an ally of the Nazis, an exterminator of Jews; from his own point of view he was simply a man obeying an order.

It may be said at once that MacMichael's remarkable coolness in the face of danger to other men's lives did not extend to himself. In that sense, at least, he was a thorough politician. It was his duty not to expose himself and so conscientiously did he do his duty in this as in all things that the repeated attempts of the F.F.I. trained assassins to kill him all failed, and happily he got out of the Middle East with nothing worse than a minor wound.

That left Lord Moyne, who, as MacMichael's master, was also the Israeli national enemy, as a target for terrorists.

*

The two young men chosen to kill Lord Moyne were, respectively, twenty-two and seventeen years of age, but they were both old terrorist hands.

Eliahu Bet Zouri† was born in Israel in 1922; his father had

---

* Quoted by Gerold Frank in *The Deed*, Simon & Schuster, New York.
† His father's name, Steinhaus (Stonehouse), was Hebraized as Bet Zouri when he reached Israel from Russia.

reached the country from Minsk in about 1900 and received an education at the French-Israel Institution. His mother came of a very old Palestinian, Sephardic family, her ancestors having taken refuge from the Spanish Inquisition in Turkish Palestine. Moshe Bet Zouri was a post office clerk in Jaffa, but he was appointed postmaster of Tiberius when Eliahu was nine.

As a boy Eliahu had fair, curly hair and blue eyes, a fearless nature and a quick, lively mind. Like his father he was a fine linguist; his mother-tongue was Hebrew, of course, but he also learned Ladino, the Sephardic dialect of old Castilian spoken by his mother's family; Arabic from some of his playmates, the town being half Arab; English, French, and Italian. By the time he was ten he had read his people's and his country's history, was accustomed to carrying illicit ammunition to Haganah guard-posts; he had had to take refuge from numerous raids, had noted that the British treated Arab raiders and Jewish defenders as equally guilty, had become a patriot and learned to hate the British. His home life was not happy; the Bet Zouris were seven in a tiny flat and his mother and father had frequent rows which derived from their different backgrounds. This state of affairs continued in Tel Aviv when Eliahu's father was posted there and where the boy was sent to the Balfour Grammar School; his conduct there was turbulent but his marks excellent.

At school he came under the influence of Adi Landau, whose family had made a fanatical Hebrew nationalist of him and who became a 'Canaanite' some years later. Both boys joined the National Cells, a sort of revolutionary debating society, and graduated from that into nationalist militancy. When the teenage *Betar* hero Shlomo Ben Josef was hanged by the British for trying to avenge an Arab murder-and-rape outrage, Eliahu was among the youths who wore black ribbons and demonstrated in the streets, and he took an active part in the serious rioting in which the whole nation demonstrated against the White Paper which Winston Churchill denounced as 'a second Munich' and which the quietist Chief Rabbi of Palestine tore into shreds in the pulpit of Jerusalem's principal synagogue.

In 1943 Bet Zouri joined the F.F.I. and his professional work as a land surveyor enabled him to be useful, for example, as an unsuspected observer of enemy movements, and in ambush operations. He had one other great advantage as a terrorist fighter; his fair colouring and his build enabled him to look like an English officer when it was expedient to do so.

By 1944 Eliahu Bet Zouri was an experienced terrorist utterly dedicated to the cause of a free and sovereign Israel.

*

The younger of the two chosen assassins was also called Eliahu. His father, Simon Hakim, had been born into the Jewish community of Damascus which had been established in that ancient city since about 600 B.C. A silk merchant by trade, he had migrated to Haifa with his family and his business in 1933, where he had prospered. At the time of this move Eliahu Hakim was six years old.

Eliahu Hakim's first act of political militancy was that of marching, at the age of twelve, in the 1939 demonstration against the White Paper. One year later he stood on the terrace of his father's house by the seaside in Haifa and watched 1,700 fugitives from the Nazi cyanide chambers aboard the s.s. *Patria* blow themselves up with their ship when the High Commissioner refused to let them land. They, at least, had followed the example of the Jews of eleventh-century York. Thereafter he soaked himself in nationalist literature. His *Diary* reveals a mind much older than his fourteen/fifteen years, deeply troubled by his inability to do anything for his martyred people and his country; it reveals, also, the direction he was to take, in a single entry for 5 August 1942: 'Today, two years ago, Vladimir Jabotinsky died in New York. His ideas are mine. Today is a day of mourning for me.' At the time he was spending the school holiday in working on a *kibbutz* and taking his turn, rifle in hand, at guard duty.

At the end of that holiday he refused to return to school, got a job in a military garage and, in this period, must have joined the youth branch of Irgun. At all events, shortly after he had been dismissed from his job following a row with the English foreman, his mother accidentally discovered that he was a member of some

extremist underground movement, when she found him using
invisible ink to write a note. Horrified and terrified, she implored
and nagged at him to do the safe thing and join the Britsh army.
He finally agreed to do so, was accepted and sent to Egypt,
regretted it and, back on leave in Palestine, sought to join the
F.F.I.

The Central Committee was not ready to accept him; the son
of a rich man, with a reputation even at sixteen as a playboy,
he was not to be trusted. They decided to test him. He was in the
British army and he was back and forth from Egypt; let him
steal and smuggle arms for the F.F.I.

Hakim passed this test with spectacular success: fearless, and
with extraordinary effrontery, he brought suitcases full of small
arms and ammunition into Israel every time he came on leave.
These weapons were stolen by F.F.I. members serving in the
British army. As a result of this success he was accepted into the
F.F.I. and ordered to desert the army and report for terrorist
duties in Tel Aviv. That was in December 1943, and the first his
family knew about it was when a posse of Military Police arrived
to search the house for the deserter. They were utterly appalled,
and determined to do something to recall the boy to his senses.
His brother Menachem put an advertisement into the Hebrew
newspaper *Haboken* begging Eliahu to come home as their father
was ill. Eliahu saw it, went to Haifa, saw the whole family, and
proved firmly resistant to their persuasions and prayers, unmoved
by his father's anger, by his mother's tears, and by his brother's
arguments. With a lack of insight which would have been
remarkable in anyone but a father, perhaps in desperation, his
father offered him a year in Paris with all the money he could
want; the boy replied, 'It is my duty to save my country. Here I
stay.' Then his brother Menachem asked him, 'What can you and
your little party do against the mighty British Empire?' to which
Eliahu answered, 'Have you read what the Irish did against it?'

Menachem Hakim realized that his brother's character had
hardened and that he had given his life to the Lohmey Heruth
Israel; thereafter he sent the young man £15 every month: at
least he should not starve. Eliahu gave this, and whatever else

he received from his family, to the F.F.I. treasury, and himself starved on the F.F.I. ration money of 1s. a day. At times he was living on stale bread soaked in hot water, but on that diet he became a weapons expert for his unit, and their best marksman. He led a hunted, comfortless life, for now the terrorists and the police were at open war in the streets. But it was what he wanted; his life now had purpose. The police were beating up suspected terrorists when they caught them, were said to be torturing Jews for information, and killing when they could. Eliahu himself shot dead two police officers while escaping from a search.

Both the Eliahus, Bet Zouri and Hakim, at that time unknown to each other,* took part in two of the attempts to assassinate Sir Harold MacMichael. After the first attempt, the High Commissioner decreed that the punishment for possessing a gun would be death. That intensified the struggle; there is no greater mistake a government can make, of course, than to punish with the supreme penalty the mere possession of weapons, for it means that the possessor might just as well use them; he cannot be any worse off. As police terrorism mounted in response to F.F.I. terrorism, the F.F.I. Central Committee published its declaration of total war in its journal *Hazit*:

'This is how you British henceforth walk the streets of Zion: armed to the teeth, prepared for anything, fear in your eyes; fear from every dark corner, in every turn of the road, at every sound in the night, fear from every Jewish boy, fear day and night because the Jewish youth have become dynamite in this country. You shall walk on burning embers, our bodies the embers and the fire our love of country. No guards, no tanks, no fines, no curfews, no tortures and no hangings, no prisons and no detention camps will help your High Commissioners,

---

* Like all successful revolutionary organizations, the F.F.I. was organized in cells whose members were unknown to each other. This is, of course, advisable where the police are using torture. All political police forces without exception use torture whether or not it gets results and simply because only a certain kind of man is attracted by political police work. These are facts of political life, not hypotheses. As far as I am able to discover no F.F.I. prisoner broke under torture and no F.F.I. member tried to earn the blood money which had been put on their leaders' heads. The British Palestine Police either invented the torture of electric shocks through the genitals subsequently used by the French army in Algeria and by the Americans in Vietnam, or copied it from the Nazis. At no time in history has the use of torture yielded any useful result, from which we may safely conclude that it is used rather to gratify the torturer than to break down the victim.

your officers, your police. Your children will become orphans as you have orphaned the children of Israel. Your mothers shall mourn their sons as you have made the mothers of Israel mourn their sons. For every cry of a child from the deck of a burning ship, for every cry of a Hebrew mother when her child embarks on a broken ship in the midst of the sea, for every Jewish tear, we shall answer you. We came in fire and we were burned; we came in water and we were drowned. We, the remnants, walk in rivers of blood, the blood reaches our necks, our mouths, our eyes, and from fire and water and blood, trembling arms are raised, voices cry out, and from the mouths and eyes and trembling arms and fingers, from the water and the fire and blood we are coming up, we are coming. Woe unto you!'*

Many will shrug this off; it is true that the style of some Hebrew writing has been as much corrupted by the more florid passages of the Bible as has that of some English writing. It is impossible to defend it. But the intention, the feeling, is certainly clear enough, and it was reinforced by a list of F.F.I. dead, tortured, and mutilated. The declaration went on:

'As was commanded by our fathers in Holy Writ, we came to you with peace. It did not help. We came to you with money. We bought our water and our earth, the very air we breathe; it did not help. We came to you with prayer, in the name of justice and honesty and fairness; in the name of mercy we prayed to you in all the languages of the earth; it did not help, not peace, nor money, nor prayer.

'Now this is the law of our war. So long as there is fear in the heart of any Jew in the world, so long as there are embers burning under our feet anywhere in the world, so long as there is a foreign policeman guarding the gates of our homeland, so long as there is a foreign master over our country, so long as we do not rule in our own land, so long shall we be in your way. You will look around you in fear day and night. You will sleep in your uniforms, you will wear your arms, your life here will be hell day and night, for we have had our fill of shame and exile, slavery and humiliation, for we are weary of waiting and waiting, begging and praying, for we have taken the oath – the freedom of Israel.'†

* *Hazit*.   † ibid.

Shortly after this was published the final attempt on Sir Harold MacMichael, about to leave for his new post in Malaya, was made. Eliahu Bet Zouri, disguised as a surveying officer in charge of a working team, took part; so did the other Eliahu, disguised as an Arab and armed with a sub-machine gun. The attempt failed because the car driven by the High Commissioner's military chauffeur went more than twice as fast as the one which the conspirators had used for the dummy run on the day before, which confused the timing. True, the car went off the road, fire was opened, there was a running fight between F.F.I. youths and Sir Harold's guards. But the High Commissioner escaped with trifling wounds in thigh and hand.

In their usual *Hazit* explanation after the attempt, the F.F.I. declared:

'We did not single him out because he is MacMichael; the punishment is not personal; the fire was aimed at the High Commissioner of a foreign rule. . . . The remnants of the Hungarian Jews have a chance to leave their country. We can save hundreds of thousands from Hungary, Rumania, and Bulgaria if only we can open the gates of the country. But the foreign ruler closes the gates in their faces. The occupier of our country sentences them to death. . . . Brothers, listen to this and listen well. We are fighting for your freedom. Let England listen, too. With blood you will pay for spilling the blood of our brothers. Let the whole world hear this. Jewish martyrs never shook the world. Now perhaps the Jewish war will.'*

*

A fortnight after this defiance was published Eliahu Hakim was summoned by Shamir,† a member of the Central Committee, ordered to resume his British army uniform, to take the false identity papers prepared for him, and to go to Cairo. There he was to ring a certain telephone number, and he would be put in the way of reporting to his new superior, 'Ezekiel'.

Hakim did not know what his new assignment was to be. When he got to Cairo and made that telephone call he was taken in hand by an F.F.I. girl in the A.T.S., Nadja Hess. She sent him

* ibid.
† Yizermitsky: 'Shamir' was his alias.

to the home of a rich Jewish dilettante in Alexandria, a man who pretended not to know that by extending hospitality to Israelis in the British services, he was letting his house be used as a meeting-place and accommodation address by F.F.I. agents; but he was useful: the rich Alexandrine Jews were so ferociously anti-Zionist and so bitterly hostile to all forms of Jewish nationalism that they were above suspicion. By this man's means Hakim was put in touch with Sergeant Joseph Galili of the Royal Air Force. This remarkably able young man was the F.F.I. chief in Egypt – 'Ezekiel'. One month before, he had been on leave in Palestine and there he had a conference with Shamir, who had told him that the Central Committee had decided to assassinate Lord Moyne and that he, Galili, would be in charge of the operation.

'The community thinks of us as outlaws bent on personal revenge. This is a perversion of our political objective, which is to oust the British. Our attack on Moyne will clarify exactly who the enemy is. . . . If we go to Cairo and liquidate the British Minister it will make clear to the entire world that the struggle in Palestine is not a mis-understanding between natives and a local administration, but a major conflict between a fighting nation which demands national freedom and an imperialist power which denies it.'*

Such was the Central Committee's reasoning, and Shamir and Galili decided to nominate Eliahu Hakim as the principal assassin because of his fearless coolness and his excellent marksmanship; later, another man would be chosen to cover him and sent separately to join him in Cairo. F.F.I. men already in Egypt could not be used because they were all in the British army and were liable to be posted, at short notice, to Sicily, as Galili's own F.F.I. predecessor, Sergeant Gefner, had been.

Hakim and Galili met in the Jewish Services canteen and talked for an hour; they had worked together in the past when Hakim was gun-running for the F.F.I. When, later, as they walked the streets for privacy, Galili asked Hakim if he knew what his task was to be, the youth replied that he did not but had a feeling that it was to be an action he must be ready to pay for with his life.

* Frank, op. cit.

When Galili told him that he was called on to assassinate Lord Moyne, Hakim was full of awed pride: 'That I, I should have been chosen!'

Hakim was given new papers in the name of Itzhak Cohen and sent to Cairo to occupy the room which had been taken for him in that name. Galili rejoined him there and introduced him to a colleague who was to help him in the preparation for the assassination. This was an A.T.S. ambulance driver, Yaffa Tuvia, a tall and graceful girl with dark hair and blue eyes, stationed at Tel el Kebir. A dedicated F.F.I. member, she was a successful smuggler of small arms into Israel and of hundreds of copies of *Hazit* into Egypt. When Galili told her the nature of her assignment, she approved it: she held Lord Moyne responsible for all the deaths in the *Patria* and *Struma* disasters and for the hundreds of thousands which need not have occurred in the death camps had Israel's gates been open. She was to appear with Hakim whenever he was seen in public, and as a courting couple they would be able to stroll and loiter in the neighbourhood of Lord Moyne's house in Zamalek or of his offices in the city proper. It was important for Eliahu to familiarize himself with the pattern of the Resident Minister's daily life.

After a thorough and prolonged study of the Minister's habitual movements, Eliahu Hakim concluded that if other lives were to be spared the assassination could be done only at the Residence; as to his chance of escaping, that was not an important consideration with him and, from the beginning, he made it clear by his silences as much as by his words that he expected to pay for Lord Moyne's life with his own.

While, assisted by Yaffa Tuvia and advised by Sergeant Galili, he was preparing for his work, the Central Committee of Lohmey Heruth Israel in Tel Aviv had asked one of their number to see Eliahu Bet Zouri, chosen for his qualities of intelligence and character, and, without asking him in so many words to take a part in the projected assassination, to sound him. The leader in question was very much attached to Bet Zouri and carried out this assignment reluctantly and sadly, for he had no doubt whatever of his friend's reaction. But the business was now urgent, for

Shamir had heard that Galili had been arrested. The sergeant had been closely questioned in such a way as to reveal that the police knew nothing of the real plot but were afraid of an imaginary one to blow up a congress of Arab leaders in Cairo. After seven days Galili was released but posted so far from Cairo that he would probably be unable to direct the assassination operation, and it was important to send Hakim an older and more experienced terrorist to cover and help him.

When, one night after dinner on the terrace of his house, Bet Zouri's friend told him, 'There is a plan being mounted to put Lord Moyne to death. One man has already been sent to carry it out, but another will be sent to help him'; Eliahu rose abruptly to his feet and exclaimed, 'This is for me! I must be the one! I must go!'

There was no particular difficulty in smuggling him out of Israel into Egypt; a rather small railway station was chosen, to avoid the stringent Military Police controls at the principal ones, and Bet Zouri travelled in a uniform and with papers 'stolen' from a soldier on leave who was bathing off one of the Tel Aviv beaches. In reality the 'victim' was an F.F.I. man with whom the theft had been arranged in advance. The affair was carefully timed so that by the time the bereft soldier, in nothing but a bathing slip, was reporting his loss to the police with great indignation, Bet Zouri was past the controls and into Egypt.

*

Bet Zouri made contact with his young namesake in a wine-shop which was used by the F.F.I. as a meeting-place, and thereafter joined Hakim and Yaffa Tuvia in studying the problem implicit in the pattern of the Resident Minister's daily life. Two bicycles were hired and the two young men rode over the possible escape route to familiarize themselves with the road and traffic, though Hakim did so without conviction. He had shown himself willing enough to kill when his enemy was armed and fighting; but from his behaviour I get the impression that he was willing to shoot an unarmed and unready man only if his own life were then to be forfeit.

Late in October Lord Moyne flew to Athens to confer with Anthony Eden. Was it then or earlier that he told Eden of the extraordinary proposition made to him by a German–Jewish agent – one million Jewish lives for 10,000 trucks – to which he is said to have answered, 'What on earth would I do with a million Jews?' What indeed? The incident, as grotesque as any in history, illustrates the manner in which great men accept the scapegoat role. If a leader finds the way to behave with splendid magnanimity on our behalf, we love ourselves for our goodness of heart and our generosity, especially if our great man's solution costs us nothing. If he fails to find an answer it may cost him his life in the sort of war-and-revolution situation which has been our case for the past seventy years.

At all events, the two Eliahus, for whom Moyne had simply disappeared, watched anxiously for his return. On 3 November he reappeared and resumed the patterns of life they were familiar with. Galili had managed to get to Cairo for the inside of a day, and, after consultation with him, 6 November was chosen for the assassination.

On that morning Lord Moyne drove to his office as usual, that is to say with his secretary, Miss Dorothy Osmonde, by his side and Captain Hughes-Onslow, his aide-de-camp, next to the driver in front. The driver on this occasion was Lance-Corporal Fuller. Arrived at the British Embassy, the Minister did a morning's work. His work was the more exacting in that being at once pro-Arab, anti-Jewish, and strictly just, that part of it concerned with Jewish affairs, the turbulence of the Palestinian Jews and the hideous fate of those in Europe, preyed on his mind.

At 12.30, again exactly as usual, Lord Moyne, Miss Osmonde, and Captain Hughes-Onslow were picked up by the official car and driven back to the Residence: work was tiresome in Cairo in November from about noon until late afternoon, with the thermometer at between 100° and 110°F. The Minister's Residence in Zamalek on Gesira Island in the Nile, reached by way of the Bulak bridge, was a large, red-brick villa belonging to a family of wealthy Egyptians. In well-kept lawns and almost hidden by shrubberies, it stood back from the road behind an iron fence with a pair of elaborate wrought-iron gates. In evidence which she eventually gave at the assassins' trial, Miss Osmonde said that as they turned into the drive that afternoon she noticed two young men, one dark and the other fair, standing and talking by the gate; there was nothing alarming about that. The car drew up at the house and Lance-Corporal Fuller got out to open the door for Lord Moyne and Miss Osmonde, while Captain Hughes-Onslow got out on the other side and went to open the front door, which was heavy and awkward. At the same time Eliahu Hakim and Eliahu Bet Zouri, having vaulted the iron fence and raced across the lawns under cover of the shrubberies, appeared suddenly by the car, both armed with revolvers. Bet Zouri got between Fuller and the car while Hakim wrenched open the door on the other side and, saying in English to Miss Osmonde, 'Don't move', shot Lord Moyne three times. Lord Moyne said, 'We have been shot . . .' and became unconscious, dying a little later. Fuller persisting in trying to go to his passengers' help, Bet Zouri shot at him, also three times, wounding him mortally. Miss Osmonde had got out of the car as the assassins made off and heard Fuller say, 'Please help me, I'm badly wounded. . . .' She went to him but almost at once he died. Meanwhile, Hughes-Onslow, turning from the door, had seen the whole lightning scene. Being unarmed, he rushed into a neighbouring house to get help but was unable to make the servant there understand him; he then ran after the assassins. They, meanwhile, had recovered their bicycles, propped against the fence, and were pedalling hard towards the Bulak bridge about 200 yards away.

It was at this moment that the thing which cannot be planned for happened. A patrolling motor-cycle policeman, Constable Abdullah, came round the corner of the street and saw the car with all its doors open, the body of Fuller with Miss Osmonde bending over it, a houseboy standing in the doorway of a neighbouring house from which he had seen everything through a window, yelling that the 'High Englishman' had been shot, and the two assassins cycling away. He did not lose his head but went in pursuit at once, caught them after a chase through some traffic,

was shot at by Bet Zouri, but was able to stop and arrest both of
them.*

★

The assassins Eliahu Bet Zouri and Eliahu Hakim were tried by an
Egyptian court in Cairo. In both court and city the atmosphere
was as favourable to them as it could have been anywhere: the
Egyptians looked on them with admiration and respect, for they
too had had to use terrorism against the British and were still deeply
resentful of the lordly behaviour of the British in their country.
This sympathy was reinforced by the conduct of the assassins
before and during the trial. In prison they were treated with gentleness and consideration, almost as if they were sacred invalids.

Refusing the legal aid which was offered them by the Egyptian
government, each wrote a confession in Hebrew and then, afraid
that a translator would unwittingly distort their meaning, translated it into Arabic. Hakim's father sent the cleverest advocate in
Israel to help them, Asher Levitsky; he could do nothing with
them and therefore nothing for them; they did not want his legal
cunning; they wanted to tell the truth. He urged that they plead
insanity; they refused angrily. He urged, equally vainly, that
Hakim plead his youth. He urged them to plead that they had
acted under threat of death from the F.F.I.,† but they laughed at
him and told him that their organization did not use such methods,
which was true. Levitsky then told them that in that case they
would surely hang, for although the Egyptians were sympathetic
and applauded them in their hearts, they could not allow premeditated murder of an English Minister on Egyptian soil to go
unpunished. To this piece of blunt talking, Eliahu Bet Zouri
answered: 'Some men live short lives in which nothing significant
happens. That is a tragedy. But to live a short life which includes
a deed for one's motherland . . . that is a triumph. . . . If it must be
so, I am happy to give my life, for I know that our nation will
benefit by our deed.'

Despite their refusal of legal aid, three of the most distinguished

---

* He was rewarded within a matter of days with a commission as lieutenant.
† He may have had the Rathenau assassins in mind. See Chapter Nine.

advocates at the Egyptian bar were appointed to defend them. On the first day of the trial the two Eliahus were brought to the court by an escort of military vehicles and troops the size and strength of which demonstrated the impression which F.F.I. operations had made on the British and Egyptian authorities.*

The court consisted of three civil and two military judges presided over by Mahmoud Mansour Bey, and when he began to read the indictment, in Arabic, he was at once interrupted by Bet Zouri, who said that he and Hakim would speak in Hebrew and would prefer the proceedings to be in 'the language of my country'. Mansour Bey pointed out that Arabic was the official language of Egypt and he asked Hakim if he would agree to plead in Arabic; he answered, in Arabic, 'I prefer to speak in Hebrew.' After some confusion and an adjournment, an interpreter was found.

Hakim pleaded guilty to killing Lord Moyne with premeditation; he denied any part in killing Lance-Corporal Fuller and expressed regret for it; he denied the charge of trying to kill police constable Abdullah – 'we have no quarrel with the Egyptians'. When both had answered the charges, Bet Zouri asked: 'We wish to request that we be tried by an international court.' They had, he said, every confidence in Egyptian justice, but

'. . . we maintain that ours is a special case and outside the competence of any single country. We are not to be compared with ordinary criminals who act against society. Our aim is to destroy a political regime after which our society will exist under a superior regime. We claim that our case should be heard before a court responsible to no one country but to the whole world – a court based on pure justice and pure ethics.'

'MANSOUR BEY: The accused must know that such a court as he describes does not exist.'
'BET ZOURI: We know it. But it should exist for the benefit of every person in the world and that is why we make this public request.'†

* A rescue-by-kidnap attempt was mooted in the Central Committee of the F.F.I., but rejected on the expert advice of Sergeant Gefner, Galili's predecessor in Egypt, who knew that it must fail.
† From the transcript of the trial quoted in Frank, op. cit.

Hakim, at the court's request, then gave a short and very exact account of the assassination. Under questioning he refused to give names, or any information whatsoever about the organization behind him. The president received this refusal with respect. Bet Zouri did exactly as Hakim had done. Then Miss Osmonde, Captain Hughes-Onslow, and Police Lieutenant (as he now was) Abdullah, gave their evidence, Abdullah insisting that Bet Zouri had shot to kill him, a claim which was not supported by the evidence of a motorist whose car had been hit by the bullet.

On the second day of the trial when the moment came for Eliahu Bet Zouri to address the court, he began by saying that since the interpreters were unable to translate his Hebrew as correctly as he wished, and because his own Arabic was not good enough, he would speak in English; and he begged that his errors in that language be forgiven him. It was immediately realized that his object was to talk, through the British and American newspapermen who were present, to the British and American people. He gave an exact account of the assassination, and, when he came to Fuller:

'I have asked myself many times why, if I did not mean to kill him, I fired three times. I cannot claim that I lost my head. . . . It seems that the answer is, habit. When members of our organization train in Palestine we are accustomed to fire three times to see how well we group our bullets in the target. I repeat that I did not mean to kill Fuller, who was engaged in a war which has nothing to do with our war and I regret it more than I can say.'*

Under questioning, Bet Zouri denied that he had meant to kill Abdullah and had only failed to do so because he was a poor shot. With conscious and deliberate theatricality:

' "If the court will place a revolver in my hand . . . yes, if the court will give me a gun, I promise to put six bullets . . ." extending his arm and pointing an imaginary revolver at Mansour Bey. . . . "Six bullets in the face . . . of that clock above your honour's head . . .".'
'MANSOUR BEY (smiling): That will not be necessary.'†

* ibid.   † ibid.

*

Eliahu Bet Zouri spoke of his motives, of how even as a boy he had often wondered to see British policemen beating Jewish demonstrators in their own country. Why, he asked, should a man leave his country and his family to come 3,000 miles to be a policeman in my country? Why should these Englishmen hit my people and they not hit back? This piece of rhetoric made an impression on the court and spectators: the then Egyptian Prime Minister, Ahmed Maher, had himself been a terrorist against the British imperial occupation and so had several members of the court. But in his next passage Bet Zouri began to make nationalist propaganda; Mansour Bey tried to silence him; Bet Zouri insisted that what he had to say was a part of his defence and, unable to stop him, the president of the court ordered that no report of the proceedings beyond that point would be allowed and he had the newspaper reporters present deprived of their writing materials.*

Bet Zouri then indicted the British administration of his country: it was full of 'injustice, graft and anarchy'. There was a law imposed on the Israelis which was whatever the English said it was; but for the police there was no law. He gave examples.† In his country, he said, the native sons were nobody while the Englishman was master, was god. Time and again Mansour Bey called him to order, until, losing his coolness at last, Bet Zouri raised his arms and shouted, 'Our deed stemmed from our motives and our motives stemmed from our ideals, and if we prove that our ideals were right and just then our deed was right and just.'

And when, after a silence, he was bidden to continue, he turned to the press table and said, 'If my words will be heard beyond the gallows it is because you will carry them with you from here.'

Bet Zouri spoke for nearly two hours. Towards the end Mansour Bey asked him, 'Was there no other way to protest but by the gun?' a question which clearly implied the court's

---

* Immediately after the session they got together, recalled and recorded all they could, and resisted British official attempts to prevent what they wrote being cabled.
† Defence attempts to call witnesses to his charges were frustrated by the British Palestine police, who held the people in question in detention camps.

acceptance of Bet Zouri's indictment of British rule in Palestine.

'To whom could we protest? In a country which has a parliament, a cabinet, freedom of press and speech, you can protest against injustice, corruption and cruelty. But these freedoms do not exist in Palestine. If we have turned to the gun it is because we were forced to turn to the gun. When we found that every other way did not help we understood that the only way to fight a rule based on violence is to use violence. . . .'*

Eliahu Hakim also spoke in English:

'If we are asked to answer for the killing of Lord Moyne, we accuse him and his government of killing thousands of our brothers and sisters, of stealing our homeland and our property. . . .'†

These pleadings were followed on the next day by those of the lawyers. So powerfully did Fattah el Said take the line that his clients were soldiers fighting for their country at war with an imperialist invader, that Egypt was treated to a brilliant apology for Zionism by her leading advocate.

'The great powers, as we know, did nothing to rescue these victims, though they had vast territories in which they could have given them refuge had they wished. I call to your mind those miserable refugees aboard the *Patria* and the *Struma* who had the sky overhead, the sea underfoot and before them Palestine. Had they been Germans or Japanese they would have been put ashore and interned. Had they been enemies of the Allied powers they would have been treated more humanely. It was easy for the Jews to conclude that England was responsible since it was she who made the rules by which Palestine was open or closed. I remind the court that even the British Parliament has often protested against the British Administration's actions in Palestine. If the British themselves revolted, how not the Jews. . . ?'‡

When Twefik Doss Pasha followed his leader, he made the point that international law distinguishes clearly between ordinary murder and political assassination, since it allows the extradition of ordinary murderers but not of political assassins. And the third

* ibid.   † ibid.   ‡ ibid.

pleader for the defence, Hassan Djeddaoui, weeping as he spoke, recalled the thirty centuries of Jewish suffering: 'Can we, after this, fail to pay heed to the state of soul of these young men? Day and night they heard of the sufferings of their brothers and sisters, day and night that lamentation rose to their ears.' And he quoted Shylock's most pathetic speech concluding with,

> '. . . and if you wrong us
> Shall we not revenge?'

Two days passed before the court passed the sentence of death in the traditional Moslem formula: 'The facts in the case have been submitted to the Mufti.'

*

Eliahu Bet Zouri and Eliahu Hakim were hanged at 8 o'clock in the morning of 23 March. The Egyptian Minister of the Interior had asked Nahum Pasha, the Chief Rabbi of Egypt, who had been doing all in his power to get them pardoned, and might have succeeded had not the country's mood been changed by the assassination of the Egyptian Prime Minister, to be with the condemned men that morning: but, very old and quite blind, Nahum Pasha could not trust himself to carry out that terrible duty and sent a younger priest in his place, Rabbi Chudar Pasha. As they sat together they were joined by a solemn and respectful giant of a man, Moalam* Mohammed Shoura, the public hangman, and Mohammed Haidar Pasha, Director-General of Prisons, who later became Commander-in-Chief of the Egyptian army. To them a guard brought the two condemned lads from another prison; and as soon as they saw the four assembled together they understood that their time had come; and smiled.

Rabbi Ochana spoke with Hakim and told him that his death was a decree from god to be accepted with love.

'I do accept it with love.'

Then the priest asked him to repeat after him the general confession, and Hakim did so. When, after this, Shoura the hangman put upon him the red hessian robe of execution, Hakim said, 'I

---

* *Moalam* means 'master craftsman'.

wear this robe with pride.' When Hakim noticed that Shoura, who later confessed to Dr Selim, the attendant physician, that for the first time in twenty years of executions he felt like a criminal, was trembling, he said to the man, 'Do not fear. I will help you.' When he felt the noose put about his neck he began in a clear and steady voice to sing the *Hatikvah*, the song of hope which became the national hymn of Israel. The hangman, head bowed, waited for the song to end, and Hakim said, 'I am ready now. Please bury me in Haifa.' The trap was sprung. It took Eliahu Hakim four minutes to die.

While he was being hanged the other Eliahu was refusing to repeat the *viddui* after the rabbi. He did not believe in gods, only in men. He thanked Rabbi Ochana for coming to him and the warden for treating him worthily, and on the trap he too sang the *Hatikvah*. Being older and heavier, he died fifteen seconds less slowly than his comrade-in-arms.

★

The assassination of Lord Moyne by the Lohmey Heruth Israel and of Mr Burke and Lord Charles Cavendish by the Invincibles were atrocious acts; no less and no more atrocious than the acts which provoked them. The violence of the ruler begets the violence of the ruled. And these acts were less atrocious than such comparable acts of war as the murderous bombing of London, of Berlin, of the Vietnamese villages; by that comparison they were merciful and sparing of lives. Only a singular moral obliquity, a double-think whose gross absurdity is concealed by its respectable anti-quity, can condemn the assassination of a Moyne, a Burke, a Franz Ferdinand, or any other servant of one's enemy, while con-doning the mass slaughter for identical motives of tens of thou-sands of his less eminent servants.

I am very well aware that this argument will not easily find acceptance. When, in Herr Hochhuth's play *Soldiers*, Sir Winston Churchill was shown to London audiences (a) ordering the burn-ing alive of tens of thousands of ordinary men, women and children in fire-storm raids, and (b) conniving at the assassination of a single Polish general who presented a serious menace to

Britain's chances of victory and therefore survival, all the outraged letters in *The Times* defended the national hero against
accusation (b), none against accusation (a). But the resistance to
my argument is partly emotive and traditional, an aspect of that
loyalty to the Leader which, for tens of thousands of years a
condition of the survival of the human race, has now become the
most deadly enemy of that survival; and in part it derives from a
totally irrational 'feeling' that war because it involves the formal
engagement of large numbers of soldiers on both sides, directed
by government – which may, of course, mean by a single maniac,
an Adolf Hitler – is respectable. But I insist that one truth of this
business is not arguable: terrorism and assassination are more
sparing of life and treasure than the full-scale war which is often
the alternative.

9

THE OFFERING-UP OF WALTHER RATHENAU

THE Irish sacrificed Mr Burke and Lord Frederick Cavendish, the Israelis Lord Moyne as proxies for the national enemies. They were condemned and put to death, as enemy soldiers are put to death, not for their own sakes, not as makers of a policy obnoxious to the assassins' party, but as its representatives. Mr Secretary Burke and Lord Moyne stood, as it were, for the armies which their assassins, soldiers on the other side, could not get at and strike at and had not the means to fight even had they been able to do so.

In the ultimate results obtained with the help of the Irish and Israeli terrorists for their respective nationalist causes, both assassinations were, in the eyes of the nationalists in both cases, fully justified.

In some ways more extraordinary than either of these cases is that of Walther Rathenau's assassination. He fell a victim to the political ideals of an opposition fiercely hostile to his policy for Germany, and which happened to have a terrorist as well as a parliamentary wing. In that respect Rathenau's assassination is

paralleled by that of President Kennedy.* But the Rathenau case
has another and much less commonplace aspect. He was sacrificed
to the racist-religious feelings of a crowd; he was removed as an
offender against very strong nationalist sentiments; but, moreover,
he was offered up as a most suitable sacrifice to national gods, the
terrible gods of Valhalla.

*

Walther Rathenau, Foreign Minister of the German Republic from
1920 to 1922, died a human sacrifice to the tutelary spirit of the
Teuton *Völk*. The offering ensured the rise to power of Adolf
Hitler, the political messiah awaited by the *Völk*, and of his fellow
exponents of the *Völkischer* ideal.

The *Völkischer* movements among the German peoples, amount-
ing in the extreme case to a total rejection of Christianity and of
the scientific-industrial way of modern life, became articulate in
the nineteenth century in the writings of Paul Bötticher. But the
feeling behind such movements is of very ancient derivation in
Bavaria, Austria, and in Prussia, whose people resisted Christian
teaching into the ninth century and later.

Bötticher, usually known by his pen name of Paul de Lagarde,
published his *Deutsche Schriften* in 1887. It called for a kind of
mystical union of the Teuton *Völk* of all Europe and a reversion
to what he imagined had been the primitive Germanic way of life.
The old religion was to be restored. Modernism, in all its forms,
he thought evil and antithetical to Germanism, the good life. It is
important that we do not make the mistake made by the Christian
Church in its strife with the Old Religion, and insist that a religion,
a mystique which rejected Christianity, must necessarily mean that
it adored the principle of Evil. Bötticher and his followers were
sincere in their belief that the combination of Christianity and
industrialism was dehumanizing mankind and could be resisted
only by a mystical pan-Germanism ruthlessly opposed to 'modern-

* The dense clouds of verbal smoke which have been generated to obscure the simple
probabilities of the Kennedy assassination cannot hide the fact that the president's death
was necessary to and has largely served the warlike and anti-democratic purpose of the
crypto-Fascist and neo-Fascist right-wing movements in and out of the two great parties
in the U.S.A.

ism'. And this antithesis to Germanism had another name, Judaeism. The Jew was responsible for Christianity, but he was also Antichrist; by means of Christianity he had weakened the German *Völk*; by denying what was good in Christianity, he would destroy Germanism. He was responsible for capitalism, but also for its derivative, Socialism; for industrialism, too; in short for the whole modern way of life. There must soon come a violent struggle to the death between these two opposed forces; and if Germanism and the light were to triumph over Judaeo-modernism and the forces of darkness, the Jews must be exterminated like vermin.

A Frenchman, de Gobineau, and a Germanized Englishman, Stewart Houston Chamberlain, were responsible for the racism which was tacked on to this stuff; it inspired the Nazi revolution and it resulted in the partial extermination of the Jews. Its exponents and followers were members of the small burgess class, petty tradesmen and artisans, students and even teachers and professors of the same class origin. It never appealed to the aristocracy, the plutocracy, or to the industrial workers, the real proletariat. In his *Warrant for Genocide* Norman Cohn says:

'It has often been remarked that artisans and small retailers were peculiarly prone to antisemitism and in due course provided the bulk of the votes that brought Hitler to power. There is nothing mysterious about this. These sections of the population were survivals from an earlier age and they were gravely threatened by the development of modern capitalism. Though the Marxist prophecy that they would inevitably be proletarianized proved wrong, they did indeed live in a state of almost perpetual crisis. Barely able to cope with the new world of giant commercial and industrial undertakings, lacking even that rudimentary understanding of it which industrial workers received from their Marxist training, struggling frantically to preserve their status, these people felt an overwhelming need for a scapegoat.'*

Why, however, make a scapegoat of the Jew? It is true that the real Jews were for the most part themselves poor and middle class; but they were identified with an imaginary Jew, a sort of arch-Jew as it were; he was at once the crucifier of Christ; the heartless

* Norman Cohn, *Warrant for Genocide*, Eyre & Spottiswoode, London, 1967.

money-manipulator of fiction; *and* the Socialist revolutionary who upset the sound ideas of all right-thinking people. In practice there were very few Jews among the great industrial and finance capitalists; yet the little burgesses identified big capitalism with Judaeism, which did not prevent them also identifying Judaeism, and with more reason, with all those disturbing and alarming revolutions in thought which had upset the stability of the old world, done away with the good old days: Jesus was a Jew, so were Marx, Trotsky, Freud, Einstein, and many lesser subversives.

Thus, to the little burgess, and to his son, the schoolteacher, and his grandson, the student, the Jew was a two-headed monster of Capitalist-Communist evil; it is the Christ-Antichrist antithesis in modern dress, only Christ, too, is the enemy of Teutonism.

By these criteria Walther Rathenau was the arch-Jew.

*

Rathenau was born in Berlin, and his father, Emil, starting as a small iron-founder after serving his apprenticeship as an engineer, was a man of genius who became one of the half-dozen greatest industrialists of the late nineteenth century. He rose to wealth and power and the friendship of the German emperor by creating the modern German (and a good deal of the European) electrical engineering industry.

Walther received both a scientific and an artistic education.

'Many a boy is divided equally between some form of romantic idealism and competing mirages of wordly success. But as a rule youthful idealism is finally disposed of by "sound common sense" when he goes into business or one of the professions. Or if his mind and spirit happen to be of a finer and rarer stuff, idealism gains the day, and unity is restored by the boy definitely turning prophet or poet. Now the case of Walther Rathenau differs from the norm by the persistence of both tendencies in him through life, each getting the upper hand in turn, each proving itself in turn a master passion, each triumphing only to be immediately challenged and defeated by its rival. The result, apart from far-reaching effects on his reputation and career, was a peculiar iridescence of Rathenau's intellect which seemed to clothe every idea it evolved in a brilliant and multi-coloured halo. He had a vast, indeed unique, store of knowledge, economic, scientific, literary, historical, political, and a no less unique store of business experience. Now all this was kept moving back and forth between two systems, introspective asceticism and shrewd wordliness, each complete in itself, each hardening rather than compromising with its rival as life proceeded, and each illuminating every idea, as it rose over the horizon of Rathenau's mind, and passed on its way, with brilliant and ever-changing hues. His intellect thus came to resemble an astonishing coat of many colours, which he displayed for the delight or astonishment of those who approached him, and behind which he concealed from himself and others, the painful hesitations of a nature torn between two mutually destructive passions.'*

Rathenau took a science degree in 1889, and having done his year of military service in the cavalry, where his Jewish birth kept him in the ranks, did a post-graduate course for a year in electro-chemistry. Declining to make use of his father's influence, he then accepted a subordinate job in a Swiss engineering firm and in 1893 took over a failing electro-chemical firm in Saxony and struggled with it for seven years, leaving it only when he had made it prosperous. He had started to write and now decided to devote himself to literature. But, although he did set about writing in earnest, the other side of his nature assert d itself and he accepted a directorship in the great A.E.G. (the German version of General Electric) and management of the power-station building department. He built power-stations for three years in places as far apart as Manchester and Baku.

To continue, before coming to his other activities, with his industrial career: from the A.E.G. and without breaking with his work there, he went into banking with the Berliner Handelsgesell-schaft, taking over the reorganization of more than a hundred of the industrial companies in which they had interests. During the decade which ended in 1910 Rathenau became one of the really great masters of the world's work and workers.

Meanwhile he was thinking and writing. Although his interests were very wide, it is correct, I think, to claim that a single problem

* Count Harry Kessler, *Walther Rathenau His Life and Work*, Gerald Howe, London, 1929.

occupied his mind as a writer; that this problem was an extrapolation of his own personal problem; and that in his books and articles, whether he was writing about industry, finance, social systems, religion, or psychology, he was really writing about this one problem: how to reconcile the boring and debasing nature of industrial labour, absolutely essential as it was in order to increase the wealth of the world, and therefore the people's standard of living, with the needs of man's mind, spirit, soul, which must be satisfied if he was to remain human and not to be degraded below the human level, and if humanity was to add to rather than subtract from its stature. That, in essence, was the subject of his *Zur Kritik der Zeit* (1912); and his *Zur Mechanik des Geistes* (1913). In his *Von kommenden Dingen* (1917), a book which became a best-seller and, unlike the others, which were treated more or less contemptuously by the critics, received great acclaim, he offered some possible solutions to the problem of reconciliation of man's two needs. In *Die Neue Wirtschaft* (1918), his second best-seller, he discussed a possible new economy which would eliminate degrading inequalities from economic life. His later books and many of his newspaper articles dealt with all the faces of the same two-fold problem, and notably a study of what he called the physiology of business.

What is surprising in all this is that Rathenau devised, far in advance of his time, since the problems are only today being dealt with in practice, and for the first time, a working system for a common European market, virtually an economic union of the whole Continent; secondly, a working system for world industry in which, for example, all valuable raw materials were to be managed by world agencies and properly rationed according to need and capacity; thirdly, national systems for the creation of democratic and economic equality within a nation's industry. He advocated confiscatory taxation of great fortunes, death duties on a scale even stiffer than the present English ones, and the application of the moneys so obtained to the making of what was, as we now know it, the modern Welfare State.

But what on earth were people to make of a man who, one of the greatest capitalists in Germany, was advocating a very advanced form of Socialism including nationalization? What were they to make of a great property-owner who agreed with the Socialists who said bluntly that property was theft? What were they to make of a man who wrote with deep feeling about the degraded lot of the working man but who was a figure of fashionable society, lived like a prince, and was an intimate friend of the Kaiser?* What were they to make of the immensely rich banker who was declaring in 1919 that the future unquestionably belonged to Bolshevism because of its moral superiority? Of the passionate patriot who fiercely opposed Ludendorff's move to obtain an armistice from the Allies, but was yet the most brilliant and convincing exponent of internationalism?

For many Germans the answer was quite simple: the man was a Jew, the enemy of mankind and especially of Germanic mankind; naturally his ways were devious.

It was towards the end of his first creative decade, that is in 1909, that Rathenau wrote in the *Neue Frie Presse* some words which, it is hardly too much to say, were to cost him his life: 'Three hundred men, all of whom know each know one another, guide the economic destiny of the Continent and seek their successors among their followers. . . .'

The context of the article makes it clear that Rathenau, with his conviction that democratic Socialism was the most desirable practicable social-economic system, was deploring the power of an hereditary oligarchy. But given a lead by the most German of the Germans, General Ludendorff,† a considerable section of the German lower middle class, guided by a number of quite eminent academics and publicists, all of the *Völkische* persuasion, read a very different and sinister meaning into Rathenau's words: Rathenau was, of course, and with the utmost effrontery, referring to the secret Jewish government of the world; to those Elders of Zion of whom he himself must certainly be one.

*

* His biographical monograph on Wilhelm II appeared in 1919. A single sentence of it was misused by Ludendorff to assert that Rathenau had been a traitor. See page 210.
† Later field-marshal. See his *Kriegführung und Politik*, Berlin, 1922, p. 51, footnote.

In 1797 a French Jesuit priest named Barruel published a long and
tedious work entitled *Mémoire pour servir à l'histoire du Jacobinisme*.*
In it he traced the origin of the French Revolution to a secret
society deriving from the Order of Templars and from its heir
(as he believed it to be), the Order of Freemasons. This society
included Voltaire, Condorcet, and Diderot, not to mention the
Abbé Sièyes, among its members, was pledged to overthrow the
Catholic religion and all monarchy everywhere and to set up a
world-wide liberal republic. Its Central Committee was com-
posed of those enemies of the human race and sons of Satan, the
Bavarian 'Illuminati' under their sinister leader, Adam Weishaupt.

Barruel's fantasy was read by an Italian who signed himself
J. B. Simonini; who or what he was nobody knows; not even
Barruel ever managed to trace him. But he wrote an admiring
letter to that author pointing out that he had overlooked a very
important point: behind all those hideous forces and devilish
conspiracies which Barruel had so admirably exposed in his
splendid book was the real directing power, the 'Judaeic Sect'.
Simonini knew that this was so because, by passing himself off as
a Jew, he had got into the confidence of their Piedmontese coven,
whereby he had been shown their wealth, their weapons, and
their plans. Some of the terms used suggest to me that Simonini,
who may have been a Catholic priest, did not distinguish between
Jews and 'Witches' and was seeing in the 'Judaeic Sect' followers
of a religion which, as we now know, was very much older than
Judaeism.

Barruel, who was making a fortune out of his book and wanted
something to keep the ball rolling, improved on Simonini's
ideas and exposed, in his later editions, a secret international
Jewish conspiracy to overthrow religion and royal government
and substitute their own. Oddly enough, Napoleon Bonaparte
inadvertently helped along this myth-making by summoning a
meeting of all the most wealthy and influential Jews in France to
ensure their support for his government and policies, and by

* In what follows I have drawn heavily on Mr Norman Cohn's *Warrant for Genocide*,
already cited, and I am anxious to acknowledge the magnitude of my debt to that remarkable book.

jokingly referring to this meeting as the Grand Sanhedrin. There were many men all over Europe who were not in the least surprised to hear that the devil Bonaparte was involved in a fiendish conspiracy, with the Sanhedrin of the Jewish Elders whose dark powers and horrible practices, such as sacrificing Christian children, were well known.*

This Barruel–Simonini work of disordered imagination, clearly influenced by 'gothik' fiction, was one of the origins of the *Protocols of the Elders of Zion*. Nothing came of it; it seemed forgotten until, in 1850, the German Catholics had recourse to Barruel in their anti-Freemasonry campaign; but in their version the Freemasons are the sole villains and the Jews have quite vanished from the scene. The Jews were put back again in 1862 by a Catholic journal called *Historich-politische Blätter*: behind the Freemasons were the Jewish Elders and their world conspiracy; among their devoted and cowed servants were Lord Palmerston and Mazzini.

Six years later a convicted Prussian forger named Hermann Goedsche published a 'gothik' novel called *Biarritz*, using the pen name of Sir John Retcliffe.† In one of the chapters the leaders of the Twelve Tribes of Israel meet in a cemetery in Prague at night and there make their report to, and receive their further orders from, their patron and master, Satan, for the furtherance of their dominion over the world. Here, again, we have the 'Grandmaster' and twelve followers – a coven. It looks more and more as if one explanation of anti-Semitism may be that the Jews have somehow inherited a measure of the terror and hatred of Christians for the Old Religion and the god of the witches. However, Russian anti-Semites, on the look out for printable stuff for their propaganda, reissued this chapter of Goedsche's novel in Russian as a pamphlet; there were several editions and the later ones were introduced as being an extract from the forthcoming memoirs of an English diplomat, Sir John Readclif. Their title was *The Rabbi's Speech*, for in them the dialogue had been rewritten as a single address by their leader and rabbi to the Elders

---

* This medieval libel persisted well into the twentieth century.
† Had he, I wonder, come across and been influenced by the novels of Ann Radcliffe?

of Israel. Later in the century a rascally Serb known as Osman-Bey carried the 'authentication' of Simonini's imaginings a stage further by transforming *The Rabbi's Speech* into the smuggled-out *Minutes of an Ecumenical Council of Jewish Elders met in Cracow to discuss the progress of the Israelitish conquest of the world.*

The tale of the *Protocols* now becomes odder than ever. In 1864 a witty French lawyer named Maurice Joly published a satirical attack on Napoleon III, disguised as a *Dialogue aux enfers entre Montesquieu et Machiavel*, an admirable piece of work in which the pair sum up the state of the world and discuss the means to world empire. A copy of this came into the hands of the brilliant and very unscrupulous head of the Ochrana, the tsarist secret police outside Russia, Rachkovsky. As a good servant of his government he was in search of anti-Semitic material for provoking pogroms; he had the work of Maurice Joly rewritten, or rather partly copied and partly plagiarized, called it *The Protocols of the Learned Elders of Zion*, and, knowing the ground already prepared by the various editions and versions of *The Rabbi's Speech* and Osman-Bey's *Minutes*, sent it to Russia.*

Whether Rachkovsky sent his forgery to Sergei Nilus and to the editors of the newspaper *Znamya*, or whether the document simply came into their hands in the course of circulation, is not clear. They, at all events, were the next propagators of the *Protocols*. The editor of *Znamya* was a militant anti-Semite named P. A. Krushevan, famous for his success in provoking pogroms. He published Rachkovsky's plagiarism of Joly's satire under the title *Minutes of the meeting of the World Union of Freemasons and Elders of Zion*. This was apparently a sort of bastard of the Osman-

---

* In 1920 *The Times* published a leader which took the *Protocols*, then circulating among politicians and newspapermen, seriously. But a year later it was able to retract when one of its correspondents, who had come across Joly's satire and was familiar with the *Protocols*, exposed the plagiarism. But the plagiarist was not identified until, in 1934, some Swiss Nazis were on trial in Berne for publishing improper (anti-Semitic) literature. Great pains were taken by the community of Swiss Jews to get effective witnesses to the non-sensical nature of the *Protocols*, the literature in question, and it was then that Rachkovsky's involvement was brought to light. For the fascinating details of this extraordinary and sinister hoax, see Cohn in op. cit. Mr Cohn has shown that 160 passages in the *Protocols*, two fifths of the text, are lifted from Joly, and has analysed the rest to show how the rewriting of Joly was done. But the plagiarist seems also to have made use of *The Rabbi's Speech* and of the Osman-Bey *Minutes*, or at least to have been familiar with them.

Bey material and the Rachkovsky–Joly forgery. It was published as 'a translation from the French', which, of course, it was, and, reprinted as a pamphlet, was used very effectively by Krushevan and his associate, C. V. Butini, in their building up of the Black Hundreds gangs of young thugs who beat up and murdered radicals, liberals, and Jews, providing a pattern and model for the Nazis.

Then there was Sergei Nilus; this pseudo-mystic was already doing very well out of his book, now in its second edition, *The Great in the Small. Anti-Christ considered as an imminent political possibility.* Nilus inserted Rachkovsky's forgery, rather clumsily, into the third edition. But according to Norman Cohn it was the version of the *Protocols* in the 1917 edition, re-entitled *He is near, At the door . . . Here comes Antichrist and the reign of the Devil on Earth*, which became a force in world history and which was one of the weapons which killed Walther Rathenau.

The *Protocols* reached Germany, carried by refugee White Russian officers, from 1918 onwards. In 1919 typescripts of them were circulating among delegates at the Peace Conference and were being taken quite seriously by even the mildly anti-Semitic in London, Paris, and Washington until *The Times* published its exposure of the forgery; but, above all, by the German Nationalist right in Berlin and other great cities of Germany; and there the exposure of their bogus nature made no impression. As a result of the work of two Russian exiles, both of them Black Hundreds men, Shabelsky-Bork and F. V. Vinberg,* *The Protocols of the Elders of Zion* were more widely read and believed in Germany than anywhere else; and, as will appear, they had a very great influence on Walther Rathenau's assassins.

*

Rathenau, who foresaw the First World War, also foresaw that the Germany he loved with all his heart ran a very serious risk of being defeated. He had long known and repeatedly said and written that the German ruling class of aristocrats and gentry knew far too little of what the world was really like and were

* For a full account of their operations in anti-Semitism, see Cohn, op. cit.

therefore incompetent to govern a country in the twentieth century, much less to fight a successful war, despite the quality of the German army.

Rathenau did not believe that a great modern war would or could be won by soldiers and armaments; it would be won by weight of economic, not military, power. That being so, he saw Germany's position as desperately dangerous, for he foresaw the blockade. His failure to impress the Kaiser and his advisers with these ideas was a source of endless distress. It should be remembered that in his feelings about his country Rathenau was far more Prussian than Jewish. In his youth he had given expression to ideas about the antithetical 'Aryan' and Jewish 'races' which would hardly have been repudiated by the egregious Herr Bötticher; and although he repented of this nonsense, he retained throughout his life a romantic admiration for the blond, Prussian Junker type; and although, unlike many Jews, he was never antisemitic, he had no illusions about the Jews and studied their faults with a cold, clear eye.*

It may surprise those of us who, because of the two world wars, have always had Germany represented to us as a mighty, bullying power abusing her huge strength to dominate her neighbours, to find Rathenau with his profound knowledge of the facts and figures envisaging her as relatively weak and vulnerable, sixty million people with very limited resources surrounded and threatened by many more, the hundreds of millions of the French, Russian, and British empires, with their inexhaustible wealth. So, when war broke out, he knew what he had to do. He went and talked to the heads of the War Department to such effect that the Minister, von Falkenhayne, gave him the powers and means to set up the War Raw Materials Department and carry out his plan for the husbanding, control, and rationing of all raw materials. It is probable that without this Germany could not have fought for two years, much less four. But that was not how the Germans

---

* See his *Staat und Judentum*, and his philosophical writings. He believed that the Jews had developed pure intelligence to a higher power than any other people, but 'The Jews are the salt of the earth; and you know what happens when you take too much salt. I have always found that people who are clever and nothing else come to grief even in business. And they richly deserve it for in themselves they are unproductive.'

saw it: they saw a Jewish businessman cornering commodities; they saw a Jew trying to starve the German people; a Jew despising the mighty German army; a Jew plotting the ruin of their country. However, for the time being, and until they could safely kick him out, Rathenau had the support of the Kaiser and of Field-Marshal Ludendorff. For some time Rathenau had great hopes of Ludendorff as an intelligent leader. But when he asked him to explain why he did not agree with Rathenau's carefully considered opinion that the policy of unlimited submarine warfare could not and would not win the war, Ludendorff replied that he could give no reasons, he just knew, instinctively, that it could and would. Then Rathenau despaired of Ludendorff and all his kind. And he came out openly and clamorously against him in 1918 when the Commander-in-Chief decided that he must ask Foch for an armstice. This, said Rathenau, was to declare oneself bankrupt instead of coming to an arrangement with one's creditors. And, calling Ludendorff's decision a loss of nerve and 'the most disastrous piece of stupidity in history' because it destroyed all possibility of a reasonable peace which might have healed the wounds of war, Rathenau made a direct appeal to the nation: he published (17 October 1918) in the *Vössische Zeitung* a call for a democratic Ministry of Defence to be set up at once and for a *levée-en-masse* under the new People's government to defend the Fatherland. 'It is peace we want, but not a peace of surrender.'

The Chancellor of the People's Government, Prince Max von Hohenzollern, put Rathenau's suggestion to Ludendorff, who turned it down flat in a reply which revealed that the old aristocrat preferred defeat to the danger of the 'disturbance' resulting from arming the workers. Rathenau's appeal had no historical consequences whatever. But for himself it had very serious ones; he had made a bitter enemy of Ludendorff and:

'. . . Rathenau incurred the bitterest hatred of the masses for "wanting to prolong the war". And so, when the Revolution broke out his position was indeed unique. For years he had been attacking the ruling system and all about it, its constitution, its policy, its economics, its social structure. He had never ceased to advocate its complete reorganization. And yet for reasons which were only too obvious – his position at the head of A.E.G., his organization of raw materials, his connexion with the "Hindenburg Programme", and finally and worst of all his appeal for a *levée-en-masse* – for all these reasons (all due in the last analysis to the dual nature of his personality), the Revolution could not but pass him by.'*

If he could not serve in office, he could write, and he continued to address his ideas to the nation in books and newspaper articles, ideas for the proper management of the peace, for the reconstruction of the European economy on lines which would benefit all the former belligerents, ideas for the internationalization of raw material, supplies, and industrial operations. He wrote as an expert who had learned his trade as a capitalist but saw how to improve the lot of all men by applying his skills in Socialist terms. Internationalist, conciliatory, he was still a German patriot. Slowly, he began to regain political influence. But while the left was learning to listen to him and be impressed by him, the right was transforming its distrust of him into bitter hatred.

In 1920 Ludendorff made his first open attack on Rathenau; misinterpreting that passage which Rathenau had written in his essay *The Kaiser*, he accused Rathenau of having wanted the German army defeated. This set the tone for the extreme right-wing and *Völkische* parties, and their abuse and vilification of Rathenau became hysterical when Dr Wirth, Chancellor after the abortive Fascist Kapp *Putsch*,† asked Rathenau to serve in the government as his Foreign Minister.

*

From the moment of his appointment Walther Rathenau grew in stature. His task was to exorcize the image of Germany as a ferocious mailed warrior, and to create a new image, that of a reformed Germany, willing and anxious to fulfil her international obligations, to be a good neighbour, to collaborate in making a new, united, and better Europe, trustworthy as a partner full of

* Kessler, op. cit.
† In 1920: an attempt made by the young Fascist parties to seize power and establish a dictatorship by force of arms. It was defeated by a general strike of the whole working class and civil service which paralysed the country.

inventiveness and good will in the work of reconstruction. Rathenau not only wanted such a role for his country because it would be worthy of the land and the people he loved; he saw that unless he succeeded in that policy then those who were on his side, Lloyd George in Britain, Briand and his party in France, the Italian government, would lose their struggle for a magnanimous policy against Poincaré's policy of revenge in France and the English right. He believed that the Poincaré line would ruin not only Germany, it would probably ruin all Europe. Despite the electorial defeat of Briand by Poincaré, Rathenau was making so much headway that he had already succeeded in restoring his country to the status of a great power talking as an equal with other great powers; and although his Treaty of Rapallo with the young U.S.S.R., signed with their Foreign Commisar Chicherin, came as a shock to Europe, it enormously increased Rathenau's bargaining power and made the world understand that the young German Republic was a force to be reckoned with.

All this was gall and wormwood to the right, whose hatred of the Foreign Minister grew in proportion to his own growth in stature. The *Deutsch-Völkische Blätter* and the Nazi *Völkischer Beobachter* made a shrill campaign of abuse and vilification; in the *Hammer*, Theodor Fritsch asserted that Rathenau was the power behind Bolshevism, and that he had secured his appointment as Foreign Minister by threatening Dr Wirth to 'sacrifice the people of Germany to Jewish world power'. All over the country public speeches were made calling for Rathenau's assassination; and all the publicists and orators invoked the *Protocols of the Elders of Zion*, accusing the Foreign Minister of being one of the Elders himself. Moreover, they had proof of this, for had it not been shown that his father, Emil Rathenau, had been one of the coven of Elders?

The 'proof' they invoked had been supplied by one Müller von Hausen in his edition of the *Protocols*. The principal reception room in Emil's Berlin house had been decorated with a frieze. This frieze, said von Hausen, beneath which the poor, misguided Kaiser had often sat with his false friend, represented 'sixty-six crowned heads resting on sixty-six dishes for receiving sacrificial blood'. The frieze was, in point of fact, a classical mask with floral decoration, repeated sixy-six times.

Now, too, Rathenau's 1909 remark about the 300 who dominated the European economy, repeated in his *Zur Kritic der Zeit* (1912), was brought up against him. No less a man than the great Ludendorff said that, clearly, the 300 were the Elders of Zion, and equally clearly Walther Rathenau, since he knew their number, was one of them. And in an article which was widely reprinted all over Germany, Graf zu Reventlow lamented that such a man as Rathenau should still be 'alive and in excellent health', while Alfred Rosenberg, for the Nazis, declared that the Foreign Minister had long been 'ripe for the gallows'.

Such incitement to assassination did not go unheard. Germany was not short of young men willing and anxious to serve their country, the youths of the young Nazi party, the lads of the Deutsch-Völkischer Schutz und Trutzbund, of the Erhardt Naval Brigade, of Organization Consul in which the armed bands of the Kapp rising had been regrouped – by these and others who marched about the streets of Berlin and Munich singing, 'Shoot down Walther Rathenau, the god-accursed Jewish sow.'

Rathenau was also, of course, receiving threats to assassinate him, every day, through the post. Special police protection was urged on him by the Chancellor and his other colleagues, but he persisted in refusing it; it would be a tedious nuisance, and if he were to be assassinated, then that was his destiny. In very superstitious minds of the mystical-Teuton cast, this indifference to his safety might be yet another sign that they had the devil himself as their enemy. The, as it were, Jungian archtype of Old Hornie, chief or Grandmaster of the Coven of Elders of Zion, was not one to fear death; there might even be memories, vague traditions, of the fact that he had, indeed, to be sacrificed at seven- or nine-year intervals; and that such sacrifices of the Man-God were being made in Germany a dozen generations ago. Yes, Rathenau's apparent indifference to his danger was probably a mark against him, and it is all the more remarkable if one recalls that at this time political assassination had become a daily commonplace in

Germany; between 1918 and 1922 the various Nationalist parties assassinated 300 liberal and left-wing politicians.*

Rathenau was attacked and abused not only in the streets and the newspapers, but in the Reichstag and the provincial Diets. The leader of this weightier assault was the former Imperial Vice-Chancellor, Karl Helferich, head of the Nationalist right in the Reichstag, whose inflammatory oratory had already led to the assassination of Mathias Erzberger, who, as negotiator of the armistice terms with Foch, was held responsible by the German right for their country's humiliation. Led by Helferrich, the Nationalist members sustained a relentless campaign against Rathenau:

'They pilloried him as the Jew responsible for the depths of shame to which Germany had been brought and for the ruin of the German middle-classes. In the imaginations of millions of impoverished Germans, Rathenau became a sort of arch-traitor, in league with the Jews, the Bolshevists and the Entente to give the death-blow to Germany.'†

*

The first young man on record to respond actively to the *Völkischer*, Nazi and Nationalist, incitements to kill Walther Rathenau was a seventeen-year-old schoolboy, Hans Stubenrauch, son of General Stubenrauch and a member of a Monarchist secret society, the Bund der Afrechten (League of the Upright). The confidant of his project was an older youth, an army deserter called Willi Gunther, who believed that Rathenau ought indeed to be put to death because, 'according to Ludendorff he was the one man in Germany who knew the membership of the secret Jewish government that caused the war'.‡ Stubenrauch's own reason for wanting to assassinate Rathenau was that, according to Ludendorff, the Jew had not wanted the German army to be victorious.

* See Gumbel, *Vier Jahre politischer Mord*, Berlin-Fichetnau, 1922.
† Kessler, op. cit.
‡ From his preliminary examination by the magistrate before trial at Leipzig in October 1922.

Günther put Stubenrauch in touch with an ex-naval officer of that blond, blue-eyed nordic type which Rathenau so much admired, Erwin Kern by name, twenty-five, a member of Organization Consul. This was a terrorist society recruited from among the young ex-service men who had made up the Kapp *putsch* fighting force. Kern approved of the project to assassinate the Foreign Minister, recruited a fellow-Consul member of his own age, Fischer, and went to Berlin.

Kern proposed to assassinate Rathenau because, as another of the conspirators, Ernst Techow, said in evidence at his trial:

'. . . Rathenau had very close and intimate relations with Bolshevik Russia so that he had even married off his sister with the Communist Radek [Rathenau's only sister was married to a Berlin banker, Herr Andreae] . . . he said that Rathenau had himself confessed and boasted that he was one of the three hundred Elders of Zion, whose purpose and aim was to bring the whole world under Jewish influence, as the example of Bolshevist Russia already showed, where at first all factories were made Jewish property, then at the suggestion and command of the Jew Lenin, Jewish capital was brought in from abroad, to bring the factories into operation again and in this way the whole of Russian national property was now in Jewish hands. . . .'*

In Berlin Kern agreed to include the originator of the plot, Stubenrauch, in the work, but decided that he was too young and unreliable to be the actual assassin. He got in touch with Ernst Techow, Consul's Berlin agent, twenty-one, son of a magistrate. He then recruited another naval officer, one Tillesen; Techow's young brother Gerd was also brought into the conspiracy.

This little group, centred on and dominated by Erwin Kern, was soon bound into a brotherhood by that peculiarly Teutonic mixture of love and fear which has played such an important part in the German youth movement – love and fear of the *Führer* – and which was to be so valuable to the Nazis. Only Techow, at his trial, pleaded that he had been forced to play his part in the assassination by Kern and had been in fear for his life. I do not think that this was true; like the others of the band, he was spellbound by Kern.

* Cohn, op. cit.

The plan of assassination was carefully rehearsed in the Grune-wald and carried out with military precision; Kern was obviously a gifted leader and a well-trained soldier. The date chosen for the operation was 24 June.

Norman Cohn, citing the *Mitteilungen aus dem Verein zur Abwehr des Antisemitissmus* (29 September 1922), has a remarkable suggestion to make touching the choice of this date:

'When the judge at Techow's trial referred to Rathenau's sacrificial death he spoke truer than he knew; for Rathenau was not assassinated simply as an Elder of Zion; he was offered up as a sacrifice to the sun-god of ancient Germanic religion. The murder was timed to coincide with the summer solstice; and when the news was published Young Germans gathered on hilltops to celebrate the turning of the year and the destruction of one who symbolized the powers of darkness.'*

While the assassins were making and rehearsing their plans, Rathenau took a characteristic step to try to relieve the pressure of hatred which was hampering his work as a Minister by giving the impression abroad that the Germans were still unrepentantly chauvinistic and aggressive. He invited the leaders of his enemies, Helferrich and his number two, a Dr Hergt, to his house in the Grunewald to dine with him and talk over their 'differences' and see whether the opposition could not be conducted in a way less damaging to the new image of Germany which Rathenau was forming. The two Nationalists accepted, talked with their host into the small hours, and agreed that while continuing to oppose him they would do so in a cooler and more rational manner. It is not recorded whether, throughout this session, they kept one hand on their genitals; or the index and little finger extended in the sign of the horns; or even, maybe, asked their host for a longer spoon. But, on the following day, 23 June, Helferich delivered one of the most violent of his abusive orations against Rathenau, in the Reichstag, on the very touchy subject of the Saar; he accused Rathenau of ruining Germany and the Germans, in subservience to the Entente powers.

At a little before 11 o'clock on the morning of 24 June,

* Cohn, op. cit.

Rathenau set out from his house to the Ministry in the rather old, slow open car which he persisted in using.* The conspirators had chosen the place for their attempt as carefully and intelligently as they had made all their preparations – 'at the corner of the Wallotstrasse where the Königsallee takes a double turn and where the cars would therefore have to slow down'.† Ernst Techow drove the powerful touring car they had borrowed for their work; Kern armed with a riflebutted automatic pistol, and Fischer with a hand-grenade, sat in the back. We have an eye-witness account of the assassination: bricklayers were at work putting up a new building in the Königsallee, and one of them, Krischbin by name, told a *Vössiche Zeitung* reporter exactly what he saw:

'About 10.45 two cars came down the Königsallee from the direction of Hundekehle. The first one, the slower of the two, kept more or less to the middle of the road and had one gentleman in the back seat. One could see exactly what he was like, as the car was quite open and the hood was not up. The second car, which was equally open, was a high-powered six-seater tourer, dark field-grey in colour, and contained two gentlemen in long, brand-new leather coats with caps to match which covered all but their actual faces. One could see that neither of them had beards and they didn't wear goggles. The Königsallee is always crowded with cars, so that one naturally doesn't notice every car that passes. But we all noticed this one because of the smart leather things the occupants were wearing. The large car overtook the smaller one, which had slowed down almost on the tramlines in order to take the double bend, on the right that is on the inner side, and made it swerve right out to the left, almost on to our side of the street. When the large car was about half a length past it, the single occupant of the other car looked over to the right to see if there was going to be a collision, and at that moment one of the gentlemen in the smart leather coats [Kern] leant forward, pulled out a long pistol, the butt of which he rested in his armpit, and opened fire on the gentleman in the other car. There was no need for him to aim even, it was such close range. I saw him, so to speak, straight in the face. It was a healthy,

---

* The Chief of the Prussian Police, Dr Weismann, had warned Rathenau as recently as the day before that if he persisted in using this car no police force in the world could guarantee his safety.

† Kessler, op. cit.

open face, the sort of face we call an officer's face. I took cover because the shots might easily have got us too. They rang out in quick succession like a machine gun. When he had finished shooting, the other man [Fischer] stood up and swung his weapon – it was a hand-grenade – and threw it into the other car, which they drove right up alongside. The gentleman had already sunk down into his seat and lay on his side. At this point the chauffeur stopped the car, just by the Erdenerstrasse, where there was a dust heap, and shouted "Help! Help!" Then the big car sprang forward with the engine full out and tore away down the Wallotstrasse. Meanwhile the other car had come to rest by the pavement. At the same moment there was a bang and the hand-grenade exploded. The impact raised the gentleman in the back some way off his seat, and even the car gave a slight jerk forward. We all ran to the spot and found nine cartridge cases and the fuse of the hand grenade lying on the road. Bits of the woodwork had splintered off. Then the chauffeur stood up again, a young girl got into the car and supported the gentleman, who was unconscious if not already dead, and the car dashed off the way it had come along the Königsallee back to the police station, which is some thirty metres further on at the end of the Königsalle towards Hundekehle.'*

The girl whom Krischbin saw was a hospital nurse, Helene Kaiser; at the trial of Techow she said that Rathenau was still alive but unconscious. He was driven back to his house, but he was dead before the doctor arrived. He had five wounds, a fractured spine, and his jaw had been shattered.

*

When, three hours after the assassination, the Reichstag met and Helferich appeared to take his place, he was greeted with such a tumult of cries of 'Murderer! Murderer!' that he was forced to withdraw, and during the following days very few Nationalists dared to take their seats in the Chamber. Nor did the Nationalists obtain from the assassination the immediate results which they had expected to get if Rathenau were assassinated. They had expected to be able to mount an immediate rising, to be followed by a Nationalist dictatorship. They were forced to wait another ten years for that; the right man, Adolf Hitler, was not yet ready.

* *Vössische Zeitung*, 25 June 1922.

They were held in check and defeated for the time being by the Berlin workers and their loyalty to the young republic. As soon as the news of the assassination was known, at about noon, the people came pouring out of their workshops and factories and even many offices, brought out the black, red, and gold flag of the republic and the scarlet banner of Socialism, formed into processions and, in their hundreds of thousands, tramped in grim and menacing silence through the streets of the upper-class West End, one dense mass of men and women, marching for hour after hour until twilight: impossible not to recall the mourning processions for Joan of Arc and Gilles de Rais. Those who saw it say that there was never a more silent but clearer warning to the enemies of the democracy that any move to take from the people what they had so hardly won would meet with instant and terrible retribution. While the police hunted the assassins, the Nationalists who had hoped so much from the assassination were cowed by the mighty and massive anger they had provoked.

It seemed, then, that far from serving the cause of the right, and helping to restore to Germany government by an aristocracy bent on revenge on the Allies beginning with the repudiation of the Versailles Treaty, Kern, Fischer, and their friends had strengthened the republic which they had sought to destroy. Whatever they had accomplished, they paid with their lives: Kern and Fischer were surrounded by the police in an old tower in Thuringia where they had taken refuge, whereupon Kern shot Fischer dead, and then took his own life. Ernst Techow ran for sanctuary to the house of his uncle, a rich landowner near Berlin; his uncle immediately handed him over to the police.

Rathenau's body lay in state in the Reichstag; by all but the Nationalist anti-Semites his supposed crimes had been forgotten and only his great services were remembered. It seemed as if, by his death, he had done his country one final service, ensuring by martyrdom (that scapegoat role again) the triumph of the parties of reason and good sense.

*

But in the event it turned out that from the purely party political point of view the Nationalist parties could hardly have taken any step better calculated to ensure the final triumph of their policy – the overthrow of the republic, the crushing of the left-wing parties, the installation of a Fascist dictatorship dedicated to the repudiation of the Treaty of Versailles and a war of revenge, than the assassination of Walther Rathenau. By that means they got rid of the one man who had a real, an excellent chance of making those things impossible.

The politician who, by his bullying of the young German republic, by his insistence on reparations payments being maintained (thus ensuring the disastrous inflation of the mark and the collapse of the franc), by his distrust and jealousy of Lloyd George, by his irrational fears of Anglo-German and German-Soviet moves towards friendly co-operation; above all by his policy of 'Separatism' for the Rhine and Saar provinces, ensured the ruin of the German Republic and the rise of Nazism with all its hideous consequences, was the French Prime Minister, Poincaré. Rathenau had succeeded, and was still succeeding, in persuading the rest of the great powers to have confidence in the integrity of the new, unaggressive, soberly radical Germany, full of good will for the future economic union of Europe. He was, moreover, probably the only European statesman at that time with not only the vision, but the knowledge and experience as a practical man in industry and finance, to understand and promote the policies of Europeanism which we are only now, half a century later, and perhaps too late, learning to apply.

From the Nationalist point of view, which was to find its expression at last in the rise of the Nazis, the assassination of Walther Rathenau was a great success. Neither Aquinas nor Locke would have approved it, certainly: but in purely political terms, the terms of power, it was justified. For it is necessary to repeat, politics is about power; and in a period of social and economic crisis, only about power.

Part Three

10

USES OF ASSASSINATION

BEFORE any useful conclusions can be drawn from these studies of a few of the more important political assassinations of the past, it is necessary to assume the correct state of mind in which to draw them: nothing in the least useful will emerge unless one dismisses from one's mind and spirit that revulsion which is educated into us against taking human life; and we must also deny ourselves all decent compassion for the victim of the assassin. In short, one can only draw useful conclusions about the political value of assassination as a political instrument in identically the same spirit and state of mind as a statesman brings to the problem of whether or not to have recourse to war, that is, to the use of mass killing, to further his policy. Conceivably such a statesman may have some moments of weakness, of compassion for the millions he is about to put to death or mutilation, for the widows and orphans he is about to make, for the countless lives he is about to deprive even of hope. But he will conceive it his duty to put these debilitating kindnesses from him and to make his decision quite coldly. And I do not think it unjust to claim that if he happens to be a 'great leader', he will, in his heart of hearts and at the prospect of giving the ultimate expression to the fullness of his power, feel intense excitement and satisfaction in the lethal quality of his mighty will. We may feel compassion for the prospective victim of the assassin; but we are trying to think politically and must, like the statesman, harden our hearts. However, before coming to a consideration of whether or not we should use assassination in our international affairs (only, of course, in a war situation), there are the other political uses of assassination to be reconsidered.

There may well be adventitious public benefits following upon party-political assassination, but it is likely that there will be more losses than gains. On the other hand, since tyrannicide may come under the head of party-political, this aspect of the subject needs very careful thought before we dismiss it.

As I have sought to show, the assassination of the father of the Roman Empire by the aristocratic and plutocratic Republican right could have had only two kinds of consequence: one, those which it did have, to wit the final destruction of the old oligarchy and the republic and the firm establishment of Caesar's new popular imperial monarchy; two, supposing Octavian to have failed, continuation of the old oligarchic misrule, punctuated by provincial and proletarian revolts, to the great injury of the empire and of the common weal. Had Caesar not been assassinated, he would have done what in the event was done for him post-humously by Octavian Augustus; true, there was this advantage in the actual event that Caesar's assassination gave Augustus the chance which only that assassination could have provided, the chance to destroy the right opposition once and for all. But this was a fortuitous and incalculable advantage and the risk was run that the right might have won the civil war and re-established its misrule. In short, we have to consider not what in the event resulted from the assassination, but what the assassinating party intended by it; by that consideration, the assassination of Julius Caesar was not in the public interest and ought to be condemned.

The assassination of Abraham Lincoln was a disaster for the country and the American people, and one from which they have not even now entirely recovered. Furthermore, had Vice-

President Andrew Johnson and Secretary of State Seward both been done to death – as, I have argued and tried to show, was the intention of the assassinating party – the disaster would have been very much greater. So that in this case there can be no doubt at all that the assassination was against the public good.

If I have not until now made any use of the assassination of President Kennedy in this book, it is because, after all the millions of words which have been published about it, we do not know why or, excepting for the identity of a man who fired a rifle, and was then murdered with what looks like the connivance of the Texan police, by whom, he was assassinated. If it be true that nobody was involved but the man Oswald, then this is a case of murder and, in our context, of no interest. In order to make use of the case to help us draw conclusions as to the proper use of assassination in politics, we must assume that this was a political assassination. But the striking result which emerges if, having made that assumption, we consider the several conceivable motives and possible assassinating parties, is that in no circumstances can this assassination be justified by the rule of public good. Whether the President was assassinated, for example, by some group of fanatical W.A.S.P.S. deeply offended by his anti-segration measure, his Catholic faith, and his Irish origin; or sacrificed as the supreme symbol of White Power by a group of Black Power Negroes; or assassinated by one of the three Communist parties; or by an industrial-financial-political cabal whose members wanted Lyndon Johnson in Kennedy's place for reasons of their own interest; or by one of the several United States crypto-Fascist parties, with Oswald playing Van der Lubbe to some para-military leader's Herman Göring – it does not matter which, if any, of these hypotheses be the correct one, the result for the nation must have been the same: the replacement of a pretty good president by a much worse one, and therefore, since the President of the United States has so much power for good and evil in his hands, a public catastrophe.

On these three very important cases alone we should be strongly inclined to treat party political assassination as common murder were this not too likely to compromise what I insist is an important right which the people must retain at all costs, the right to commit tyrannicide. And this reservation still has to be made even if we take into consideration not only the great and lamentable cases of Caesar, Lincoln, and Kennedy, but such lesser ones as the murder of the liberal and generous-hearted Matteoti by Benito Mussolini's thugs, or of the noble-spirited Socialist, Jean Jaurès, by the Royalist right in Paris in 1914.

The difficulty is that tyrannicide may also be party political, and that one man's tyrant is another man's hero. They were surely political partisans who did away with the Tsar Paul I by strangling him with a scarf, and it would be ridiculous and also very dishonest to pretend that this assassination had any but the happiest consequences for the Russian people at all levels and even for Russia as a great power. Cases of the kind are not uncommon; and even such assassinations as that of the Tsar Alexander II can have valuable consequences in the long run.

Half a century ago it might plausibly have been argued that, the people having at long last succeeded in imposing a measure of popular control over government in all civilized countries, and therefore having the means to get rid of bad rulers without actually killing them, could well afford to give up the right to tyrannicide which Aquinas, Locke, the British Parliament, and British justice all allowed them. But this is now very far indeed from being the case: not only have numerous democracies collapsed into dictatorships since the 1920s, but the hypertrophy of the party system in the western democracies has rendered their democracy more nominal than real. British Members of Parliament vote as their party bosses bid them and not as their constituents would like. France is ruled by her President and a clique of rich men. Power in the United States is in the hands of the great industrial companies; and in Germany the party system is even more vicious than in Britain. Moreover, in the successor states of the old European colonial empires, there is a marked distaste for parliamentary systems and a marked tendency in the direction of some kind of autocracy or oligarchy. I know of no country in the world, or at least no great power, where it is now possible to get rid of a bad government quickly by constitutional means. The people have lost whatever small measure of control over government they had won.

For these reasons, not only can we not give up the right to use assassination against a tyrant – dictator or committee or cabal – but we ought, perhaps, bearing Mazzini's great invocation in mind, to be making far more use of assassination in modern political life; that we fail to do so may simply mean that we no longer care much whether we are free or not, and that, bribed with the bread-and-circuses of consumer goods and cheap entertainment, having lost our nerve as free men, we deserve the half-servile role we play. But if we really should make more use of assassination in the preservation of our liberties or to prevent ugly crimes being committed in our name, we must, of course, do so coolly and with good sense. Assassination, in the terms we have agreed to consider it – that is, regardless of our feelings against taking life and of compassion for the victim – should be used as the vote should ideally be used, that is, bearing in mind only the public good and regardless of personal interest. Assassination for personal interest in merely common murder, just as casting a vote in Parliament for personal interest is merely common fraud. But that having been said, it would clearly be very wrong indeed to deny the common man the right to assassinate, for example, a new Adolf Hitler.

So that despite such cases as those of Caesar, Lincoln, and possibly John Kennedy, we cannot absolutely condemn party political assassination, since only some kind of political party can organize and carry out a justifiable political assassination, that of a Hitler, for example.* By 'political party' in this context I understand any group of citizens, even a small one, bound together in the service of a political policy. Against this assertion might be argued the cases of Charlotte Corday and her victim Marat, of the Honourable Violet Gregory's attempt to assassinate Benito Mussolini, and others in that category. But it would be going too far to allow individuals, albeit activated by the noblest motives, to act alone, emotionally and unsupported by a consensus of decent

* Owing to the laws of libel and against incitement to murder I am unable to name living examples.

opinion, to exterminate even such political criminals as those I have named. It ought to be clearly understood that assassination, to be useful and meaningful, must be based on principles and on reason and not on a state of unwholesome excitement.

Our cases of the sacrifice of scapegoats cannot be considered in the same way. It is quite clear that in common equity the citizens of a state unable to wage war on a national enemy (but only so long, of course, as war remains one of the means of furthering political aims), and who make use of assassination as a substitute for war, should, if caught, be treated as prisoners of war and not as common criminals. No people can possibly have the right to hold another in subjection against its will, but it often happens that an imperial people is so strong, the subject people so weak, that conventional warfare is not open to the subject people; in that case, assassination must be allowed them. Thus Bosnia and Hercegovina had not the means to wage war on the Habsburg Empire, but their young men could do so by confining themselves to killing the great men of the enemy side: the assassination of Franz Ferdinand was a legitimate act of war. And the assassins of the Permanent Secretary for Ireland, Thomas Henry Burke, were soldiers of the Irish Republic, to which they had taken a solemn oath and which had frequently been in a state of conventional war with the British, even as late as 1798. The young men of Lohmey Heruth Israel were, likewise, soldiers of a republic at war with an imperial power which was denying it life, and helping to enable its own worst enemy to massacre Jews.

I should be wholly and passionately against such assassins as these, should deny them the right to assassinate, and should punish them as common murderers, on one condition only and one which I hold to be fair and reasonable: it is that war, whether waged by a handful of assassins or by an army of a million men, be outlawed and all the civilized nations repudiate violence as a means of furthering policy and combine to punish whichever nation refuses to do so. By all means let all men be denied the right to kill for political reasons; 'all men', however, must be understood literally, and while rulers, governments retain the right, then it is out of the question to deny it to opponent factions or parties.

It will doubtless be pointed out that it is all very well to talk and write about treating governments, that is to say the politicians who compose them, resorting to war, as common criminals – but where is the policeman to arrest, the court to try, the prison to punish the criminals? In the absence of the sort of peace-keeping world empire that Caesar created or the British at one time ruled, no power exists to enforce the peace, as we know to our cost.

Which does not mean that nothing whatever can be done. We have before us the example of the Old Man of the Mountains: and that leads back to the proposition that the principal object of any nation at war ought to be to kill the enemy's leading men.

I concede at once the argument that these leaders may not necessarily be solely to blame for the state of war. They are, after all, trying to rule creatures of whom few truer words have ever been spoken than those which the King of Brobdingnag used to Lemeul Gulliver after hearing that traveller's account of ordinary mankind:

'But by what I have gathered from your own relation, and the answers I have with much pain wringed and extorted from you, I cannot but conclude the bulk of your natives to be the most pernicious race of little odious vermin that nature ever suffered to crawl upon the surface of the earth.'

But then the Brobdingnagian monarch was a Platonic philoso-pher-king who rejected with the utmost horror Gulliver's offer to show him how to make guns and gunpowder, of which he said that some evil genius, enemy of mankind, must have been the first contriver. No doubt rulers have sometimes been forced into war by the quarrelsome and vainglorious ruled. But there has lately been far too much inclination among men in places of power to wriggle off the hook of responsibility with some para-phrase of this kind of argument. Moreover, as a general rule, governments have been more responsible for war than have their peoples. Can it be doubted that the Nazis deliberately led the Germans into war and involved the world in it? That Japanese governments rather than the Japanese people were responsible for the decades of war in which they involved their country and several others? That Mussolini rather than the Italian people insisted on going to war against Britain and France? That in 1914 the German government could have prevented war by declaring against it? That the United States government wages war in Asia against the will of at least half the American people?

But taking the other case for a moment, that of a people forcing its rulers into war: it is the business of rulers to give a lead, and the flat refusal of a government to go to war, and its resignation on being required to do so despite this refusal, could not but make a very great impression on the bellicose population. We have an Act against incitement to race hatred; how about an Act against incitement to war? Furthermore, when a man accepts the role of leadership he accepts the role of scapegoat and cannot complain if he is blamed for what his people do. In short, the argument that not our rulers but ourselves are to blame when the Four Horsemen of the Apocalypse threaten to ride us down, is in part nonsense which politicians are naturally industrious in propagating and circulating; and in part beside the point.

What follows from this is a proposal which is meant in all seriousness but will probably be dismissed as a piece of facetiousness. It is that as well as armed forces trained and equipped to kill the citizens of other nations, we should also have Assassination Commandos especially trained and equipped to kill their leaders. In the past it would have been possible and even desirable to insist that such commandos ought to confine their murderous attention to the other side's military chieftains. But now that all civilized nations have taken to making war principally on civilians by the bombing of cities and villages, no such magnanimous policy is possible and the Assassination Commandos would have to give priority to eliminating the enemy's ablest political leaders and military scientists. (In the early 1940s the assassination of the leading Nazis would have shortened, if not have stopped, the war.) The men composing the commandos would have to be picked for brains, cunning, force of character, and higher education: because of the difficulties of assassinating a well-guarded chieftain or technologist, they would have to be capable of living not only in the enemy's cities as one of himself, but of entering his services and rising high in them; and, of course, they would have to be equipped with every resource of modern science. But these are merely technical problems; the thing is to get the principle accepted, the principle of the Old Man of the Mountains, that by assassinating the enemy's leaders you have a good chance of saving the lives of his ordinary citizens as well as those of your own.

The temptation to use Assassination Commandos in the way that the Intelligence services already use murder against the alien crowd's lesser but troublesome agents would have to be resisted – the temptation, that is, to use them in any circumstances short of a war situation. For example, Mr Harold Wilson and Mr Ian Smith must not be allowed to have each other assassinated, for no important result would be achieved by that. And although there are many who believe that the human condition in general, and local conditions in particular, would be improved if, say, Mao Tse-tung or Charles de Gaulle, and half a dozen other troublesome old men were put down, that is not the use of assassination which I am discussing and even advocating here. It would be going too far. No, I am supposing a war situation actually to exist; it is at that moment that the Assassination Commandos would go into action, and as swiftly as possible, against the principal political leaders, military commanders and military scientists of the opposing crowd or crowds. The object, of course, would be to paralyse the enemy by depriving him of trained leadership; and, by so doing, to stop the war before irreparable damage had been done. There might also be a case for an Assassination Commando at the disposal of the United Nations secretary-general, to be used instantly against any great leader anywhere who was striking dangerously belligerent attitudes.

It is surely not taking a too cynical view of our nature to argue that, if this were done, if the statesmen composing governments knew themselves to be the principal targets in case of war, they would strive harder than ever to avoid particular wars, and would be spurred to apply themselves with much more enthusiasm and

persistence to the task of outlawing war completely, and disarm-
ing. I do not suggest that these happy results would be immediate:
men are incapable of believing that they are going to be killed and
I daresay it would be necessary to make a few examples before the
lesson was learned. Consequently some way must be found, if
we are to avoid the danger of our assassins becoming mere
governmental goon-squads, of ensuring that the assassins must be
of and for the people, and not of and for the state.

This proposal to train and equip Assassination Commandos for
use against the enemy leadership in war should not be dismissed
as not serious. As a matter of fact we have already taken one step
in that direction with our war-crimes trials and punishments.
But there is not really much point in putting an enemy leader to
death after the damage has been done. It is a well-known fact that
fear of capital punishment does not deter would-be murderers
and there is even less reason to believe that it would deter men
from the crime of war. No; the enemy leader must be killed as
quickly as possible after the war begins, and not after he has
succeeded in killing millions on both sides of the quarrel.

There is, of course, a corollary which will at once cross the
reader's mind: if the war leaders on both sides are to be assassinated, precisely the same result could be achieved with much less
trouble and expense if each side assassinated its own leaders.
Something of this sort is unquestionably the right solution. This
is mere common sense, however, and men are not reasonable
creatures. It would be asking the Commandos to outrage their
loyalty to and love of the chief who, upon the outbreak or even
at the threat of war, at once comes to personify the crowd in a
single individual and to become the vehicle for the crowd's
violent feelings. Nor would the Assassination Commandos be
imbued with the necessary feelings of heroic abnegation, so that
they could despise their own lives in the attempt to take the
chieftain's, unless that chieftain embodied the alien crowd's
hatefulness in his person. If only we still believed in the leader as
the incarnation of the Dying God, we should, with grief and
lamentation, but ruthless determination also, sacrifice him for the
people. But we are too near to being rational beings; and yet not

near enough to destroy our own leaders on purely rational grounds excepting in the course of a great revolution. It would, for that matter, have made no difference to the citizens of London and Berlin in the 1940s had London been bombed by the Royal Air Force, Berlin by the Luftwaffe, instead of the other way round; and it would have been much cheaper in aircraft, aircrews, and petrol. And the results would have been identical, that is each high command would have had the great satisfaction of maiming, mutilating, and killing just as many men, women, and children, and of destroying just as much valuable property. But however much we seek to rationalize warfare, for example by the use of my Assassination Commandos, the elements of traditional war must be retained; the thing is still not simply an industrial operation, lives must be risked and lost, there must be fierce competition, blood must be let among the attackers as well as the attacked. These conditions would be met if my proposal were adopted; I imagine that the casualties among the Assassination Commandos would be high; and I can see them becoming the heroes of their countrymen.

To sum up the conclusions again: party political assassination should be discouraged as being rarely in the public interest, but we should be careful to distinguish and exempt the case of tyrannicide, to which we must retain the right. Secondly, that no man or woman who has not given painful proof of outright pacifism by suffering the penalties for open conscientious objection to war, has the faintest shadow of a moral right to disapprove of the nationalist terrorist variety of assassination. For they who take the sword shall perish by the sword and we are entitled to make sure that this is literally and specifically true.

ENVOI

I have done my best in the course of writing this book to be fair and merciful to the mighty men, the leaders, whose violent death the theme has obliged me to discuss so cold-heartedly. Reflecting on my own perhaps excessive care in this respect, I wonder now whether I have not, from the point of view of ordinary men, women, and children, suffering horribly and dying uselessly in war as I write, war into which they have been led by just such men as sometimes fall victim to the assassin, been too kind. Even as I write these words, such mighty men as the President of the United States, President Ho Chi Min of North Vietnam and their advisers, are continuing with their leaderly work of slaughtering their own and each others' citizens. And while, in Nigeria, General Gowan persists in leading his people in the extermination of the Ibos of Biafra, the Biafran chieftain Colonel Ojukwu, condemns thousands of his people's children to death by refusing the medical aid and food offered by Britain because Britain's leaders are arming the Nigerians. Meanwhile, the Soviet army occupies Czechoslovakia in order to deny freedom, or any measure of it, to the Czech people. Stern fathers, are they not?

Perhaps, by the time this is in print their chastisements of their children will have been forgotten; quite certainly those they now put to death with their implacable and fatherly will at the rate of several thousand a day, will have been forgotten. To those, then, who are so suffering and dying to satisfy their great men, I address, as a plea for forgiveness for my mildness, the words which Shakespeare put into Mark Antony's mouth as he stood over Caesar's corpse:

> Oh, pardon me thou bleeding piece of earth
> That I am meek and gentle with these butchers.

INDEX